From Pioneer Home to the White House: Life of Abraham Lincoln

William Thayer

CHAPTER I

BIRTHPLACE

The miserable log cabin which the artist furnishes further on in this chapter, tells the tale of poverty and lowliness into which Abraham Lincoln was born. It was a floorless, doorless, windowless shanty, situated in one of the most barren and desolate spots of Hardin county, Kentucky. His father made it his home simply cause he was too poor to own a better one. Nor was his an exceptional case of penury and want. For the people of that section were generally poor and unlettered, barely able to scrape enough together to keep the wolf of hunger from their abodes.

Here Abraham Lincoln was born February 12th, 1908. His father's name was Thomas Lincoln; his mother's maiden name was Nancy Hanks. When they were married, Thomas was twenty-eight years of age, and Nancy, his wife, twenty-three. They had been married three years when Abraham was born. Their cabin was in that part of Hardin County which is now embraced in La Rue County, a few miles from Hodgensville—on the south fork of Nolin Creek. A perennial spring of water, gushing in silvery brightness from beneath a rock near by, relieved the barrenness of the location, and won for it the somewhat ambitious name— "Rock Spring Farm."

"How came Thomas Lincoln here?" the reader will ask, "Whence did he come?" "Who were his ancestors?"

Thomas Lincoln was born in Rockingham County, Virginia, in 1778. Two years later (in 1780), his father lured by the stories of the remarkable fertility of the soil in Kentucky, and the rapid growth of the population, removed thither for a permanent abode. He had five children at the time—three sons and two daughters—and Thomas was the youngest child but one. He settled in Mercer, now Bullitt County.

Then, a hundred years ago, the Indians in that region, and throughout the whole north-west territory, were deadly hostile to the whites. The pioneer "took his life into his hands" by removing thither. His rifle was his constant companion, that he might defend himself against the savage foe, whether at home or abroad. If he went to the field to plough or build fence, or into the woods to chop, his rifle was indispensable. He knew not when or where the wily Indian would surprise him.

Four years after the father of Thomas Lincoln moved into Kentucky, he went into the field to build fence. He took Thomas, who was then about six years old, with him, and sent his two older sons, Mordecai and Josiah, to work in another field not far away. While busily engaged in putting up fence, a party of Indians in ambush fired at the father and he fell dead. The sons were terribly frightened, and little Thomas was well-nigh paralyzed. Josiah ran to a stockade two miles off, and Mordecai, the eldest, ran to the cabin, from the loft of which, through a loop-hole, he could see the Indians. A savage was in the act of lifting his little brother from the ground, whereupon Mordecai, aiming his gun through the hole in the loft, fired, and killed the "redskin." The latter fell to the ground instantly and Thomas ran for his life to the cabin. Mordecai continued at his post, blazing away at the head of every Indian who peered from the underbrush. Soon, however, Josiah arrived from the stockade with a party of settlers and the savages fled, leaving their dead comrade and a wound td one behind them. Mordecai had done good execution with his rifle.

That was the darkest day that the family of Abraham Lincoln's grandfather ever knew. The lifeless form of their strong protector, borne into their humble cabin, made it desolate indeed. Who would defend them now. To whom would they look for bread. A home in the wilderness was hardship enough, but the fatal shot of the savage multiplied hardships an hundred fold.

Abraham Lincoln often listened, in his boyhood, to this tale of woe in his grandfather's cabin. It was a chapter of family history too startling and important to be passed over with a single rehearsal. It was stereotyped and engraved upon Abraham's young heart, with many other reminiscences and facts connected with life in Kentucky at that early day. His father was a great story-teller, and was noted for his "yarns," and besides, a sort of pride prompted the recital of this exciting chapter of family history, with scenes that preceded it.

"It would take me a week," he would say, "to tell you all I have heard your grandpa say about those dark days. The very year he came here, 1780, the Indians attacked the settlers in great force. All the men were ordered to organize into companies, and Daniel Boone, 'the great hunter of Kentucky,' who settled there five years before the Lincolns did, was made a lieutenant-colonel, and all the forces were put under the charge of General Clark. They started to meet the enemy, and found them near the Lower Blue Licks. Here they fought a terrible battle, and the Indians beat, and cut up the whites badly, Boone's son was wounded, and his father tried to carry him away in the retreat. He plunged into the river with him on his back, but the boy died before he reached the other side. By the time Boone got over the river, he looked around and saw that the Indians were swimming after him; so he had to throw down his dead son and run for his life. He got away and reached Bryant's Station in safety. Before that, the Indians captured three little girls and carried them off. They belonged to the fort at Boonesboro, and one of them was Boone's daughter. They were playing with a canoe in the Kentucky river and crossed over to the other side, when a party of Indians rushed out of the bushes into the river and drew the canoe ashore. The girls were scared almost to death, and screamed so loud that they were heard at the fort. The men in the fort ran out to help them, but by the time they reached the canoe, the savages had fled with the girls. It was almost night—too late to organize and pursue them, and so they spent the night in mustering all the men they could and started after them at break of day. But it was well nigh the 'close of the next day when the settlers came in sight of the Indians, forty miles off. They had camped for the night, and were cooking their supper. Fearing that the Indians would kill the girls rather than give them up, it was the plan of the settlers to shoot them so suddenly that they would have no time to kill the girls. So they banged away at the savages, all of them together, as soon as they came in sight of them, taking good care not to hit the children. Not one shot hit an Indian, but the at tack was so sudden and uproarious, that the red skins were scared half out of their wits; and they ran away as fast as their legs could carry them, leaving the girls and their weapons behind."

Abraham's young life was regaled with many such "yarns"—real facts of history—belonging to the times and experience of his ancestors. Whatever may have been the effect of these "harrowing tales" upon his mind, it is quite certain that he must have seen, by contrast, that his own condition, with all its want and woe, was a decided improvement upon that of his grandfather's family.

But to return to our story, Abraham's grandmother removed after her husband was shot and Thomas, his father, was compelled to shift for himself as soon as he was old enough to work for his living. Being a rover by nature, and under the necessity of supporting himself, he wandered about from place to place in search of jobs, and took up his abode wherever there was a chance to earn his bread and butter. He was not very enterprising or particularly industrious at this period of his life. He loved a roving life too well and was too well satisfied with jolly companions to mean business. His wandering career, however, showed him much of the world, and furnished the opportunity to store his mind with anecdotes and some useful information, which he made frequent use of in after years, and by reason of which, he became very popular with his associates.

When Thomas Lincoln was about twenty-six years of age, he went to live with Joseph Hanks, a carpenter, of Elizabethtown, Kentucky, to learn his trade. It was here that he met Nancy Hanks, niece of Joseph Hanks, whom he courted and afterwards married, thereby getting, not only a trade, but a wife, also. The latter, however, was much more of an acquisition than the former; for he was never competent to do any but the roughest work at his trade. When he was married to Nancy he set up housekeeping in a more miserable abode at Elizabethtown than the log cabin on Nolin Creek. From this shanty, into which he took his bride, he soon removed to the other shanty on the aforesaid Creek.

This is how and why Thomas Lincoln, father of Abraham, became the proprietor of the rickety habitation in Hardin county that we have described to the reader. Here three children were born to him; Sarah, the eldest, Abraham next, and Thomas the third. The latter died in infancy.

Thomas Lincoln could neither read nor write. He had not been to school a single day in his life. His wife could read passably, but she could not write sufficiently to undertake a letter. She could sign her name to a document, and perhaps do a little more in the same line; while her husband could only make his mark.

"You can learn," said his bride to him, soon after the twain became one flesh. "Never too old to learn."

"That's a question," responded her husband, who was one of the easy bodies, who could scarcely think it worth while for a man to go to school, even to his wife, at twenty-eight years of age.

"It's not a question at all," responded Mrs. L. "You can learn to write your name, if nothing more, and that will be a great improvement over making your mark. I can teach you as much as that."

At length the good-natured husband consented to take lessons of his wife in penmanship and he actually set to work to accomplish his purpose. The most that he accomplished, however, was to learn to write his name so that ingenious people could read it. He lifted himself out of that ignorant and unambitious class who are content.

At this time Thomas Lincoln and his wife were members of the Baptist Church, showing that they cast in their lot with the best people of the county and aspired to a Christian life. Mrs. Lincoln was a more devout follower of Christ than her husband, and was more gifted mentally. Dr. Holland says: "She was a slender, pale, sad, and sensitive woman, with much in her nature that was truly heroic, and much that shrank from the rude life around her." Lamon says: "By her family her understanding was considered something wonderful." There is no doubt that she was a bright, sensible, brave Christian woman, whose father removed from Virginia into Kentucky about the time that the father of Thomas Lincoln did. Thomas appears to have been satisfied with his choice, and her influence over him war strong and elevating.

When Abraham was four years old, his father removed to a more fertile and picturesque spot on Knob Creek, six miles from Hodgensville. This creek empties into the Rolling Fork, the Rolling Fork into Salt River, and Salt River into the Ohio, twenty four miles from Louisville. How so poor a man could purchase so much of a farm (two hundred and thirty-eight acres) for one hundred and eighteen pounds, seems mysterious, until we learn the fact that, at the end of the year, he sold two hundred acres for one hundred pounds, reserving but thirty-eight acres for himself. But even this condition of his affairs shows a decided advance in contrast with the pitiable poverty that inducted him into wedded life. Then, too, the fact that he aspired after a more fertile and attractive location, and actually planted from six to eight acres the first year of his residence on Knob Creek, proves that the spirit of a larger enterprise possessed his soul. Somehow his marriage to Nancy Hanks had raised him above that restless, thriftless, aimless life that characterized his youth and early manhood.

It was on Knob Creek that Abraham, or "Abe," as he was familiarly called by his parents and other people, was initiated into fishing and other sports. On Nolin Creek he hunted "ground-hogs" with a precocious boy, Johnnie Duncan, who afterwards became quite widely known as Rev. John Duncan. On Knob Creek, he played in the water, took long tramps, and enjoyed himself generally with one Billy Gallaher. For a boy of his age (but six or seven at that time) he was adventurous and enterprising. One of his venturesome sports was, to catch hold of a branch of a sycamore tree and swing over the water. One day, when indulging in this risky sport, with his no less venturesome Billy, he lost his hold of the limb and plunged into the water. If Billy had not been a cool, smart, efficient boy, Thomas Lincoln would have lost a good son on that day, and the United States of America a good President. But Billy was equal to the occasion, and, by brave efforts, succeeded in delivering "Abe" from a watery grave.

Another boy, Dennis F. Hanks, his cousin, was one of his boon companions, though a little older than himself. Thomas Sparrow, who reared Nancy Hanks to womanhood (Mrs. Lincoln), had given Dennis a home in his family, and Sparrow was now a neighbor of Thomas

Lincoln, and Dennis and "Abe" playmates. Dennis was a great lover of hunting and fishing, and "Abe" accompanied him upon many a long tramp, though he was not old enough to use fire-arms; nor did he ever become expert in either hunting or fishing.

The Lincoln cabin on Knob Creek was very little better than the one on Nolin Creek. It was a doorless log-house, with one room below and a loft above, and the usual accompaniment of stools, skillet, and Dutch oven. Here "Abe" began to show signs of remarkable brightness, as evinced by his tact, intelligence and aims. It was noticeable that he was more precocious than other children of his age and his parents were not slow to perceive and appreciate the fact. The next chapter presents him in a new role.

CHAPTER II
A SCHOOLBOY

Biney is going to keep school," remarked Mr. Lincoln to his wife, one day, "and he wants to know if Sarah and Abe will go." "I hope so, certainly, though lie can't be much of a teacher any way," replied Mrs. Lincoln. "A poor school is better than none."

"There can be no doubt about that," continued Mr. Lincoln. "It won't take Riney long to tell the children all he knows but that is better than nothing."

"He can't write nor cipher," added his wife, "and a man who can't do that can't be much of a reader."

"Well, reading is all he claims," said Mr. Lincoln. "He has nothing to do with figures or writing. He proposes to teach boys and girls what he knows, and nothing more."

"That's about all the best of them can do—teach what they know,"—Mrs. Lincoln answered. "To attempt more would be foolish indeed."

This Hezekiah Riney was a new comer, and he had settled within a half mile of Lincoln's cabin. He was a rough, ignorant man, with scarcely one qualification for a teacher, even in that wild untutored country. But he wanted to eke out a miserable subsistence by adding a few dollars to his pitiable income and so he proposed school-keeping as about the only thing possible in that barren country. Parents accepted the proposition because there was nothing better and here the hero of this volume began to be a schoolboy, accompanying his sister Sarah daily to Riney's cabin. "Abe" made some progress at this school —he began to read. A dilapidated copy of Dillworth's spelling-book was the only volume the two children of Tom Lincoln had between them at this Riney institution, and they appear to have made good use of it. The brightness of the pupils was a pleasant offset to the stupidity of the teacher.

Riney's school, for some reason, was of short duration it closed in five or six weeks. Perhaps the fountain ran dry in that time. Possibly some of the scholars knew more than their master at the end of that period, which is not claiming very much for the pupils. At any rate, "Abe" and his sister transferred their destiny to another "pioneer college," as, forty years afterwards, Abraham Lincoln facetiously called those cabin-schools of the woods.

"Mr. Hazel knows a heap more than Riney," said Mr. Lincoln, "and we must try to have the children go to his school, though it is a long way off."

"Yes; it is time that ' Abe knew something about writing,' and Hazel can learn him that," Mrs. L. replied. "The children won't mind the distance. If we can scrape together enough to pay for their schooling, they ought to go."

The last remark touched upon a subject that was often uppermost in Tom Lincoln's mind—how to get money enough to pay for the necessaries of life. Although he was satisfied with corn-cake and milk for daily food, yet it would require considerable ingenuity and economy to produce the extra money to pay for the schooling; so he replied—

"I've counted the cost, and I guess we can raise the money some way. Hazel can start Abe off on writing, and that will be worth everything to him. Some day I hope to live in a country where I can earn something at my trade."

"That will be some distance from here, I'm thinking," replied Mrs. L. "We can't expect much growth in this part of the country at present. If Indiana comes into the Union a free State, there may be a better chance there." The question of admitting Indiana into the Union as a free State was then agitating the country. The subject was before the American Congress, and the slave power was doing every thing possible to prevent such an event. The slaveholders of Kentucky were especially exercised about it, because another free State so near would be an additional invitation to their slaves to find an asylum there. The subject was discussed, pro and con, in every Kentucky cabin where white men dwelt. The Lincolns were in favor of making Indiana a free State. They knew full well that the curse of slavery blighted the prosperity of every slave State.

"There's a better chance for every thing in a free State," was Mr. Lincoln's only answer.

The reader must understand that schools were very scarce in Kentucky in Tom Lincoln's day and the few in existence were very poor, scarcely deserving the name of schools. They would not be tolerated now. Teachers were no better than the schools for it is always true, "like teachers, like schools." Hazel's school was better than Riney's for Hazel could give instruction in "reading and writing." True, his acquisitions in these several branches were small indeed they compared well with his surroundings. But he could give such a boy as Abraham a start in the right direction.

Hazel's school was four miles distant and it was kept in a log schoolhouse, the only one in all that region. To this pioneer institution Sarah and Abraham traveled daily, carrying their dinner of corn-bread, without varying it a single day during the eight or ten weeks of their attendance. Here Abraham really began his career. Here he acquired the art of penmanship, very imperfectly, of course but he learned to form letters, and became enthusiastic over the acquirement. Here, too, he made rapid progress in reading. Mr. Hazel discovered the elements of a noble character in the boy, and predicted that he would not always live in the woods as his father had. The best evidence we can find proves that Abraham learned about all Hazel was able to teach in the few weeks he was his pupil.

All the books the Lincoln cabin could boast, at that time, were the Bible, Catechism, and the copy of Dillworth's Spelling-Book that Sarah and Abraham shared between them. This was a very small library even for a pioneer, but it was good as far as it went. Any library that begins with the Bible begins well. The Catechism and Spelling-Book were suitable companions for the Book of books. "The three safeguards of our country are the Bible, Sabbath, and Public School and here they were in the Lincoln cabin—elements of family and national growth. Other things of like value followed in due time.

The religious advantages of that day and region were smaller, if possible, than the educational. There was no worship, nor place of worship, within many miles. "Parson Elkins" embraced that part of Kentucky in his circuit, so that occasionally he preached in the Lincoln cabin, where he was a favorite. Indeed, he was a favorite in all that region, and was cordially welcomed by all settlers who had any respect for religion. With this exception, public worship was unknown among the pioneers of that time, and Christian families were obliged to depend upon themselves chiefly for Bible study and Sabbath observance. As Mrs. Lincoln could read, and the Bible was the only reading-book in the family, Abraham often heard it read upon the Sabbath, and other days. Before he learned to read, he became familiar with many of the narratives of the Bible. He delighted in Bible stories in his childhood, and never tired of listening to their rehearsal. As soon as he could read, the Bible became his reading book, in the absence of all others. Over and over again its narrative portions especially were read, until his mind became stored with Scriptural knowledge. As he grew older, and other reading books occupied his attention, he neglected the Bible for them. Still, his familiarity with it in his childhood made an impression for life. Though he was not a Christian man when he entered upon his public career, yet he evinced a remarkable familiarity with the Scriptures. His conversation and public addresses were often envied by quotations and figures from the Bible. In the sequel it will appear that this one book must have been the source of that honesty, noble ambition, adherence to right, and dependence upon Providence, which signalized his public career.

Three incidents of his life in the White House show his familiarity with the Bible. At one time he was very much annoyed by men who complained of prominent officials. To one of these parties, he said, one day, "Go home, my friend, and read attentively the tenth verse of the thirteenth chapter of Proverbs." That verse is, "Accuse not a servant to his master, lest he curse thee, and thou be found guilty." General Fremont, whom he had relieved of his command, consented to run against him for the Presidency, after Lincoln's re-nomination for the office. A small following of disappointed politicians and military aspirants rallied around Fremont. About the time the latter withdrew his name,—satisfied that his candidacy would make more enemies than friends,—Mr. Lincoln said to a public man, who introduced the subject, "Look here hear this;" and he proceeded to read the following from the First Book of Samuel, "And every one that was in distress, and every one that was in debt, and every one that was discontented, gathered themselves unto him, and he became captain over them, and there were with him about four hundred men."

At one time Henry Ward Beecher criticized his administration sharply in the "Independent," of which he was the editor-in-chief. Several editorials of this character were published in that journal, and some one cut them out and forwarded them to Mr. Lincoln. One day he took them out of the envelope and read them all through, when he flung them upon the floor, exclaiming, "Is thy servant a dog that lie should do this thing." The criticisms were based on falsehoods, and were therefore unjust and cruel; hence his apt quotation from the Bible.

It has been said by one of Abraham Lincoln's biographers, that his father had no interest in his education. The facts already cited prove such a conclusion to be incorrect. A father and mother whose poverty compelled them to live upon "hoe-cake," must have had a decided interest in the education of their children, to try to scrape together a few dollars for their tuition at school, and then send them four miles on foot daily to enjoy the coveted boon! If that be indifference to culture, then the more we have of it the better. That Thomas Lincoln and his pious wife cherished a strong desire for the education of their children, there can be no doubt; that they saw in their son, Abraham, early evidence of remarkable mental powers is certain but that they expected he would ever become distinguished as a public man is not true; for there was no prospect whatever that he would lift the incubus of want and obscurity, and step out into the world of renown. Such an anticipation could not possibly have been indulged by them.

It was the autumn of 1816. Indiana had been admitted as a free State into the Union, and immigration thither had already set in as a consequence. The excitement over freedom in Indiana had reached Kentucky, as we have said already, and Thomas Lincoln and wife became interested parties. They discussed the question of removing thither, and finally decided in the affirmative, provided their farm could be sold.

"As soon as the fall work is through," was Mr. Lincoln's decision.

"If you can sell," added Mrs. L., with a significant emphasis upon the if. "It's a hard place to sell anything here. Perhaps we shall have to stay a while longer."

"There'll be somebody to buy," added Mr. L.,, with a confident air.

"Heard anything from the man Gallaher told about?"

"Not a word; but there's time enough yet."

Neighbor Gallaher had met a person who desired to purchase a small farm like Lincoln's, and he had told him of Lincoln's desire to sell in October, "after the fall work was through." The man's name was Colby; and Mr. Lincoln really expected the would-be purchaser would make his appearance. His wife had little faith in the enterprise, although she really desired to remove to Indiana. The difficulty of selling a farm at such a time and in such a place appeared far greater to her than to her husband.

"We must go soon or not at all this year," added Mrs. L. "Winter will overtake us in the wilderness before we are ready for it."

"It will not take long to pull up stakes and locate in Indiana when we once get started," responded Mr. Lincoln.

"Perhaps not; but it will be time enough to think of that after we sell," suggested his wife, as if she had little faith that a purchaser of their farm could be found. "We must learn to labor and wait."

"We've got that lesson pretty well learned now," responded Mr. Lincoln. "About all I've ever done is to labor and wait and if I wait much longer I may lose what title I have to my land now, as others have."

"That is not impossible, as everybody about here knows," added Mrs. Lincoln.

"The chances are that the title to this place may prove worthless, judging from the experience of others," continued Mr. Lincoln. "A man doesn't know whether he owns an acre of land or not about here."

Great excitement prevailed in Kentucky relative to land-titles. Many settlers, after toiling for years for a livelihood, found their titles to their farms defective. The heirs of Daniel Boone were cheated out of every acre of land purchased by their illustrious ancestor. So many had experienced trouble and heavy losses in this way, that almost every landholder feared his title might prove invalid. Thomas Lincoln shared this fear in common with others. One of his biographers maintains that he removed to Indiana solely on this account— that the curse of slavery in Kentucky, or the advantages of freedom in the new State of Indiana, had nothing to do with his decision. But we beg leave to dissent from this conclusion. There can be no doubt that the uncertainty of land-titles in Kentucky was one important reason for his removal, but it was by no means the only reason. Another reason, without doubt, was his love of change. His roving disposition was not entirely eradicated. But, more than all, the excitement over the making of another free State, with the rose-colored views promulgated concerning the advantages of a free State to poor men like himself, influenced him to make the change. It is positive that he would not have removed to Indiana at all had it come into the Union as a Slave State. The general enthusiasm over its admission in the interest of freedom, lured him thither as it did hundreds of others. The very rapid immigration to that State, commencing immediately after its admission, is conclusive proof of this statement. The reason of his locating just where he did in Indiana was, probably, because a former acquaintance— Thomas Carter—had removed thither. But the next chapter will disclose the details of this affair.

CHAPTER III

THE OLD HOME SOLD

About the middle of October (1816) a stranger appeared at the cabin. It was Colby.

"You want to sell your place, I hear," he remarked, after introducing himself.

"I'm thinking of it," answered Mr. Lincoln. "Gallaher told me that you would come to see me about it. So we've been expecting you, and rather making arrangements to sell the farm. This is about what you would like?"

"Yes, from Mr. Gallaher's description of it. I can't handle much of a place; I'm too poor for that."

"In the same boat with the rest of us, then," suggested Mr. Lincoln. "Not much money in these diggings. How much money can you put into a place?"

"Not much, just now. I must make a barter trade if I buy now. What's the damage for such a place as this?"

"Three hundred dollars," answered Mr. Lincoln promptly. "That is the price I've settled on."

"Cash."

"Yes; that's what I've been expecting, though I might take something else for part of the pay."

"Well, I haven't much money," continued Mr. Colby; "but I have what is good as money in the market."

"What is it?"

"You see I've been speculating a little since I gave you a call in the summer. I used up my grain for whiskey, and I bought some, too, thinking that I should make a spec out of it but I ain't sold but a trifle won't yet. Now, if I could pay you mostly in whiskey, I would strike the bargain at once and may be that over in Indiana you'll find a ready market for it."

"I hadn't thought of taking pay in such an article," answered Mr. Lincoln; "and I don't know as I could ever sell it. I'm going to strike right into the wilderness."

"That may be; but you'll have neighbors within a few miles and over there they ain't got the knack of manufacturing it, I suppose, and this would make it easier to sell it."

"It's awkward stuff to carry on such a trip, though I expect to move on a flat-boat."

"Just the easiest thing in the world to carry this; you can carry it as well as not on a boat. You won't have half a load of other stuff. And it will bring you double there what it will here, I'm thinking."

"That's all guess-work."

"But don't it stand to reason that whiskey would bring more where they can't make it, as they can here?"

"Yes, I admit that it may probably bring more there, and it ought to bring more to pay for the trouble of taking it there. But can't you turn it into money some way?"

"I don't see how I can; I've done the best I could about it. The fact is, the folks in this part of Kentucky have laid in largely for whiskey. I can sell it in time, I have no doubt, at a stiff price, but that won't help me just now."

"Of course not; but this is unexpected, though I 'm determined to sell out at some rate. You look over the place; it 's all in a stone's throw, and I will talk with my wife, and see what we can do."

So Lincoln left Colby to examine the premises, after having shown him the limits of the place, and proceeded to consult his wife. Mrs. Lincoln looked surprised and amused over the proposition to turn the farm into whiskey. "A queer bargain," she said. "Something I never dreamed of."

"Nor I; but I must sell the place, and this may be my last chance this season."

"That is very true, and the matter must be looked at carefully. It may be that the whiskey can be sold in Indiana more readily than we expect. I scarcely know what to say. You must do as you think best."

"Well, I think it is best to sell out at some rate, and if I thought that this was my last chance to sell this fall, I should take the whiskey, and run the risk."

"As to that, I think it likely that you won't have another chance this fall. It isn't often that you can sell a place in this part of the country."

"I'm inclined to think, then," continued Mr. Lincoln, musing, with his eyes fastened upon the earth floor of their cabin, as if scarcely knowing what to do, "that I shall take the whiskey if I can't do any better with him."

"Just as you think best," answered his wife. "You can judge better than I can whether it will do or not."

After going to the man, and satisfying himself that he must take the whiskey, or fail to sell, Mr. Lincoln introduced the subject of the price of it, about which nothing had been said.

"How much a gallon?" he inquired. "You'll of course sell it at a discount, seeing I take such a quantity."

"Certainly; I shall sell it to you for five cents a gallon less than the wholesale price of a barrel; and you can't ask anything better than that."

"That's fair, I think and now let me see, how much will it take." The reader must remember that Mr. Lincoln never studied arithmetic, though he could solve such a problem as this, only give him time. He had been obliged to think and act for himself from boyhood, and, of course, contact with men and things had given him some knowledge of figures, or, at least, the ability to perform some problems mentally.

Mr. Lincoln continued: "Seventy cents a gallon—that will be—let me see—seventy cents a gallon—that will—"

"Why, one hundred gallons would come to seventy dollars," interrupted Colby, "and four hundred would come to two hundred and eighty dollars."

"Yes, I see it—four hundred gallons, and the rest in money."

"That is it; it will make just ten barrels of forty gallons each and twenty dollars in money."

"I see it. I will agree to that. Ten barrels and the balance in money. And when shall we close the bargain?"

"Just as soon as you propose to leave."

"That will be about the first of November. I shall want the whiskey and money, though, a week before that, so as to be all ready to start."

"A week before that it is, then. I agree to that, and shall be here promptly at the time. Perhaps I shall bring the whiskey before that, if it comes right."

"Just as well—as soon as you please."

So the bargain was struck, and Colby left.

Let the reader stop here to ponder this trade. A homestead sold for ten barrels of whiskey and about twenty dollars in money! Surely Abraham's father could not boast much of this world's goods! And then what an article to take in exchange for a homestead! What a prospect for his son! Many a homestead is now bartered away for whiskey, or some other intoxicating beverage, and haggard want is all that remains. But not so in this case. Mr. Lincoln did not countenance immoderate drinking. He used whiskey to some extent, in common with everybody else, but he frowned upon intemperance.

Such a transaction as the above was not thought singular at that day. Good people sold and drank whiskey. There was no temperance movement in Kentucky at that time. Indeed, it was not until about that time that the subject of temperance attracted attention in New England, and then it did not assume the form of total abstinence. The pledge required persons to abstain from immoderate drinking. It was not till fifteen years thereafter that the pledge of total abstinence was adopted.

At the present day the sale of a place for whiskey would excite surprise and amazement, and subject the character of the recipient of the whiskey to suspicion, at least. People would make remarks about it, and strongly suspect that the man loved whiskey more than real estate. But not so at that time, when the sale and use of it was regarded as right and proper in every part of the country.

It was necessary to hasten preparations for removal, as Colby desired to take possession as soon as he could. Mr. Lincoln must take his goods to Indiana by flat-boat, and return for his family, which would require time as well as dispatch. He had no flat-boat, and, therefore, was under the necessity of building one. This would require several days of hard labor. He was competent for such an emergency for he had constructed and run a flat-boat, on one or two trips, to New Orleans, in the company and employment of Isaac Bush. His trade and experience served him a good purpose now.

Arrangements were completed for the flat-boat trip. Colby had arrived with the whiskey and made a settlement with Lincoln and the singular cargo was loaded. The heavy wares, like his carpenter's tools, pots, kettles, stools, puncheon-table, axes, etc., were loaded upon the boat with the whiskey and the many other things necessary to be done before "pulling up stakes," as Lincoln called it, were attended to.

Mrs. Lincoln, Sarah, and Abraham, who had watched the progress of the boat-building with peculiar interest, and seen the boat launched and loaded, waited upon the bank as the homely craft was pushed out into deep water and floated down the river.

We cannot stop to detail much that occurred on the voyage. One incident, however, deserves attention.

He had floated down the Rolling Fork into the Ohio River, and proceeded quite a distance on his voyage, experiencing no perils of wind or storm and he was congratulating himself upon his success, when he met with an accident. By some mishap, the boat tilted, and the whiskey rolled from its position to the side, causing him to upset. He sprung forward to the other side in order to save his boat, but it was too late. The whiskey was heavy, and, once started from its position, there was no saving it or the boat. In a moment he was tipped into the water, with all his cargo. It was a good place for the whiskey, but not so pleasant for him. However, he clung to the boat, and made the best of it.

"Hold on there!" shouted a man who was at work with three others on the bank of the river. "Hold on, and we'll come to your help." He was not more than three rods from the bank.

"Quick as you can," replied Mr. Lincoln.

"We'll be there in a jiffy," bawled one of them, and all ran for a boat that was tied about twenty rods below.

One of the number leaped into it, and, plying the oar with all his might, he soon reached the craft that was upset, and took Mr. Lincoln on board.

"Bad business for you," said the man.

"Not so bad as it might be," answered Mr. Lincoln. "Rather lucky, I think, to meet with such an accident where help is close by."

"But you've lost your cargo, though we may save some of it if we set about it."

"Won't save much of it, I'm thinking. The water is ten or fifteen feet deep there."

"Hardly that."

"Pretty near it, I'll warrant."

By this time they had reached the bank of the river, and the men were consulting together about righting Lincoln's boat and saving his cargo. Such accidents were not uncommon on the Ohio, and those who lived along the bank had lent a helping hand to many unfortunate adventurers. This was the case with the men who came to Lincoln's rescue. They were not long in laying their plans, nor dilatory in executing them.

In a short time they secured his boat, and succeeded in putting it in good trim. They proceeded, also, to save so much of his cargo as they could. They called other men in the neighborhood, and, with such apparatus as the vicinity afforded, they raked the river, and recovered a part of his carpenters' tools, axes, a spider, and some other articles. By much perseverance and hard labor they succeeded in saving three barrels of the whiskey. All these articles were reloaded upon Lincoln's boat, and, with many thanks to the kind-hearted men for their assistance, he proceeded on his way.

Before starting again, however, he consulted the men who aided him with regard to the future of his way and he decided, in view of the information derived from them, to land at Thompson's Ferry, and there secure a team to convey his goods into the interior. He had previously settled in his mind, as we have said, what part of Indiana he should make his home.

Accordingly he took his boat and goods to Thompson's Ferry, and there he found a man by the name of Posey, whom he hired to take him eighteen miles, into what is now Spencer County. This Posey owned a yoke of oxen, and was quite well acquainted with that section of country.

"No road into that county," said he. "We shall have to pick our way, and use the ax some at that."

"I am sorry for that," answered Lincoln. "Are there no settlers in that region?"

"Yes; here and there one and they'll be right glad to see you. We can put it through, if you say so."

"Put it through, then, I say," replied Lincoln.

The man agreed to carry his goods to his place of destination, and take his boat for pay. Lincoln would have no further use for his boat, so that it was a good bargain for him, and equally good for Posey, who wanted a boat.

Accordingly, the team was loaded with his effects, and they were soon on their way. But, within a few miles, they were obliged to use the ax to make a road.

"Just as I expected," said Posey. "I have been through the mill."

"How far do you expect we shall have to cut through places like this?" inquired Lincoln.

"Far enough, I have no doubt; this is a real wilderness."

"Then, we must go at it, if we'd see the end soon."

"Yes; and hard work, too, it will be." And, without wasting time or breath on words, they proceeded to cut a road before them.

"I've cut through miles of just such a wilderness as this," said Posey "and I shouldn't be surprised if we had to cut a road half the way."

"I hope not," answered Lincoln. "If I thought so, I should almost wish myself back in Kentucky."

"Should, hey?"

"Yes; it would be an everlasting job to cut through to where I am going."

"Well, I don't suppose it will be as tough as this much of the way, but bad enough, no doubt."

So with the resolution of veteran pioneers they toiled on, sometimes being able to pick their way for a long distance without chopping, and then coming to a stand-still in consequence of dense forests. Suffice to say, that they were obliged to cut a road so much of the way that several days were employed in going eighteen miles. It was a difficult, wearisome, trying journey, and Mr. Lincoln often said that he never passed through a harder experience than he did in going from Thompson's Ferry to Spencer County, Indiana.

Some two or three miles south of their place of destination they passed the cabin of a hospitable settler, who gave them a hearty welcome, and such refreshments as his humble abode contained. He was well acquainted with all that region, too, and suggested to Mr. Lincoln the spot upon which he decided to erect his cabin, and also volunteered to accompany them thither.

The settlers at that day delighted to see others coming to their vicinity to dwell, thus increasing their neighbors, and removing somewhat the loneliness of pioneer life. They were ever ready to lend a helping hand to new-comers, and to share with them the scanty blessings that Providence allowed them.

Mr. Lincoln was glad to reach the end of his journey and he found the spot suggested by his new friend in the cabin, whose name was Wood, a very inviting one.

"Better than I expected," said Lincoln. "I wouldn't ask for a better place than this."

"I've had my eye on it some time," replied Wood.

"Chance for more settlers, though," continued Lincoln. "One cabin in eighteen miles ain't very thick."

"That's so," added Posey. "There's elbow-room for a few more families, and it won't be long before they'll be here."

"But you've neighbors nearer than that," said Wood. "There's one family not more than two miles east of here."

"Then I shall have two neighbors," said Lincoln.

"And there are two other families within six or eight miles,—one of them is north, and the other west," continued Wood. "The fact is, people are flocking into this free State fast."

We must not dwell. Posey returned with his team to Thompson's Ferry, and Mr. Lincoln, having deposited his goods, and secured Mr. Wood's promise to look after them, directed his steps on foot back to his family. It was about one hundred miles from his old home in Kentucky to his new one in Indiana. This was the distance, in a direct line. It was twenty-five miles further, the way Mr. Lincoln came. It was a part of his plan to return on foot. A direct line, about southeast, would bring him to Hardin County—a three days' journey.

His family gave him a cordial welcome, and Abraham was somewhat taken with the story of his father's adventure, particularly the part relating to his plunge into the Ohio River.

Hasty preparations were made to remove the family and such things as he did not take with him on the boat. He took no bedding or apparel with him on the boat. These were left to go with the family, on horseback. Two horses were provided, and on these were packed the aforesaid articles,—Mrs. Lincoln, her daughter, and Abraham sometimes riding and sometimes walking.

They were seven days in performing the journey, camping out nights, with no other shelter than the starry skies over them, and no other bed than blankets spread upon the ground.

It was a novel experience even to them, nor was it without its perils. Yet they had no fears. In that country, at that day, neither men nor women allowed themselves to cower in the presence of dangers.

Females were not the timid class that they are now. They were distinguished for heroism that was truly wonderful. Inured as they were to hardships and perils, they learned to look dangers steadily in the face, and to consider great privations as incidental to pioneer life. Experiences that would now destroy the happiness of most of the sex then served to develop the courage and other intrepid virtues that qualified them for the mission God designed they should fulfill.

Many facts are found in history illustrating the heroism of Western females in the early settlement of that part of our country. Soon after Abraham's grandfather removed to Kentucky, an Indian entered the cabin of a Mr. Daviess, armed with gun and tomahawk, for the purpose of plundering it, and capturing the family. Mrs. Daviess was alone with her children. With remarkable presence of mind she invited the Indian to drink, at the same time setting a bottle of whiskey on the table. The Indian set down his gun to pour out a dram, and at once Mrs. Daviess seized it, and, aiming it at his head, threatened to blow his brains out if he did not surrender. The Indian dropped the bottle, sat down upon a stool, and promised to do no harm if she would not fire. In that position she kept him until her husband arrived.

In another instance, about the same time, the house of a Mr. Merrill was attacked in the night by several Indians, and Mr. Merrill was seriously wounded as he went to the door. The savages attempted to enter the house, when Mrs. Merrill and her daughter shut the door against them, and held it. Then the Indians hewed away a part of the door, so that one of them could get in at a time. But Mrs. Merrill, though her husband lay groaning and weltering in his blood, and her children were screaming with fright, seized an ax, when the first one had got partly into the room, and dealt upon him a mortal blow. Then she drew his body in and waited for the approach of another. The Indians, supposing that their comrade had forced an entrance, were exultant, and proceeded to follow him. Nor did they discover their mistake until she had dispatched four of them in this way. Then two of them attempted to descend the chimney, whereupon she ordered her children to empty the contents of a bed upon the fire and the fire and smoke soon brought down two Indians, half suffocated, into the room. Mr. Merrill, by a desperate exertion, rose up, and speedily finished these two with a billet of wood. At the same time his wife dealt so heavy a blow upon the only remaining Indian at the door that he was glad to retire.

Volumes might be filled with stories that show the heroism of Western women at that day. We have cited these two examples simply to exhibit their fortitude. Mrs. Lincoln was a resolute, fearless woman, like her pioneer sisters, and hence was cool and self possessed amidst all exposures and dangers.

We said they were seven days on the journey. Two miles from their destination they came to the cabin of their nearest neighbor, Mr. Neale, who treated them with great kindness, and promised to assist them on the following day in putting up a dwelling. It was a pleasant proffer of assistance, and it served to make them happier as they lay down in their blankets on the first night of their residence in Spencer County, Indiana.

We have been thus particular, in this part of the narrative, because this experience had much to do with the development of that courage, energy, decision, and perseverance for which Abraham was thereafter distinguished.

CHAPTER IV
A NEW HOME MADE

It was in the new home in Indiana that Abraham began to be a genuine pioneer boy. The ax was the symbol of pioneer life; and here he began to swing one in dead earnest. From the time he was eight years old until he had past his majority, he was accustomed to the almost daily use of the ax. His physical strength developed with wonderful rapidity, so that he became one of the most efficient wood-choppers in that region. After he became President, and the "War of the Rebellion" was on his hands, he visited the hospitals at City Point, where three thousand sick and wounded soldiers were sheltered. He insisted upon shaking hands with every one of them and, after performing the feat, and friends were expressing their fears that his arm would be lamed by so much handshaking, he remarked— "The hardships of my early life gave me strong muscles." And, stepping out of the open door, he took up a very large, heavy ax which lay there by a log of wood, and chopped vigorously for a few moments, sending the chips flying in all directions and, then pausing, he extended his right arm to its full length, holding the ax out horizontally, without its even quivering as he held it. Strong men who looked on—men accustomed to manual labor— could not hold the same ax in that position for a moment. When the President left, a hospital steward gathered up the chips, and laid them aside carefully, "because they were the chips that Father Abraham chopped."

It was necessary for the Lincoln family to erect a habitation as soon as possible, and "a half-faced camp" could be more easily and quickly built than a cabin, because it could be constructed of "poles" instead of logs. For this reason, Mr. Lincoln decided to erect the "camp" for a temporary abode, and the next year build a substantial log-cabin. He could cut the logs and prepare slabs during the winter, so that the labor of erecting a cabin would not be great after the planting of the next spring was done.

A "half-faced camp" was "a cabin enclosed on three sides and open on the fourth," a very poor habitation for the cold winters of Indiana. But pioneers accepted almost any device for a shelter, and made the best of cold, hunger, and hardship.

Abraham began pioneer life by assisting his father in erecting the "camp." Cutting "poles" was an easy method of initiating him into the hard work of chopping wood. It was not, however, until the following summer when the more substantial cabin was erected, that Abraham engaged in the enterprise with all his heart. A severe winter and unusual exposure caused him to appreciate a better habitation.

After "clearing some land, and planting corn and vegetables," in the spring of 1817, and the summer work was well under way, Mr. Lincoln proceeded to erect his log-cabin. His nearest neighbor rendered him essential aid, and Abraham proved himself very efficient for a boy of eight years. One who often found shelter under the hospitable roof of this cabin has furnished the following description of it:—

"It was sixteen by eighteen feet in size, without a floor, the unhewn logs put together at the corners by the usual method of notching them, and the cracks between them stopped with clay. It had a shed-roof, covered with slabs or clapboards split from logs. It contained but one room, with a loft, slabs being laid on the logs overhead, so as to make a chamber, to which access was had by pins driven into the logs in one corner. It had one door and one window. The latter, however, was so ingeniously constructed, that it deserves particular attention. Mr. Lincoln made a sash of the size of four six-by-eight squares of glass and, in place of glass, which could not be obtained in that region, he took the skin that covers the fat portion of a hog, called the leaves, and drew it over the sash tight. This furnished a very good substitute for glass and the contrivance reflected much credit upon the inventive genius of the builder."

The cabin was furnished by Mr. Lincoln and Abraham, and we will give some account of the way of doing it.

"Bring me the auger, Abe," said his father, "and that measure, too; we must have a bedstead now."

"I can bore the holes," answered Abraham, at the same time bringing the auger and measure.

"No, you can't. It's tough work to bore two-inch holes into such logs as these. But you can go and find me a stick for a post, and two others to lay on it."

"That all?"

"Yes, that's all. I'll just make it in that corner, and then I shall have but two holes to bore, and one post to set up. It's not more than an hour's work."

By making the bedstead in the corner, the work was but small. He measured off eight feet on one side, and bored one hole, then four and a half feet on the end, and bored another hole. Then, setting up the post in its place, two sticks from each auger hole would meet on the post, thus making the framework of the bed. This was soon done.

"Now for the bed-cord, Abe," said his father, jocosely. "We must have something to lay the bed on."

"I thought you laid on slabs," answered Abraham, not exactly comprehending the drift of his father's remark.

"We haven't any other bed-cord, so pass me some of those yonder." The slabs used to lay over the bed frame were like those on the roof.

"How many shall I bring?" and he began to pass the slabs.

"About six, I think, will do it."

They were soon brought, and the bed was complete.

"Now, a sackful of straw on that will make a fine bed." Dry leaves, hay and husks were sometimes used for this purpose. Few had feathers in that region.

"You must keep on with your cabinet-making," said Mrs. Lincoln. "We need a table as much as a bed."

"Of course. That comes next," replied her husband "The legs for it are all ready."

"Where are they?" inquired Abraham.

"Out there" pointing to a small pile of limbs, sticks, and slabs, Abraham went after them, while his father sawed off a puncheon of the required length for the table. A puncheon was made by splitting a log eighteen inches, more or less, in diameter, the flat side laid uppermost. Puncheons were used in this way to make tables, stools, and floors.

By the time Abraham had brought the sticks for the legs of the table, his father had the table part all ready, and was proceeding to bore the holes for the legs.

"Now you may bring some more of those sticks in the pile,— the shortest of them I shall want next."

"What for?"

"Oh, we must have some chairs now; we've sat on the ground long enough. I want the sticks for legs."

"Enough for one stool each now will do. We'll make some extra ones when we get over our hurry. Four times three are twelve; I shall want twelve."

"Must they be just alike?"

"No; you can't find two alike, hardly. If they are too long, I can saw them the right length."

All this time the work of making the table went on. As Abraham had so large a number of stool-legs to select and bring from the pile, the table was nearly completed when his part of the work was done.

"A scrumptious table, I'm thinking," said Mr. Lincoln, as he surveyed it when it was fairly on its legs. "Pioneer cabinet-work ain't handsome, but it's durable."

"And useful, too," said his wife. "Two of them wouldn't come amiss."

"No; and when I get time we'll have another. Perhaps Abe can make you one some time. Can't you make a table, Abe?"

"I can try it."

"Well, you ought to succeed now you have seen me do it. You can try your hand at it some day. But now for the stools."

A good slab was selected, of which four stools could be made and before night the house was furnished at small expense. A bed, table, and stools constituted the furniture of this pioneer home, in which Abraham spent twelve years of his eventful life.

Abraham occupied the loft above, ascending to his lodgings by the ladder. It was his parlor-chamber, where he slept soundly at night on the loose floor, with no other bedding than blankets. Here, year after year, he reposed nightly with as much content and bliss as we usually find in the mansions of the rich. He had never known better fare than this and perhaps, at that age, he did not expect a larger share of worldly goods.

By this time the loss of the family by the accident on the Ohio River was nearly made good, except one or two iron kettles, and a little very poor crockery. The puncheon table and stools were replaced by better ones. Through the winter and spring, the family had got along as they could, anticipating an improved condition in the autumn.

The pioneer families of that day needed the means of converting their corn into meal. Meal was a staple article of food, without which they could scarcely survive, but there were few grist mills in all the region for many miles around. The nearest was Thompson's Ferry, where Lincoln landed on his way to Indiana. They were hand-mills, and could grind but little faster than corn could be pounded into meal with mortar and pestle.

"I'll have a mill of my own," remarked Mr. Lincoln.

"How?" inquired Abraham.

"You'll see when it is done. This going eighteen miles to mill don't pay we must have one right here."

"And it won't take you longer to make one than it would to go to the ferry once and back," said Mrs. Lincoln.

"It's an all-day job to go there, and a pretty long day at that." She knew what kind of a mill he referred to, for she had seen them.

"We'll have one before to-morrow night," added Mr. Lincoln, with a shrug of the shoulder.

"How will you make it?" inquired Abraham, who was growing interested.

"You'll see when it's done: I shall need some of your help, and if you do first rate, you may try the rifle some day." The boy had been promised before that he should learn to shoot.

" I like that," said the lad.

"And so shall I, if you make a marksman. You can be a great help to us by killing game to cook. When you get so that you can pop over a turkey or a deer, I ain't need to hunt any."

"Will you let me do it?"

"Yes, and be glad to have you. The woods are full of game, and you shall have a chance to make a good shot."

Abraham was delighted with the prospect of making a gunner, and he went to his hard bed that night with glowing thoughts of the future. The morrow's sun found him up and ready to assist his father in making a grist-mill.

"The first thing is a log," said his father; and he proceeded to look for a tree of suitable dimensions nor was he long in finding one.

"When I get it ready, I shall want you to make a fire won't, Abe," he continued.

"What! Burn it up!" screamed the boy, not understanding what his father meant.

"Ha! not quite so bad as that. It wouldn't be worth much for a mill if 'twas burnt up."

"Didn't you say make a fire on it!"

"Yes, on the top of it ; we must burn a hole in it a foot deep, to put corn in ; so get your fire ready."

It was not long before the tree was prostrate, and a portion of the trunk cut off about four feet long. Setting it upon one end, Mr. Lincoln continued, "Here, Abe, that's what I mean by making a fire won't. You must make a fire right on the top of it, and burn a hole in it well nigh a foot deep. I'll help you."

The fire was soon kindled, and Abraham's curiosity was at the highest pitch. What was coming next was more than he could tell— and no wonder.

"Now, bring some water; we must keep it wet."

"And put out the fire?" said Abraham, inquiringly.

"No, no; we must keep the outside of it wet, so that the whole of it won't burn. We don't want to burn the outside—only a hole in the centre."

Abraham saw through it now, and he hastened to get the water. The fire was kept burning while Mr. Lincoln looked up a spring-pole, to one end of which he attached a pestle.

"What is that for?" asked Abraham.

"You'll see when I get it into working order," replied his father. "Keep the fire a-going till its burnt deep enough."

"It'll never burn as deep as you say."

"Yes, it will, only keep doing. That's the way pioneers have to make grist mills."

"It'll take more than one day to burn it anyhow, at this rate."

"No, it won't. It will burn faster when it gets a little deeper. We'll have it done before night. You must have patience and keep at it."

And they continued at the work. Mr. Lincoln prepared the spring-pole somewhat like an old-fashioned well-sweep and it was ready for use before the hole was burned deep enough in the log. Then, with his additional help, the log was ready before night, and the coal was thoroughly cleaned out of the hole, and the pestle on the pole adapted thereto.

This was all the mill that he proposed to have. It was the kind used by many settlers at that day. It was a mortar and pestle on a large scale, and, on the whole, was much better than to go twenty miles to a real mill that could grind but little faster. About two quarts of corn could be put into the hole in the log at once, and a few strokes from the pestle on the spring-pole would reduce it to meal. In this way the family could be provided with meal at short notice. The apparatus, too, corresponded very well with all the surroundings. For a Dutch oven and spider constituted the culinary furniture of the cabin. All their other articles of iron-ware were at the bottom of the Ohio River. The spider was used for griddle, stew pan, gridiron, kettle, and sundry other things, in addition to its legitimate purpose; proving that man's real wants are few in number. It is very convenient to be provided with all the modern improvements in this line but the experience of the Lincoln family shows that happiness and life can be promoted without them.

This mill served the family an excellent purpose for several years. It was so simple that it needed no repairs, and it was not dependent either on rain or sunshine for the power to go. Any of the family could go to mill here. Abraham could carry a grist on his arm and back, and play the part of miller at the same time.

The Lincoln family was not fairly settled in Indiana until they moved into their new log-cabin in the autumn of 1817. By that time, Abraham had become a thorough pioneer boy. He had made considerable improvement, too, in "reading and writing." The impulse that Hazel gave him in Kentucky was not lost in Indiana. The three books of the family library continued to supply his intellectual wants.

During the long winter evenings of that first winter in Indiana, he read by the light of the fire for they could not afford the luxury of any other light in their cabin. This was true, very generally, of the pioneer families: they had no more than was absolutely necessary to supply their wants. They could exist without lamp-oil or candles, and so most of them did without either. They could afford the largest fire possible, since wood was so plenty that they studied to get rid of it. Hence the light of the fire was almost equal to a good chandelier. Large logs and branches of wood were piled together in the fireplace, and its mammoth blaze lighted up every nook and corner of the dwelling. Hence lamps were scarcely needed.

He practiced penmanship with a charred stick on the bark of trees and on slabs. In the winter, he wrote his name in the snow with a stick and, in the summer, he wrote it on the ground in the garden. In this way he increased his ability to write, along with his ability to read. Still, we can scarcely conceive of a more unpromising situation for a bright boy.

The exact location of Mr. Lincoln's cabin was between the forks of Big Pigeon and Little Pigeon Creeks, one mile and a half from what is now the village of Gentryville. His cabin was surrounded with a dense forest of oaks, walnuts, sugar-maples, and other varieties of trees found in the woods of North America. The trees were of the largest growth, affording a refuge and shelter for birds and beasts, which abounded here. Deer and wild turkeys furnished abundant food for the settlers, whose experience with the rifle was their assurance of enough to eat. Lincoln was expert with the rifle, and in the forests of Indiana game met him on every hand. There was a small open space, or prairie, within a short distance from his cabin, where the deer resorted and here he made many a good shot to supply his larder with venison.

The situation of his cabin was all that Mr. Lincoln could desire. There was one drawback, however—there was no spring of water within a mile. One of the most fatiguing "chores" that Abraham and his sister did, in those days of hardship, was to bring water from the spring, one mile away. This need was subsequently supplied in some way. Dennis Hanks says that Mr. Lincoln "riddled his land like a honeycomb" in search of water and, perhaps, he found it through this "riddling" process. There is a story that he employed a Yankee with a divining-rod, who directed him to excellent water for five dollars but it is only a story.

How he obtained possession of this farm is explained by Dennis Hanks, who says, "He settled on a piece of government land,—eighty acres. The land he afterwards bought under the Two-Dollar Act; was to pay for it in installments; one-half he paid, the other half he never paid, and finally lost the whole of the land."

We have said that Mr. Lincoln settled in Spencer County. The location of his cabin was in Perry County; but, within a few years, through increasing immigration and rapid changes and improvements, he found himself in Spencer County, with the court-house at Rockport and the village of Gentryville springing up about a mile and a half distant. Nine years after he settled in Indiana, a post-office was established at Gentryville.

David Turnham, who was a boy with Abraham in Spencer County, furnishes an interesting account of that country when he first removed thither, as follows:

"When my father came here in the spring of 1819, he settled in Spencer County, within one mile of Thomas Lincoln, then a widower. The chance for schooling was poor but, such as it was, Abraham and myself attended the same schools.

"We first had to go seven miles to mill and then it was a hand-mill that would grind from ten to fifteen bushels of corn in a day. There was but little wheat grown at that time and, when we did have wheat, we had to grind it on the mill described, and use it without bolting, as there were no bolts in the country. In the course of two or three years, a man by the name of Huffman built a mill on Anderson River, about twelve miles distant. Abe and I had to do the milling on horseback, frequently going twice to get one grist. Then they began building horse-mills of a little better quality than the hand-mills.

"The country was very rough, especially in the lowlands, so thick with bush that a man could scarcely get through on foot. These places were called Roughs. The country abounded in game, such as bears, deer, turkeys, and the smaller game.

"At that time there were a great many deer-licks and Abe and myself would go to these licks sometimes, and watch of nights to kill deer, though Abe was not so fond of a gun as I was. There were ten or twelve of these licks in a small prairie on the creek, lying between Mr. Lincoln's and Mr. Wood's.

"The people in the first settling of this country were very sociable, kind, and accommodating; but there was more drunkenness and stealing on a small scale, more immorality, less religion, less well-placed confidence."

Mr. Turnham's allusion to the prevalence of drunkenness, at that day, renders it necessary to state that the prevalence of this evil was the source of much anxiety to Mrs. Lincoln. The danger to her boy was imminent and many a word of warning and counsel dropped from her lips into his young ears. When Abraham began his public career, and he fearlessly and firmly avowed his total abstinence principles, he said that he owed much to one counsel of his mother; viz., "Men become drunkards because they begin to drink; if you never begin to drink, you will never become a drunkard."

The sagacity and wisdom of the mother in this striking remark v/ill not appear to the reader until it is remembered that, at that day, there was not a total abstinence society or pledge in the world. Mrs. Lincoln had never heard of a temperance movement for, indeed, there had been none, except on the smallest scale, in a few localities. Yet, she proposed the only safeguard to her boy—one that proved of inestimable value to him, as he publicly and privately acknowledged many years thereafter.

We have given in detail the time, place, and circumstances of Abraham's discipline in early life, that the reader may appreciate the force of character which lifted the incubus of poverty and obscurity, and made him famous in the world.

CHAPTER V

AFTER GAME

It was in the spring of 1817, when Thomas Lincoln was preparing to put his first seed into the soil of Indiana, that Abraham made his first shot at game. His parents were discussing the old subject—their loss on the Ohio River; when Mrs. Lincoln remarked—

"I'm thoroughly convinced that our loss was all for the best. I think I can see it."

"Glad if you can," replied Mr. Lincoln, "you're pretty good for seeing what nobody else can;" and he uttered this sentence rather thoughtlessly, as his mind was really absorbed in another subject.

"I don't know about that; but what in the world would you have done with all the whiskey, if we had not lost any of it in the river." Never could sell it all here—and what a job it would have been to get it here from the Ferry!"

"Well, if I didn't sell it, we should be about as well off as we are now."

"Except the cost of getting the barrels here."

"That wouldn't be much."

"Then there's the danger of the evil it might do. Its dangerous stuff any way, as the case of many men shows."

"I know that; but I don't fear for myself."

"Neither do I fear for you; but I was thinking of Abe. You know how it is with boys in these times, and how much misery whiskey makes in a great many families. And I can't help thinking that it is all for the best that most of it is in the river."

"I can't say but what it is; I hope it is. It makes mischief enough, if that's all and if I dreamed it would make any in my family, I should wish that all of it was at the bottom of the river."

"You may as well be glad now; for we have less to fear and perhaps the Lord thought it was best to put so much of it where it could injure no one."

"So be it, then; but I must go to my work. This weather is too fine to be lost in doing nothing. The stuff is all sold now, so that there is no fear on that score." He sold a barrel to Posey, the teamster, who hauled his goods from the Ferry, and the remainder he disposed of in the course of the winter.

Mr. Lincoln arose and went out to his work, and within ten minutes afterwards Abraham came rushing into the cabin in a state of great excitement.

"Mother," he exclaimed, "there's a flock of turkeys right out here that I can shoot. See there, and he directed her to look through a crack in the cabin where the clay had fallen off. "Let me shoot, mother."

"Sure enough, Abe, there is a flock," responded his mother, as she caught sight of the turkeys; "a fine shot it is," and she hastened for the rifle that was always kept loaded.

"Be quick, mother, I'll fire right through the hole," continued Abe, under increasing excitement.

His mother was not long in bringing the rifle, and adjusting it through the loop-hole between the logs, when, with a few quick words of caution, she allowed him to fire.

"Bang!" went the rifle, and resounded through the forest with unusual volume, as Abraham thought in his intense earnestness. Both mother and son ran out to discover the result of the shot, and by the time they reached the spot, the smoke had cleared away, and there lay one of the flock dead.

"Killed one," shouted Abraham, as he lifted an extra large turkey from the ground.

"So you have," answered his mother, under almost as much excitement as her son.

"A monster!" continued the lad, surveying the lusty fellow with boyish pride. "Did you ever see such a big one."

"It is a very large one," replied his mother; "that was a good shot, Abe."

By this time Mr. Lincoln had reached the spot. Hearing the report of the gun, he left his work, and hurried back to learn the cause.

"What's the firing for?" he asked hurriedly.

"I've killed a turkey," answered Abraham, exhibiting in triumph the dead bird.

"Did you do that, Abe?"

"Nobody else did it," was the boy's rather characteristic reply.

"A capital shot, Abe; you'll make a good one with the rifle if you keep on," his father added, intending to praise the boy. The fact was it was not a capital shot at all: he accidentally killed the turkey. He did not understand the use of a gun well enough to make a "capital shot." The turkey happened to sit in the way of the bullet, and was killed in consequence—that was all there was of it.

We have already said that pioneer families were dependent upon game for food. On this account fathers and sons became good marksmen, and even females were often expert with the rifle. Mrs. Lincoln could load and fire off a gun if necessary. In common with her sex, she was accustomed to such things, and adapted herself to circumstances.

Marvelous stories are told about the skill of the pioneers in the use of the rifle, and good authority substantiates their truthfulness. One writer says: "Several individuals who conceive themselves adepts in the management of the rifle, are often seen to meet for the purpose of displaying their skill and they put up a target, in the centre of which a common-sized nail is hammered for about two-thirds its length. The marksmen make choice of what they consider a proper distance, and which may be forty paces. Each man clears the interior of his tube, places a ball in the palm of his hand, and pours as much powder from his horn as will cover it. This quantity is supposed to be sufficient for any distance short of a hundred yards. A shot that comes very close to the nail is considered that of an indifferent marksman: the bending of the nail is of course somewhat better; but nothing less than hitting it right on the head is satisfactory. One out of three shots generally hits the nail and should the shooters amount to half a dozen, two nails are frequently needed before each can have a shot."

The same writer continues: "The snuffing of a candle with a ball I first had an opportunity of seeing near the banks of Green River, not far from a large pigeon-roost, to which I had previously made a visit. I had heard many reports of guns during the early part of a dark night, and knowing them to be those of rifles, I went forward toward the spot to ascertain the cause. On reaching the place, I was welcomed by a dozen tall, stout men, who told me they were exercising for the purpose of enabling them to shoot under night, at the reflected light from the eyes of a deer or wolf by torchlight. A fire was blazing near, the smoke of which rose curling among the thick foliage of the trees. At a distance which rendered it scarcely distinguishable, stood a burning candle, but which, in

reality was only fifty yards from the spot on which we all stood. One man was within a few yards of it to watch the effects of the shots, as well as to light the candle, should it chance to go out, or to replace it, should the shot cut it across. Each marksman shot in his turn. Some never hit either the snuff or the candle, and were congratulated with a loud laugh, while others actually snuffed the candle without putting it out, and were recompensed for their dexterity by numerous hurrahs. One of them, who was particularly expert, was very fortunate, and snuffed the candle three times out of seven, while all the other shots either put out the candle or cut it immediately under the light."

Such was the skill of riflemen at that day. Hence it was of considerable importance that boys should learn how to fire accurately. Not as a pastime was it valued, but as a means of gaining subsistence. In addition to procuring game for the table, furs were in great demand, and there were many animals valuable on this account. It was necessary, therefore, that Abraham should learn the art.

The summer of 1817 passed away, and early in the autumn the loneliness of their wilderness-life was somewhat relieved by the coming of old friends. Thomas and Betsy Sparrow, who reared Nancy Hanks (Mrs. Lincoln), came to settle by their side. Mr. Lincoln had just removed into his new cabin, so the Sparrows at once began housekeeping in the half-face camp. Dennis Hanks, also, had a home with the Sparrows, and Betsy was his aunt; so Dennis removed to Indiana with them.

It was a happy day for the Lincolns when the Sparrows became their neighbors.

"Sparrows on the house-top," had often regaled them with song, but the human Sparrows from Kentucky were to them more than song—they were society. To Abraham especially was their coming a real godsend for now he had an intimate and constant companion in his jolly cousin, Dennis Hanks. Such an acquisition to a boy in the woods was more of a boon than language can describe.

CHAPTER VI

DARKER DAYS

Abraham continued to peruse the three books of the family library, — the Bible, Catechism, and Spelling-Book. There was no prospect that another book of any sort would be added to the number. The thirst for knowledge begotten in his soul already was forced to find its aliment in this narrow compass. The result was, that he knew the Spelling-Book and Catechism by heart and he could repeat much of the Bible. His mind was hungry for knowledge but could not find enough to eat. It was daily put upon "short allowance."

In these circumstances he longed for other books. He began to tire of the Bible. "I don't want to read the Bible all the time," he often remarked; "I wish I could have some other book to read." He did not know what other books were in existence. His parents were not wiser than he in that respect. But his mind was ravenous, and would have accepted almost any sort of a literary dish, good, bad, or indifferent. It pleaded for books.

While he was in this famishing intellectual state, a fearful disease broke out among the settlers, called "the milk disease." Cows that gave the milk, and the people who drank it, became sick, suffered, and died. The first case was fifteen or twenty miles away, but near enough to create alarm in the Lincoln cabin. It was not long, however, before the dreaded visitor came to their door. Mr. and Mrs. Sparrow were stricken down by the disease nearly at the same time. It was in the summer of 1818. Consternation now turned the attention of Abraham from books to the perils of the hour. His longing for other books was exchanged for fear of sudden death.

The Sparrows were very sick, and no doctor within thirty or forty miles. Mr. Lincoln and his wife, together with other settlers, rendered all the assistance in their power to the ill-fated couple. Week after week their sufferings were prolonged, sometimes worse, sometimes better, hope rising or waning accordingly--

"We must remove them into our cabin," said Mrs. Lincoln to her husband; "they must have better quarters and care," Mr. and Mrs. Sparrow were as father and mother to Mrs. Lincoln, and her love for them was like that of a daughter.

"Perhaps it will be best; they can't live long any where in my opinion," Mr. Lincoln replied.

"I can look after them much better here," continued Mrs. Lincoln; "and whether they live or die, we shall have the satisfaction of knowing that we did everything in our power for them."

The sick couple was removed into the Lincoln cabin in September, and no one was more rejoiced over the event than Dennis Hanks, to whom, also, the Sparrows were as father and mother. Dennis emphasized his joy over the removal by saying he was glad "to get out of the mean little half-face campy."

The removal brought no relief to the sinking patients. In a few days both of them died, spreading gloom over the neighborhood, and creating the saddest experience Abraham and Dennis ever knew.

A spot was selected for the burial-place of the dead, about one half mile from the cabin, on a beautiful know that nestled under the shadow of mammoth trees. Mr. Lincoln was the only settler in the vicinity capable of making a coffin and he set about the sorrowful work, making them out of "green lumber, cut with a whipsaw." They were rough and heavy, like everything else connected with pioneer life but answered their purpose well. Without funeral ceremonies, the neighbors gathered from far and near, and tearfully committed their deceased friends to the dust.

A few days only elapsed after the burial, before Mrs. Lincoln was attacked, much more violently than the Sparrows, with the same dreaded disease. It was about three o'clock in the morning. Abraham was awakened out of a sound sleep, and hurried away for the nearest neighbor, Mrs. Woods, and, at the same time, Dennis, who became a permanent member of Lincoln's family after the death of the Sparrows, and was Abraham's bed-fellow in the loft, made his appearance, to render any assistance within his power. In the absence of physicians, a strong bond of sympathy united pioneer families, and the feminine members were always ready to tender their best nursing abilities to the sick. Nor were they altogether unsuccessful in their treatment. Some of them exhibited much skill in managing diseases, having been thrown upon their own resources for a long period, reflecting and studying for themselves. As physicians could not be had, they were compelled to do the best thing possible for themselves.

Mrs. Woods was not long in coming to her relief, and before the close of that day several other neighbors, who were notified of Mrs. Lincoln's sickness, came to proffer assistance. The tidings of her sudden attack spread so rapidly, that, within two or three days, all the pioneer families in the vicinity heard of it, and their proffers of assistance were prompt and tender. But the patient steadily grew worse, and soon became satisfied that her sickness would prove fatal. Some persons attacked with that singular disease lingered for weeks, as the Sparrows did; but Mrs. Lincoln's sickness was violent and brief. On the fifth day of October, she expired, leaving the Lincoln cabin more desolate than ever. Coming so speedily after the Sparrows passed away, death had additional terrors to the living. Dennis Hanks remembers the woe-begone appearance of Abraham from the time his mother's life was despaired of until weeks after she was laid in her grave. He was nine years old, thoughtful and sensible, not much inclined to talk about the event, but ever looking as if a pall were draw over his heart. The reader can imagine, perhaps, what no language can convey, the loss of a good mother to a bright, obedient, and trusting boy, hid away in the woods, where a mother's presence and love must be doubly precious. The bitter experience was well suited to make the loneliness of pioneer life vastly more lonely, and its real hardships vastly harder.

Preparations were made for the burial. With his own hands, Thomas Lincoln constructed a rough coffin for his wife, and she was laid beside the Sparrows on the knoll. One party thinks that one neighbor read the Scriptures and another offered prayer; but it is probable that she was buried, as her foster-parents were, without any ceremonies — silently deposited in the ground with no special tribute, save honest tears.

Here, better than elsewhere, we can describe an event that is worthy of record. It occurred several months after the death of Mrs. Lincoln.

"You must write a letter for me, Abe, to Parson Elkins," said his father, one evening. "You can write well enough now to do that." Abraham had passed his tenth birthday.

"If you can tell me what to write, I can do it," answered the boy.

"That I will do. It will be your first letter, you know, and you must remember that your father never wrote one—never knew enough to write one."

"What do you want I should write about?" inquired Abraham.

"Write about the death of your mother. He knows nothing about it yet and I want to ask him to visit us, and preach a funeral sermon."

"When do you want he should come?"

"When he can, I suppose. He'll take his own time for it, though I hope he'll come soon."

"He may be dead," suggested Abraham.

"What makes you think so."

"He's as likely to die as mother, ain't he and he may be dead when we don't know it, the same as she's dead when he don't know it."

"Well, there's something in that," answered his father; "but we'll see how you can make out writing a letter."

Pen and paper were provided, and Mr. Lincoln proceeded to dictate the letter. He directed him to write about the death of Mrs. Lincoln, when it occurred, and under what circumstances, and to invite him to visit them, and preach a funeral sermon. He also gave a description of their new home, and their journey thither, and wrote of their future prospects.

"Now read it over," said Mr. Lincoln.

"The whole of it?"

"Of course; I want to hear it all. I may think of something else by that time."

Abraham commenced to read it, while his father sat the very picture of satisfaction. There was genuine happiness to him in having his son prepared to write a letter. Never before had there been a member of his family who could perform this feat. It was a memorable event to him.

"See how much it is worth to be able to write," said he, as Abraham finished reading the letter. "It's worth ten times as much as it cost to be able to write only that one letter."

"It ain't much work to learn to write," said Abraham; "I'd work as hard again for it before I'd give it up."

"You'd have to give it up, if you were knocked about as I was when a boy."

"I know that."

"You don't know it as I do and I hope you never will. But it's worth more than the best farm to know how to write a letter as well as that."

"I shall write one better than that yet," said Abraham. "But how long will it take for the letter to go to Parson Elkins?"

"That's more than I can tell; but it will go there some time, and I hope it will bring him here."

"He won't want to come so far as this," suggested Abraham.

"It ain't so far for him as it was for us."

"Why ain't it?"

"Because he lives nearer the line of Indiana than we did. It ain't more than seventy-five miles for him to come, and he often rides as far as that."

The letter went on its errand, and Abraham was impatient to learn the result. On the whole, it was rather an important event in his young life,—the writing of that first letter. Was it strange that he should query whether it would reach the good minister to whom it was sent? Would it be strange if the writing of it proved one of the happy influences that started him off upon a career of usefulness and fame? We shall see.

Mr. Lincoln had much to say to his neighbors about the letter that his son had written, and they had much to say to him. It was considered remarkable for a boy of his age to do such a thing. Not one quarter of the adults in all that region could write and this fact rendered the ability of the boy in this regard all the more marvelous. It was noised abroad, and the result was, that Abraham had frequent applications from the neighbors to write letters for them. Nor was he indisposed to gratify their wishes. One of his traits of character was a generous disposition to assist others and it prompted him to yield to their wishes in writing letters for them. Nor was it burdensome to him, but the opposite. He delighted to do it. And thus, as a consequence of his acquiring the art of penmanship, far-distant and long-absent friends of the pioneer families heard from their loved ones.

The letter brought the parson. After the lapse of about three months he came. The letter reached him in Kentucky, after considerable delay, and he embraced the first opportunity to visit his old friends. Abraham had almost concluded that his letter was lost, as the favorite minister did not come. But one day, when the lad was about two miles from home, who should he see coming but Parson Elkins, on his old bay horse! He recognized him at once, and was delighted to see him.

"Why, Abe, is that you?" exclaimed the parson. "Am I so near your home?"

"Yes, sir; did you get my letter." Abraham thought of the memorable letter the first thing. He had good evidence before him that the letter reached its destination, but he would know certainly.

"Your letter!" exclaimed Parson Elkins, inquiringly. "I got your father's letter." Abraham did not stop to think that the letter went in his father's name.

"I wrote it," he said.

"You wrote it! Is that so?"

"Yes, sir; father can't write, you know."

"O, yes; I do remember now that he couldn't write and so you did it? Not many boys that can write like that."

"It was the first letter I ever wrote."

"Better still is that, —the first one? Well, you needn't be ashamed of that."

They were advancing towards the cabin during this conversation, Abraham running alongside the horse and the parson looking kindly upon him.

"There's our house!" exclaimed Abraham, as they came in sight of it. "We live there," pointing with his finger.

"Ah! that's a pleasant place to live. And there's your father, I think, too."

"Yes, that's he. He'll be glad to see you."

"And I shall be glad to see him."

By this time they came near Mr. Lincoln, who recognized Parson Elkins, and gave him a most cordial greeting. He was really taken by surprise, although he had not relinquished all expectation of the parson coming.

"You find me in a lonely condition," said Mr. Lincoln. "Death has made a great change in my family."

"Very great indeed," responded Mr. Elkins. "I know how great your loss is but whom the Lord loveth, he chasten."

Assenting to this, Mr. Lincoln continued—

"Now, let me say, that, while you are here, I want you should preach a funeral sermon. You know all about my wife. You will stay over next Sunday, won't you." "It was now Wednesday."

"Why, yes, I can stay as long as that, though I must be about my Master's work."

"You will be about your Master's work, if you stay and preach a funeral sermon and it may do a great sight of good."

"Very true and I shall be glad to stay for if any one ever deserved a funeral sermon, it is your wife. But where shall I preach it?"

"At her grave. I've had that arranged in my mind for a long time and we'll notify the people; there will be a large attendance. The people thought a deal of her here."

It was arranged that Mr. Elkins should preach the funeral sermon at the grave of Mrs. Lincoln on the following Sabbath. Accordingly, notice was sent abroad to the distance of twelve or fifteen miles, and a platform was erected near the grave. Every preparation was made for the solemn event. Although nearly a year had elapsed since Mrs. Lincoln died, yet a sermon to her memory was no less interesting to her surviving friends.

In the mean time, Mr. Elkins busied himself in intercourse with the family and he visited some of the neighbors, and conversed with them on spiritual things. Abraham, too, received his special attention. The boy had improved rapidly since he left Kentucky, and his remarkable precocity was suited to draw the attention of such a preacher.

The Sabbath arrived, — a bright, beautiful day. From a distance of twelve or fifteen miles, the settlers came to listen to the sermon. Entire families assembled parents and children, from the oldest to the youngest. Hoary age and helpless childhood were there. They came in carts, on horseback, and on foot, any way to get there. As they had preaching only when one of these pioneer preachers visited that vicinity, it was a treat to most of the inhabitants, and they manifested their interest by a general turn-out. The present occasion, however, was an unusual one, as the funeral sermon of Mrs. Lincoln was to be preached.

Parson Elkins was an earnest man, and the occasion inspired him with unusual fervor. None of the people had ever listened to him before, except the Lincoln family, and they were delighted with his services. His tribute to the memory of Mrs. Lincoln was considered just and excellent. None thought that too much was said in her praise. On the other hand, the general feeling was rather, as one of the number expressed it, that, "say what he might in praise of her, he couldn't say too much."

Abraham was deeply interested in the sermon, and it brought all his mother's tenderness and love afresh to his mind. To him it was almost like attending her funeral over again. Her silent dust was within a few feet of him, and vivid recollection of her worth was in his heart.

He drank in the sentiments of the discourse, too. He usually did this, as he was accustomed to think for himself. A few years later he often criticized the sermons to which he listened, much to the amusement of those with whom he conversed. He sometimes called in question the doctrines preached. This was one of the things in which his precocity appeared. It was at this point that his mental activity and power were often seen. But the sentiments of the aforesaid funeral sermon especially impressed his mind.

At this time of his life he was a close listener to the conversation of the neighbors and he would become almost vexed over the conversation of some of them, who talked so unintelligibly through ignorance, that he could not understand them. His active brain labored to compass every subject, and he sometimes fretted over unlettered talkers whose meaning he failed to comprehend. After he came into the possession of additional books, he was wont to discuss their subject-matter, and express his own views freely.

In this respect he was unlike most boys, who are superficial in their views of things. They read, and that is the end of it. They think no more about it—at least, they do not inquire into the juvy and wherefore of matters stated and so the habit of sliding over things loosely is formed. They do not think for themselves. They accept things as true, because others say they are true. They are satisfied with knowing that things are, without asking juvy they are. But Abraham was not so. He thought, reflected and this developed his mental powers faster than even school could do it.

The reader should understand more about these pioneer preachers, in order to appreciate the influences that formed Abraham's character, and therefore we will stop here to give some account of them.

They v/ere not generally men of learning and culture, though some of them were men of talents. Few, if any of them, were ever in college, and some of them were never in school. But they had a call to preach, as they believed, and good and true hearts for doing it. Many of them preached almost every day, traveling from place to place on horseback, studying their sermons in the saddle, and carrying about with them all the library they had in their saddle-bags. They stopped where night overtook them, and it was sometimes miles away from any human habitation, with no bed but the earth, and no covering but the canopy of heaven. They labored without a salary, and were often poorly clothed and scantily fed, being constrained to preach by the love of Christ. The following account of two pioneer preachers, by Milburn, will give the reader a better idea of this class of useful men than any description of ours, and it will be read with interest:—

"One of these preachers, who traveled all through the Northwestern Territory, a tall, slender, graceful man, with a winning countenance and kindly eye, greatly beloved by all to whom he ministered, was presented by a large landholder with a title-deed of three hundred and twenty acres. The preacher was extremely poor, and there had been many times when he received scarcely enough support to keep soul and body together. Yet he labored on, and did much good. He seemed pleased with his present of land and went on his way with a grateful heart. But in three months he returned, and met his benefactor at the door, saying, ' Here, sir, I want to give you back your title-deed.'

"What's the matter?" said his friend, surprised. "Any flaw in it?"

"No."

"Isn't it good land?"

"Good as any in the State."

"Sickly situation?"

"Healthy as any other."

"Do you think I repent my gift?"

"I haven't the slightest reason to doubt your generosity."

"Why don't you keep it, then?"

"Well, sir,' said the preacher, 'you know I am very fond of singing, and there's one hymn in my book the singing of which is one of the greatest comforts of my life. I have not been able to sing it with my whole heart since I was here. A part of it runs in this way:—

"No foot of land do I possess
No cottage in the wilderness;
A poor wayfaring man,
I lodge awhile in tents below,
And gladly wander to and fro,
Till I my Canaan gain;
There is my house and portion fair,
My treasure and my heart are there,
And my abiding home."

"Take your title-deed, he added; 'I had rather sing that hymn with a clear conscience than own America."

"There was another preacher of the pioneer class so intent upon his work that hunger and nakedness did not affright him. He was more scholarly than most of the preachers around him, and often sat up half the night, at the cabins of the hunters where he stopped, to study. These cabins were about twelve by fourteen feet, and furnished accommodations for the family, sometimes numbering ten or twelve children and, as the forests abounded in war mints the hens and chickens were taken in for safe keeping. Here, after the family had retired, he would light a pine knot, 'stick it up in one corner of the huge fireplace, lay himself down on the flat of his stomach in the ashes,' and study till far into the night.

"Many a time was the bare, bleak mountain-side his bed, the wolves yelling a horrid chorus in his ears. Sometimes he was fortunate enough to find a hollow log, within whose cavity he inserted his body, and found it a good protection from the rain or frost.

"Once, seated at the puncheon dinner-table with a hunter's family, the party is startled by affrighted screams from the door-yard. Rushing out, they behold a great wildcat bearing off the youngest child. Seizing a rifle from the pegs over the door, the preacher raises it to his shoulder, casts a rapid glance along the barrel, and delivers his fire. The aim has been unerring, but too late, —the child is dead, already destroyed by the fierce animal.

"That same year he had a hand-to-hand fight with a bear, from which conflict he came forth victor, his knife entering the vitals of the creature just as he was about to be enfolded in the fatal hug.

"Often he emerged from the wintry stream, his garments glittering in the clear, cold sunlight, as if they had been of burnished steel armor, chill as the touch of death. During that twelvemonth, in the midst of such scenes, he traveled on foot and horseback four thousand miles, practiced four hundred times, and found, on casting up the receipts, —yarn socks, woolen vests, cotton shirts, and a little silver change—that his salary amounted to twelve dollars and ten cents.

"Yet he persevered, grew in knowledge and influence, became a doctor of divinity, and finally was made president of a university. He is known on the page of history as Henry Bidleman Bascom."

Such were the pioneer preachers of the West of simple-hearted piety, lofty faith, a fiery zeal, unwavering fortitude, and a practical turn of mind, through which they did a great work for God.

We have made this digression from the thread of our story, to show what influences of the ministry were thrown around Abraham's early life. It is true the preachers to whom he listened were not "circuit riders," as traveling preachers were called. They were Baptist ministers, who lived within twenty miles, and who occasionally preached in that neighborhood. During the first few years of Abraham's residence in Indiana, there was one Jeremiah Cash, who sometimes preached in the vicinity, and the young listener became much interested in him. A few years later, two others came to that section of country to live. Their names were John Richardson and Young Lamar. One of them dwelt seven or eight miles from Abraham's home on the north, and the other eight or ten miles to the south and both of them were wont to preach at Mr. Lincoln's cabin, and at other cabins, as they had opportunity. Sometimes they preached in the open air, as Mr. Elkins did the funeral sermon. This was always the case when more people attended than could crowd into a log-house.

Such was all the pulpit influence that reached the boyhood and youth of Abraham. Yet it left indelible impressions upon his mind. Though it was small and inconstant, apparently, in comparison with the pulpit advantages that boys enjoy at the present day, it imbued his soul with sentiments that were never obliterated. He was much indebted to the unpolished eloquence of those pioneer preachers, whose sterling piety caused them to proclaim the truth with fidelity and earnestness. This was one of the few influences that contributed to make him a remarkable man.

CHAPTER VII
BRIGHTER HOURS

Abraham deeply felt the change that death had wrought in his cabin home, and, for weeks, his mind was absorbed in his loss. Perhaps his oppressive sense of loneliness and his grief would have continued, but for an unexpected blessing that came to him in the shape of a book. His father met with a copy of The Pilgrim's Progress, at the house of an acquaintance, twenty miles away or more and he borrowed it for Abraham. The boy was never more happily surprised than he was when his father, on his return, said:

"Look here, Abe, I've found something for you," at the same time exhibiting the book.

"Found it!" exclaimed Abraham, supposing that his father meant that he picked it up in the woods or fields.

"No, no; you don't understand me. I meant that I came across it at Pierson's house, and I borrowed it for you."

"Pilgrim's Progress," said Abraham, taking the book and reading the title; "that will be good, I should think." He knew nothing about the book; he never heard of it before.

"I shall want to hear it," said his father. "I heard about that book many years ago, but I never heard it read."

"What is it about?" asked Abraham.

"You'll find that out by reading it," answered his father.

"And I won't be long about it neither," continued Abraham. "I know I .shall like it."

"I know you will, too."

"I don't see how you know, if you never heard it read."

"On account of what I've heard about it."

And it turned out to be so. Abraham sat down to read the volume very much as some other boys would sit down to a good dinner. He found it better even than he expected. It was the first volume that he was provided with after the spelling-book. Catechism, and Bible, and a better one could not have been found. He read it through once, and was half-way through it a second time, when he received a present of another volume, in which he became deeply interested. It was sops Fables, presented to him, partly on account of his love of books, and partly because it would serve to occupy his mind and lighten his sorrow.

He read the fables over and over until he could repeat almost the entire contents of the volume. He was thoroughly interested in the moral lesson that each fable taught, and derived therefrom many valuable hints that he carried with him through life. On the whole, he spent more time over Aesop's Fables than he did over The Pilgrim's Progress, although he was really charmed by the latter. But there was a practical turn to the fables that interested him, and he could easily recollect the stories. Perhaps his early familiarity with this book laid the foundation for that facility at apt story-telling that distinguished him through life. It is easy to see how such a volume might beget and foster a taste in this direction. Single volumes have moulded the reader's character and decided his destiny more than once, and that, too, when far less absorbing interest was manifested in the book. It is probable, then, that Aesop's Fables exerted a decided influence upon Abraham's character and life. The fact that he read the volume so much as to .commit the larger part of it to memory adds force to this opinion.

With two new books of such absorbing interest, it was not strange that Abraham was disposed to neglect his daily labor. His father could readily discover that Aesop had more attractions for him than ax or hoe. Nor was he inclined to break the spell that bound him until he actually feared that the books would make him "lazy."

"Come, Abe, you mustn't neglect your work; we've lots to do, and books must not interfere," was his father's gentle rebuke.

"In a minute," answered the boy, just like most other boys of that age, who are "book-worms."

"That's what makes boys lazy, waiting to play or read, when they ought to be at work," continued his father. "All study and no work is 'most as bad as all work and no study."

"Only a minute, and I'll go," added Abraham, so absorbed in his book that he scarcely knew what answer he made.

"It must be a short minute," retorted his father in a tone of injured authority.

"I'll work hard enough to make it up when I get at it," said Abraham, still delaying.

"I don't know about that. I'm afraid that your thoughts will be somewhere else; so put down the book and come on."

With evident reluctance the young reader laid down his book, preliminary to obeying orders.

"Good boys obey at once," continued his father; "don't have to drive 'em like cattle."

"I only wanted to had a minute longer," answered Abraham, by way of palliating his offence.

"And I only wanted you shouldn't," exclaimed his father angrily. "I know what is best for you. I'm willing you should read and write, but you must work when work drives."

It was altogether new for Abraham to exhibit so much disobedience as he did after he became enthusiastic over The Pilgrim's Progress and ^sop's Fables. Nor was he conscious of possessing a disobedient spirit; for no such spirit was in his heart. He was simply infatuated with the new books.

We must not conceal the fact that his father had been somewhat annoyed by the boy's method of improving his penmanship by writing with chalk or a charred stick upon almost any surface that came in his way. But for his paternal pride over this acquisition of his boy, he might have checked him in this singular way of improvement. One incident occurred that served to reconcile his father in the main to his scrawls here and there, although he may have thought still that Abraham was carrying the matter too far.

An acquaintance came into the field where father and son were at work, when his eye was arrested by letters cut in the mellow soil.

"What's that?" he inquired.

Abraham smiled, and let his father answer.

"What's what?"

"Why, this writing, —it looks as if somebody had been writing on the ground."

"Abe's work, I suppose."

"Abe didn't do that!" answered the neighbor.

"I did do it with a stick," said the boy.

"What is it.?" The man couldn't read.

"It's my name."

"Your name, hey? Likely story."

"Well, 'tis, whether you believe it or not;" and he proceeded to spell it out, — "A-b-r-a-h-a-m L-i-n-c-o-l-n."

"Sure enough, it is and you certainly did it, Abe?"

"Yes, sir; and I will do it again, if you want to see me;" and, without waiting for an answer, he caught up a stick, and wrote his name again in the dirt.

"There 'tis," said Abraham.

"I see it, audit's well done," answered the neighbor.

And there, on the soil of Indiana, Abraham Lincoln wrote his name, with a stick, in large characters—a sort of prophetic act that students of history may love to ponder. For, since that day, he has written his name, by public acts, on the annals of every State in the Union.

From the time, however, that Abraham became absorbed in The Pilgrim's Progress and Aesop's Fables, he was subject to the charge of being "lazy." The charge gained force, too, as he grew older, and more books and increasing thirst for knowledge controlled him. Dennis Hanks said: "Abe was lazy, very lazy. He was always reading, scribbling, ciphering, writing poetry, and such like." John Romine declared that "Abe was awful lazy. He worked for me; was always reading and thinking; I used to get mad at him. He worked for me pulling fodder. I say Abe was awful lazy. He would laugh and talk, and crack jokes, and tell stories all the time; didn't love work, but did dearly love his pay. He worked for me frequently, a few days only at a time. He said to me one day, that his father taught him to work, but never learned him to love it."

Mrs. Crawford, for whose husband Abraham worked, and in whose cabin he read and told stories, said: "Abe was no hand to pitch into work like killing snakes." At the same time, Mr. Crawford could find no man to suit him as well as Abraham, when the latter was but fifteen years of age.

We protest, here and now, against this charge of laziness which some biographers have made so prominent. Nothing was ever more common than to charge studious boys and girls with laziness. A great many men and women, who know no better, bring the same charge against professional gentlemen. Any person who is not obliged to work on the farm, or at the forge, or engage in some other manual labor, for a livelihood, they pronounce lazy and aristocratic.

Through sheer ignorance, studying and literary aspirations are regarded as proof of laziness. It was so in Abraham's time. Because he possessed talents that craved knowledge as the appetite craves food, leading him to snatch fragments of time for reading, and perhaps to devote hours to the bewitching pastime that ought to have been given to hard work, careless, ignorant observers called him "lazy." It is a base slander. There was not a lazy bone in him. The boy who will improve such bits of time as he can save from his daily toil for study, and sit up nights to read the Life of Washington, or master a problem in mathematics, is not lazy. He may love a book more than he loves chopping or threshing, just as another may love the latter more than he does the former; but he is not lazy. Laziness wastes the spare hours of the day in bringing nothing to pass, and gives the night to sleep instead of mental improvement. As many of the busiest and most cheerful workers in our country are its scholars, without a particle of the element of laziness in their composition, so many of the most industrious and noble boys are those who prefer a book to the plow, and would rather go to school than to harvesting. That was true of Abraham Lincoln. His heart was set on books; but his hands were so ready for hard work, that any farmer was glad to hire him at the age of fourteen or fifteen years of age, because he would do more work than any youth of his age. He would chop more wood in a day, lift larger logs, and "pull more fodder," boy as he was, than half the men who hired him.

True, from the time that John Baldwin, the blacksmith, came into the neighborhood, when Abraham was about ten years old, he would steal away to the smithy's shop to listen to his stories. John was a great story-teller, and he was fond of children also, and these were attractions enough for such a precocious boy. His mind yearned for thoughts; it was desperate for entertainment and the blacksmith's stories, and incidents of his life, supplied both thoughts and entertainment. He spent much time with this jolly son of Vulcan before he began to tell stories himself, and, after that, he exchanged them with the smutty toiler at the forge. But there was no evidence of laziness in those visits to the blacksmith's shop. And when we place this freak of a singularly bright boy, together with all his other acts that denoted laziness to the ignorant pioneers, beside the fact, that in manhood, to the day of his death, Abraham Lincoln was one of the hardest workers who ever lived, both at manual and intellectual labor, ignoring all ten hour systems, and toiling fifteen, sixteen, and even eighteen hours a day, to satisfy his honorable ambition, the charge of laziness is branded as slander on the part of those who make it. "The boy is father to the man,"—the lazy boy makes the lazy man, and vice versa. If Abraham was a lazy boy, his manhood completely belied his youth, and the old maxim is exploded.

We have seen that they who called him lazy coupled the charge with the statement that he was always "reading and thinking," evidently considering that his love of books was proof of a disposition to shirk labor. Their ignorance is the explanation of and excuse for, their charge.

We have made this digression, at this point, in order to direct the attention of the reader to an important element of Lincoln's character that will find ample support in the sequel.

Now that we are speaking of Abraham's books, we may record the facts about two other volumes that came into his hands within two years after Aesop's Fables. They were Ramsay's Life of Washington and Robinson Crusoe,

Dennis Hanks came home one day and said to Abraham—
"Don't you want to read the life of Washington?"
"Of course I do," was his reply. "What do you ask me that for?"
"Because I've seen one."
"Where?"
"Down at Anderson's Creek."
"Whom did it belong to?"
Dennis told him, adding, "He offered to lend it to me."
"Then I can borrow it?"
"Any time you are there; there's no doubt of it."

Without recording the details of this affair, it will answer our purpose to say that Abraham embraced the first opportunity to secure the loan of that valuable biography. He knew that Washington was called the "father of his country" —that he was commander-in-chief of the army in the American Revolution. He had been told, also, of the part his grandfather took in the "war of independence." This was all he knew of the illustrious statesman whose life he purposed to read but this was quite enough to awaken his enthusiasm over the volume. It was read and re-read with the deepest interest, and its contents discussed with his father and Dennis, both of whom learned more about Washington and his times from Abraham than they ever knew before.

It is not known how he came into possession of Robinson Crusoe. Doubtless the book was borrowed and it proved a source of genuine satisfaction to him. Once reading it only created the desire to read it a second time, and even a third time. There was a kind of witchery about the book to his active mind different from that exerted over him even by The Pilgrim's Progress. He could scarcely command language to express his admiration of the volume.

CHAPTER VIII
A NEW MOTHER AND SCHOOLS

Mr. Lincoln remained a widower until December, 1819. During this time his only housekeeper was his daughter Sarah. Abraham was a "handy boy" about the cabin, and often rendered timely aid to his sister in her daily work. He became so expert in household matters, that, a few years later, when he "worked out" among the farmers, their wives pronounced him the "best hand" because he was so "handy," and was willing to make fires, bring wood and water, or tend the baby. It was evidently a good school for him, since his manhood was characterized by being "handy about the house." A dweller in Springfield, Illinois, where Abraham commenced his public life, in 1837 remembers how he "used to draw the baby back and forth in front of his house, early in the summer morning, while his wife was getting breakfast, at the same time reading a book that he held in one hand."

But Thomas Lincoln needed a wife, and his son needed a mother. Household affairs had been left "at loose ends," as they are likely to be where there is no mother to superintend. There was not that neatness and order necessary to make even a cabin home attractive and what clothes the children had were in a very dilapidated condition. It was both wise and necessary for Lincoln to go in search of a wife.

He remembered Sally Bush, of Elizabethtown, Kentucky, to whom he once proposed, but who preferred another, one Johnson by name. She married the latter instead of Lincoln. Her husband died three years before Mrs. Lincoln did, and Thomas Lincoln knew that she was a widow. Where would he be so much inclined to go as there for a good wife? Where could he go with more hope of success?

Lincoln posted away to Kentucky, found Widow Johnson, proposed, and was accepted. On the following day they were married. Mrs. Johnson possessed a good supply of furniture for that day, so much as to require a four-horse team to remove it to Indiana. She owned a bureau that cost forty dollars, a clothes-chest, table and six chairs, together with a quantity of bedding, crockery, tin-ware and iron-ware. Ralph Browne, Mr. Lincoln's cousin, removed both goods and bride, with her three children—John, Sarah and Matilda—to Indiana. With this rather large accession for one match, Thomas Lincoln numbered eight souls in his household—all to dwell in a cabin with a single room and loft. Still, it was, on the whole, as the sequel will show the best bargain that Thomas Lincoln ever made.

Abraham was filled with wonder on the arrival of his new mother and her goods. Such a quantity of "household stuff" his eyes never beheld before; and he could scarcely believe that his home would boast, henceforth, a "bureau, clothes-chest and real chairs." His stepmother, too, won his heart at once. He thought she was just the woman to own such a bureau —the latter was a fitting accompaniment to the former.

The second Mrs. Lincoln was better educated than the first. She could not only read and write, but she was reared in girlhood under more favorable circumstances than Nancy Hanks. In her teens she was rather the belle of the town, or, at least, she was one of them. One person said, "she was the best and proudest of the Bushes." She dressed better, was more tidy and brighter than most of the girls around her. The girl was mother to the woman, so that Thomas Lincoln found he had a wife in her who was ambitious for personal appearance and comfort. One of the first things she set her husband about, after settling in Indiana, was to make a floor to the cabin. Then she posted him away to the only place where he could buy window-sashes and doors, twenty or thirty miles distant, for these indispensable articles. When the Lincoln cabin had a floor, a real door and real windows, and was furnished with a veritable bed, bureau, chairs, crockery, etc., it presented quite a respectable appearance. It was certainly a much neater, more orderly and attractive abode than it ever was before. The change which Mrs. Lincoln wrought in the habitation, in a very short time, was indicative of a smart, enterprising woman, possessing much executive ability.

It was a glorious day for Abraham when a faithful and intelligent stepmother was installed over his dreary home. Her advent brought such cheerfulness to him as he had not known since his own mother was laid in her grave. He gave her a hearty welcome and a large place in his heart. Her son and daughters, too, he received as a true brother. They v/ere better clad than himself and more tidy; but soon, under his good stepmother's care, he was made as neat and prim as they. The two families of children became as one family soon, and no discord ever rose among them. Abraham became strongly attached to the two Johnson girls, who were bright and social and they came to regard him, not only as a brother, but also as a prodigy. Their coming lifted Abraham into a higher plane of social life.

Dennis Hanks, who was a member of the family at the time, says, "In a few weeks all had changed and where everything was wanting, now all was snug and comfortable. She was a woman of great energy, of remarkable good sense, very industrious and saving, and also very neat and tidy in her habits, and knew exactly how to manage children. She took an especial liking to young Abe. Her love for him was warmly returned, and continued to the day of his death. But few children loved their parents as he loved his stepmother. He was encouraged by her to study, and any wish on his part was gratified when it could be done. The two sets of children got along finely together, as if they had been children of the same parents. Mrs. Lincoln soon discovered that Abraham was a boy of uncommon natural talents, and that, if rightly trained, a bright future was before him, and she did all in her power to develop those talents."

We may add, here, once for all, that Dennis Hanks subsequently married one of the Johnson girls, and Allen Hall, another cousin of Abraham, the other. A granddaughter of Dennis Hanks, Mrs. H. A. Chapman, says of Mrs. Lincoln, "My grandmother was a very tall woman, straight as an arrow, fair complexion, and was, as I first remember her, very handsome, sprightly, talkative, and proud; wore her hair curled till gray; was kind-hearted, and very charitable, and also very industrious."

A new mother was not the only boon that Abraham received in that winter of 1819-20. For the first time in Indiana a school opened for him.

"I hear that a man by the name of Dorsey is going to keep school," said Mr. Lincoln to his son;" and you can go, and the other children too." He learned the news of a neighbor whom he met on that day.

"Who is Dorsey?" inquired Abraham.

"I don't know, only he is a man who is going to keep school down by Little Pigeon Creek; and he's good in reading, writing, and ciphering."

"A good chance for you, Abe," remarked his stepmother, whom we shall know hereafter only as mother. "You want to know something about arithmetic as soon as you can; the sooner the better."

"Where shall I get an arithmetic to study?"

"As to that, I can find one somewhere," replied his father. "I shall go to market before the week is out, and I will see what I can find among the settlers there on the way. You must study arithmetic somehow."

"A good day for you, Abe, when you learn to cipher," added his mother. "Even a poor chance to learn that is better than none. Two miles will be just far enough for you to walk to keep your legs limber."

Settlers had come into that region rapidly, and had put up a log-house, two miles from Lincoln's, to serve as a schoolhouse whenever an occasion might arise. It was a poor affair. Dorsey could just stand up under the roof, and he was no taller than Abraham. It had "holes for windows," in which greased paper was used instead of glass. A large fire-place, that would admit logs four feet in length, was the only cheerful object within and the boys appeared to think so for they piled on the fuel by the half cord, and made the biggest blaze possible.

To this pioneer school Abraham went with a glad heart. His father found an old arithmetic somewhere, in a damaged condition, and he bought it for him. His mother made him a new suit of clothes, for his old suit was much the worse for wear. It was not made of broadcloth or cassimere but of such material as could be obtained. It consisted of a linsey-woolsey shirt, buckskin breeches, low shoes made of leather tanned in the family, and a cap of coon-skin. Overcoats were unknown.

Here Abraham became particularly interested in arithmetic and "spelling for places." In reading and writing, he was fully equal to his teacher, and, also in spelling. But he never spelled in classes before for places, an exercise which the boys christened with the name, "trapping up and down." Abraham always "trapped up," so his contestants said. He never missed a word, and was always found at the head of his class, except when he took his place at the foot, according to the custom, to "trap up" again.

This school continued but a few weeks and, as Abraham never had but two more opportunities to attend school, we shall devote the remainder of this chapter to the details of his experience.

Four years later— in 1823 —one Andrew Crawford, who lived in Spencer County, opened a school in the same log-house in which Dorsey taught. He was much better educated than any of Abraham's previous teachers. He was first-class for that day and place. He was a master, too, with whom boys could not trifle. He was "great on thrashing" one boy said.

Abraham attended this school, and became more enthusiastic than ever over his studies. He had found a more congenial teacher; and Crawford appeared to understand him thoroughly, and to know how to lead him. Teacher and pupil were never on better terms than were Crawford and Abraham. Crawford saw in the lad the foreshadowing of a great man. He had no doubt of it, and he did not hesitate to express his admiration of the boy. He said to Mr. Lincoln one day:

"Abe is a wonderful boy— the best scholar I ever Ind. He's never satisfied without knowing all about his lessons. He wants to know every thing that anybody else knows, and he doesn't see why he can't.

"That's Abe exactly," responded Mr. Lincoln. "He cares more for a book than anything else. I sometimes wish he liked work as much as he does a book."

"He couldn't like both equally well," continued Crawford; "that's impossible. If he liked work with all his soul, he would not be so great a scholar—he could not be such a scholar."

"Maybe; but work is more necessary to backwoods life than books," said Mr. Lincoln, who failed to look into the future as Mr. Crawford did. "Pioneers ought to know more than I do, but they needn't know everything."

"But Abe will not live in the backwoods all his days. Even if he should continue to live in Spencer County, he will not be a backwoodsman long. As immigration is going on now, by the time he is thirty years old he will be out of pioneer life. But such a boy will rise above such a life. His ability and perseverance will overcome obstacles, and he will make his mark. Abe is as good, too, as he is bright."

"Yes; Abe's a good boy," responded his father. "We can't expect boys will do right always, you know but Abe's good to mind. His mother thinks there never was such a boy." And this last testimony was a confirmation of what we have said of his filial love and obedience.

"I was struck with his honesty the other day," added Mr. Crawford. "I saw that a buck's horn that was nailed on the schoolhouse was broken off, and I concluded that some of the boys did it. So I asked them the next day, when they had all got still, which of them broke it, and Abe answered promptly, "I did it."

"Just like him," said his father.

"I said, how happened that, Abe?"

"I didn't mean to do it," he replied. "I hung on it and it broke. I wouldn't have done it if I had thought it would break."

"I dare say he spoke the truth," said his father.

"I have no doubt of it but few boys would own up like that. Most boys would try to conceal what they had done, and wouldn't own it till they were obliged to."

"That's so and I've thought that it might be owing a little to the Life of Washington that he read some time ago. He seemed to think a sight of his owning up that he cut the cherry tree with his new hatchet and he spoke of it ever so many times."

"Well, this was certainly like that," said Mr. Crawford; "and I took occasion to say that it was a noble trait to confess a wrong that was done, instead of trying to conceal it."

"He never was disposed to conceal his wrongdoings. He takes all the blame to himself, and don't try to put it on to anybody else."

"I should think so and such truthfulness is worthy of all praise," said Mr. Crawford.

Nat Grigsby attended Crawford's school, and he says: "Essays and poetry were not taught in this school, but Abe took them up on his own account. He first wrote short sentences on 'cruelty to animals,' and finally came out with a regular composition on the subject. He was very much annoyed and pained by the conduct of the boys, who were in the habit of catching terrapins and putting coals of fire on their backs. He would chide us, tell us it was wrong, and would write against it."

This statement shows that Abraham's teacher encouraged him in just those exercises that contributed to his rapid mental growth. Evidently he understood the boy, as we have said, and gave him an impulse, onward and upward, that he never ceased to feel. Here he first attempted the role of poet, as well as essayist and, also, played the part of orator. He possessed a remarkable memory, and could repeat long paragraphs from the books he had read and the sermons he had heard. He was wont to recite these for the amusement of his companions and, one day, he was displaying his oratorical powers upon a stump, when one of the boys threw a terrapin against a tree near the speaker, crushing the poor animal so cruelly that he writhed upon the ground, exciting the tender sympathies of Abraham, and causing him to strike out upon an oration or sermon (whatever we may call it) against cruelty to animals, denouncing the act as inhuman, and holding up the boy who did it to scorn until he writhed under the scorching rebuke well nigh as much as the terrapin did through his thoughtless act.

At another time he became the counsel for a terrapin on whose back the boys were putting coals of fire.

"Don't," exclaimed Abraham, as if he felt the burning coals upon his own back.

"Don't what?" responded a boy, at the same time giving the terrapin a punch with a stick.

"Don't be so cruel," continued Abraham; "how would you like to have coals put on your own back?"

"Try it, and see," shouted one.

"Well, it is cruel to treat him so—and mean, too," persisted Abraham.

"Why, Abe, it's nothing but a terrapin," interjected a boy.

"Don't terrapins have feelings?" responded our hero.

"I don't know whether they do or not," replied the first named boy, at the same time adding another coal of fire to the animal's back.

"You shan't do it, Nat, unless you are stronger than I am," exclaimed Abraham, knocking the last coal from the animal's back, and pushing the boy with the stick aside.

"You're a chicken-hearted feller, Abe, as ever lived," continued Nat. "I should think the terrapin was your brother."

"Whether he is or not, you won't burn him any more while I'm 'round."

"That's it," said Dave Turnham, who stood looking on. "I go in for Abe. He wouldn't hurt a fly."

"He would if he trod on it," retorted Nat, aiming to be funny.

Mr. Crawford had witnessed a part of this scene, and he came out at this stage of the affair, and rebuked the cruelty of the boys who were torturing the terrapin, while he commended Abraham for his tenderness.

"We are coming to the Rule of Three now," said Mr. Crawford to Abraham, "and that will be all you can learn of me."

"Is it hard." asked the boy.

"It won't be for you. I think you can get through it by the time your father wants you this spring."

"Why is it called the Rule of Three?"

"I hardly know. Some call it Simple Proportion and that is the true name for it. You will see a reason for it, too, when you come to master it."

"What if I don't master it?"

"I'll risk you on that. It won't be of so much use to you as what you have been over already. Some people don't study it."

"My father never studied arithmetic," said Abraham.

"Nor mine. Not half the folks about here have studied it."

"Father never had a chance to study it when he was a boy."

"That's the case with a good many."

"Well, I can cipher now in Addition, Subtraction, Multiplication, and Division."

"Yes, you understand these rules well, and you will always find use for them."

Encouraged by his instructor, Abraham grappled with the so-called "Rule of Three." It was somewhat more difficult for him to comprehend this rule than it was the previous ones yet he was not discouraged. His discriminating mind and patient labor did the work for him, and he enjoyed the happiness of understanding Proportion by the time his school-days were over. We do not mean that he comprehended it fully, so as to be complete master of it, but he understood it, as we arc wont to say that pupils understand the rules they have been over at school. At least, he made such progress that he was prepared to become master of all the rules he had studied, by devoting his leisure moments to them thereafter.

We must stop here to relate another incident of those school-days, because it illustrates a trait of character for which Abraham was well known in his youth. We often find the key to a boy's character by observing his intercourse with companions at school.

It was near the end of his term of school at Crawford's. Several boys were on their way home at the close of school in company with Abraham, when a difficulty arose between two of them about spelling a word.

"You didn't spell it right," said John.

"Yes, I did spell it right," replied Daniel. "I spelt it just as Mr. Crawford did."

"He said you didn't spell it so."

"I know he said so, but he didn't understand me. I spelt it just as he did."

"I know you didn't," continued John.

"And I know I did," retorted Daniel. "You are a liar, if you say so."

"Don't call me a liar!" exclaimed John, doubling up his fist. "You'll get it, if you say that again!"

"I stump you to do it, old mad piece!" said Daniel, putting himself in an attitude of defiance.

"Come, Dan, don't," said Abraham, throwing one of his arms over his neck.

"Let him come, if he wants to," said John, in a great rage; "I'll give it to him: he's a great coward."

"What's the use, John." interrupted Abraham, throwing his other arm around John's shoulders, so as to bring himself between the two wrathy boys; "that ain't worth fighting about."

"Yes, it is, too," answered John. "You wouldn't be called a liar by anybody I know, and I won't neither." Abraham was now walking along between the two boys, with his arms over their shoulders.

"Yes, I would, too; and I shouldn't care neither, if it wasn't true."

"Nobody would think of calling you a liar," added John.

"They wouldn't call you so, if you didn't care anything about it," answered Abraham and there was much truth in the remark.

By this time the two combatants had cooled off considerably and Daniel put out the last spark of fire by adding, "I'll take it back, John."

"That's a good fellow," said Abraham, while John was mute. Five minutes thereafter the two vexed boys were on good terms, their difficulties having been adjusted by Abraham, "the peace-maker," as he was often called. He could not endure to see broils among his companions, and he often taxed all his kind feelings and ingenuity to settle them. This trait of character was prominent through all his life. Last, though not least, we had an exhibition of it, when, at the outbreak of the Rebellion in 1861, he put his arms around the neck of both North and South, and attempted to reconcile them. But his effort proved less successful than it did in the case of John and Daniel for the southern combatant was fully determined to fight.

Abraham was by far the best speller in Crawford's school. It was not expected by teacher or pupils that he would miss a word. More than that he sometimes taxed his ingenuity to help others out of difficulty in their spelling classes. One day a class was spelling, and Crawford put out the word defied. The girl to whom the word was given spelled it de-f-i-de. The next one, d-e-f-y-d; the third, d-e-f-y-d-e; the fourth, d-e-f-y-e-d ; and soon, not one spelling the word correctly, Crawford became angry.

"What!" he bawled out, "these big boys and girls not able to spell the simple word defied! There shan't one of you go home to-night if you don't spell it, you lazy, ignorant louts."

Just then, a girl in the class by the name of Roby, to whom Abraham was somewhat partial, looked up, and took a valuable hint from his smiling face. To use her own language, as she described the scene many years thereafter:—

"I saw Abe at the window; he had his finger in his eye, and a smile on his face. I immediately took the hint, that I must change the letter j into an i. Hence I spelled the word— the class was let out. I felt grateful to Abe for this simple thing."

Notwithstanding Crawford's was a "pioneer college," he taught "manners." He rather prided himself on teaching his pupils etiquette, at least, as far as he knew. Imparting to his scholars some idea about cultivated society in thoroughly civilized places, he converted his school-room into a parlor of "ladies and gentlemen." One pupil was required to go out, then re-enter in the role of a gentleman or lady stranger, whom another pupil introduced to every one in the room. Imagine Abraham, almost six feet high, though but fifteen years of age, homely as he could well be, clumsy and gawky in his appearance, clad in pioneer style, with legs and arms out of all proportion to his head and body, going through this ordeal of refinement! Nat. Grigsby describes Abraham, at that time, thus: "He was long, wiry and strong; while his big feet and hands, and the length of his legs and arms, were out of all proportion to his small trunk and head. His complexion was very swarthy, and his skin was shriveled and yellow even then. He wore low shoes, buckskin breeches, linsey-woolsey shirt, and a cap made of the skin of an opossum or coon. The breeches clung close to his thighs and legs, but failed by a large space to reach the tops of his shoes. Twelve inches remained uncovered, and exposed that much of shin bone, sharp, blue, and narrow." It must have been a comical sight, when this overgrown and awkward boy was required to play the gentleman, and was put through a course of "manners" indispensable to pioneers, as Crawford thought. It did him good, however, as we judge from the words of Mrs. Josiah Crawford, for whose husband Abraham subsequently worked. She said, "Abe was polite; lifted his hat on meeting strangers and always removed it from his head on coming into the house."

Three years after Abraham attended Crawford's school, he attended another, nearly five miles distant, taught by one Swaney. He continued but a short time at this school, since the great distance consumed too much of his time. But John Hoskins, who was a fellow-pupil, declares that "Abe took the lead, and was big in spelling," when "we would choose up, and spell every Friday night."

Here, Abraham's school-days ended and all his schooling amounted to less than one year. Nevertheless, according to David Turnham, he completely drained his teachers. We have his word for it that "Abe beat all his masters, and it was no use for him to try to learn any more from them."

We may add, in closing this chapter that about this time, Levi Hall, a relative of the Lincolns, removed from Kentucky with his family, and settled near them. Also John Hanks, cousin of the first Mrs. Lincoln, and son of Joseph Hanks of Elizabethtown, of whom Tom Lincoln learned the carpenter's trade, came to live with the latter. John had no education could neither read nor write but he was a temperate, upright, truthful man, without a particle of Abraham's wit, and none of his extreme awkwardness. He lived four years with Mr. Lincoln; then returned to Kentucky whence he removed to Illinois, where we shall meet him again.

CHAPTER IX
BORROWING AND WHAT CAME OF IT

The greatest man that ever lived!" said Abraham, as he sat upon a log in the woods, conversing with David Turnham, "This country has a right to be proud of Washington."

"That is your opinion but I guess the British won't say so," answered David.

"And that is just because they were whipped by him and they don't want to own up."

"How do you know so much about Washington, Abe?"

"Because I have read about him and I always heard that he made the red-coats run for life."

"Who do you mean by the red-coats?"

"Why, the British, to be sure. They were called 'red-coats,' because they wore coats of that color, I expect that they looked splendidly, though they didn't feel very splendidly, I guess, after they got whipped."

"Have you read the Life of Washington?"

"Of course I have, a good while ago. I read Ramsay's Life of Washington, and that shows that he was the greatest man who ever lived."

"Is that like the one Josiah Crawford has?"

"I didn't know that Mr. Crawford had a Life of Washington."

"Well, he has for I heard him talking with father about it."

"How long ago?"

"Not more than two or three weeks ago."

"You don't know the name of the author? There are lives of Washington written by different men."

"I don't remember who wrote this. I didn't mind much about what they were saying."

"I can find out," added Abraham; and he did find out. He embraced the first opportunity to inquire of a neighbor, and learned that it was Weems's Life of Washington that Mr. Crawford owned.

"Can I borrow it?" he inquired of his parents, for he was very anxious to read it.

"Perhaps he won't like to lend it," answered his mother.

"I shall find that out when I ask him," said Abraham.

"And you should tell him that you will not take it unless he is perfectly willing to let you have it."

"Then I may ask him, may I?"

"If you are very desirous to read it."

"Well, I am, and I will go there to-night when I get through work."

Abraham was elated with the idea of getting hold of this new work. He viewed the character of Washington with admiration, and he would know what different biographers said of him. He was not a little impatient for his day's work to be done. He toiled as usual, however, with a good degree of interest in his work, until night, when he prepared himself to call on Mr. Crawford.

The family gave him a cordial welcome, and Mrs. Crawford said: "I wonder what has brought you out tonight. I haven't seen you here for a long time."

"Perhaps you won't be so glad to see me after you learn what I came for," replied Abraham.

"And what did you come for, that makes you think so?" asked Mr. Crawford.

"I came to borrow a book."

"A book, hey! That is a good errand, I am sure."

"But I did not know as you would be willing to lend it."

"What book is it?" asked Mr. Crawford. "I have no doubt that I can accommodate you."

"It is the Life of Washington. I was told that you had it, and I want to read it."

"I wish all the boys wanted to read it," said Mr. Crawford. "I will lend it to you, Abe, with great pleasure. I am glad to see that you like to read."

"I will not take it unless you are perfectly willing to lend it," said Abraham.

"If I did not want you should have it, I should tell you so. I am not one of those persons who are afraid to tell what they think. I am glad that I have the book to lend you."

"I will take good care of it, and return it to you all safe," responded Abraham. This was just like him. So considerate a boy would not ask the loan of a book without some diffidence, and when it was borrowed, he would feel that great care must be used to preserve it. He valued the few books which he himself possessed so highly as to lead him to think that other people held their volumes in equal estimation. It was really an excellent trait of character that caused him to use so much discretion in borrowing books, for the borrowing of this single article has been the occasion of much trouble in neighborhoods. In consequence of thoughtlessness and less regard for the interests of others than their own, many persons have borrowed books and never returned them, or else returned them in a much worse condition than when they were received. Frequently books are lost in this way from Sabbath-school and other libraries. Borrowers do not return them. They think so little of their obligations, that the books are forgotten and lost. Book borrowers are very apt to be negligent, so that when we see a lad so particular as Abraham was, it is worth while to take note of the fact.

"It will take me some time to read so large a work," said he, as he took it from Mr. Crawford. "Perhaps you will want it before I get through with it."

"Oh, no; you are such a great reader that you will finish it in short metre. Keep it as long as you want it, and I shall be suited."

"I thank you," Abraham replied, as he arose to leave. "Good night."

"Good night," several voices responded.

It was a very joyful evening to Abraham as he bore that Life of Washington home, and sat down about the middle of the evening to read the first chapter therein.

"Keep it nice," said his mother. "Remember that it is a borrowed book."

"I will try," he replied. "Mr. Crawford was perfectly willing to lend it, and I shall be none the less careful on that account."

Those were pleasant hours of leisure that he devoted to reading Weems's Life of Washington. Every evening, after his day's labor was completed, he read the work with absorbing interest, and at other times, when he could find a spare moment, it was in his hand. He had nearly completed it, when the following mishap caused him many unpleasant thoughts and feelings.

A driving storm was raging, so that he could perform little labor except what could be done under cover. Of course his book was in his hand much of the time, and the whole of the dreary evening, to a late hour, was his companion. On going to bed, he laid it down directly under a large crack between the logs, and the wind changing in the night, the rain was driven into the house, and the book was wet through. The first sight that met Abraham's eyes in the morning was the drenched book, and his feelings can be better imagined than described.

"O dear!" he exclaimed. "That book is spoiled!" And he could scarcely restrain the tears that welled up to his eyes.

"How did you happen to lay it there?" asked his mother.

"I never thought about its raining in there. But only look at it is completely soaked!" and he lifted it up carefully to show his mother.

"Oh, I am so sorry! it is ruined!" she said.

"I can dry it," answered Abraham, "but that will not leave it decent. See! the cover will drop off, and there is no help for it. What will Mr. Crawford say." I told him that I would keep it very carefully, and return it to him uninjured."

"Well, it is done, and can't be helped now," added his mother; "and I have no doubt that you can fix it with Mr. Crawford."

"I have no money to pay him for it, and I don't see how I can make it good to him. He ought to be paid for it."

"Of course he had, and he may want you to do some work for him, which will be the same as money to him. You'd better take the book to him today and see what you can do."

"I am almost ashamed to go. He will think that I am a careless fellow."

"Never be ashamed to do right, my son."

"I am not ashamed to do right. I was only saying how I felt. I told him that I would keep it nicely."

"And so you meant to; but accidents will happen, sometimes, even if we are careful."

"He shall be paid for it somehow," continued Abraham. "I will see him today."

The volume was exposed to the heat of the fire that day, and when Abraham was ready to go to Mr. Crawford's in the evening, it was dry enough for transportation. The storm had passed away, and the stars were looking down from the skies, as he took the book, carefully wrapped in a cotton handkerchief, and proceeded to Mr. Crawford's. His heart was heavy and sad, and he dreaded to open the subject to him.

"Good evening, Abe! Got through with the book so quick?" said Mr. Crawford.

"Good evening," responded Abraham, in his usual manly way. "I have brought the book back, although I have not finished it."

"Keep it, then, keep it," replied Mr. Crawford, before the lad could tell his story. "I told you to keep it as long as you wanted it."

"Perhaps you won't want I should keep it when you hear what has happened to it." And he proceeded to untie the handkerchief in which it was wrapped.

"There," continued Abraham, exhibiting the book; "it is ruined. I laid it down last night where the rain beat in and wet it through, and it is spoiled. I'm very sorry indeed, and want to pay you for it in some way."

Josiah Crawford was a hard man by nature, and an excess of whiskey made him harder. He was not a relative of Andrew Crawford, the teacher, although he was like him in one particular—he had an ungovernable temper. At sight of the ruined volume his countenance changed, and he snapped out in his wrath.

"Carelessness! Pretty mess for a borrowed book."

Had he not been a good friend of Abraham, there is no telling what abuse he might have heaped upon the boy. As it was, with all his regard for Abraham as an uncommon youth, he poured out large vials of wrath upon him, the boy all the while declaring that he was willing to pay for it.

"I've ruined the book, and I'll do any work you say to pay for it. Have you any work I can do?"

Crawford's wrath abated somewhat when he heard the word work. The idea of getting work out of the lad was tempting to him for he was an unscrupulous, avaricious, stingy man, and now was his time to take advantage of Abraham's generosity.

"Yes, work enough," he growled, angry as a panther that prowled about the forest at night.

"How much was the book worth?" asked Abraham.

"Mor'n I'll ever get," Crawford growled again.

"I'll work to pay its full value, and keep it for my own, if you say so," continued Abraham.

After further parleying, Crawford, seeing his opportunity to make something out of Abraham, cooled down to ordinary heat, and proceeded to say:

"I tell you what it is, Abe, I'm in great trouble about my corn. You see the whole of my corn has been stripped of the blades as high as the ear, and is now ready to have the tops cut off for winter fodder but my hands are full of other work, and how it is to be done is more than I can tell. Now, if you can help me out of this scrape, we can square the account about the book."

"I'll do it," replied Abraham, with emphasis. "How much of it shall I cut?"

"All of it, of course," answered Crawford, unpleasantly; "you can't expect to get such a book for nothing."

Abraham v/as taken somewhat by surprise by this exorbitant demand; nevertheless, he was equal to the occasion, and promptly responded:

"Well, then, I'll cut the whole of it; when shall I begin?"

"Tomorrow morning;" and the exacting manner in which he thus proceeded awakened Abraham's contempt for him. Still he answered:

"Tomorrow morning it is, then; I'll be on hand as early as you want to see me."

Abraham hastened home and reported. His parents united with him in the opinion that it was one of Crawford's acts of extortion. Still, they were glad that their son could settle the affair in some way.

Abraham undertook to redeem his pledge on the next day, and, bright and early, he was in Crawford's cornfield. There were several acres of the corn, and several days of very hard work would be required to finish the job. Abraham bent himself to the task with more than usual determination, and completed it in about three days, although ordinarily, a man would have needed nearly five days in which to perform the work. Abraham never forgot the extortion which Crawford practiced upon him, and he always despised his overreaching propensity. Still, he was glad to own another volume, especially one of so much value as Weems's Life of Washington. That Crawford forgot his own meanness, is quite evident from the fact, that, subsequently, he sought Abraham's services, and those of his sister to assist his wife. Both Abraham and Sarah were glad of the opportunity to earn an honest dollar, and accepted his proposition. They lived with Crawford several months during that year, and pleased the crabbed old fellow mightily. Abraham finished his log house by "daubing it," that is, filling the interstices between the unhewn logs with clay, especially the loft in which he lodged.

He split many rails for Crawford during that season, planted, sowed and harvested, receiving only twenty five cents a day. If he lost only a few minutes from hard work, as he would on some days, his employer deducted it from his small wages, thereby exposing his contemptible spirit, though Abraham never protested.

Abraham might not have remained at Crawford's during the whole season, but for the presence of his sister there, and his high respect for Mrs. Crawford, who was an excellent woman; "nothing that her husband was, and everything that he was not."

He found several books there which he had never seen before and these he read over and over at night. One of them was the Kentucky Preceptor, which he pored over with unusual interest, because it contained dialogues and declamations. Many of these he committed to memory; indeed, when his time was up at Crawford's, he had no need to carry away the books, for the contents of them were in his head. Although his employer paid him little more than half of what the boy ought to have had, it proved to be a good place for him on account of the books that he used for his own personal improvement.

Josiah Crawford was as homely as he was ill-tempered. The lids of his eyes were red as a lobster's claw, and his nose was considerably longer than it should have been for symmetry and beauty and what was worse yet, a bad habit had pimpled and reddened the end of it as if purposely to make him ugly-looking. Abraham celebrated the characteristics of Crawford's nose in verse, sometime after he ceased laboring for him, perhaps the following winter. Afterwards when he was indulging his gift for "Chronicles," he embalmed the memory of it in that style of composition. These literary efforts spread both the fame of Crawford's nose and the talents of the writer. How widely the subject-matter of his "verse" and "chronicles" were discussed and enjoyed, is learned from the fact that one of his biographers says, that the fame of Crawford's nose spread "as wide as to the Wabash and the Ohio." We cite the incident only to show that Abraham wielded a facile pen at that early day, and that the people regarded him as a marvelous boy.

Mrs. Josiah Crawford records a curious incident concerning Abraham. During the season he worked for her husband, he frequently lingered after dinner to have a frolic with the girls in the kitchen. One day he became unusually boisterous, when Mrs. Crawford reproved him for "fooling," and asked, "What do you think will ever become of you?" Abraham replied promptly, "be President of the United States." Nor was this the only occasion of his making a similar remark. He often used it in his boyhood and youth. As his miserable surroundings absolutely precluded any such idea, and he was wont to joke about his homeliness, poverty and future promise, some of his friends suppose that he made the remark in a vein of pleasantry. But whether so or not, the fact is worthy of record.

Long before this time, Mr. Lincoln had discontinued the use of his domestic grist-mill, for Hoffman built a mill to run by water, on Anderson's Creek, twelve miles away. To this mill Abraham and David Turnham carried their guests, until Gordon built a horse mill within a few miles of Lincoln's cabin. Then their patronage was transferred to Gordon's. To the latter place Abraham carried a grist one day, and safely tied the "old mare" while waiting for the grinding.

When the time came to start for home, he untied the mare, jumped on, and started the animal so suddenly with a "cluck," and stroke of a stick, that she kicked furiously, and knocked him head over heels, from the cart to the ground. He was picked up in a state of insensibility, the bystanders fearing that life was extinct. For several minutes he remained insensible, and when consciousness returned, he finished the "cluck," that was only half uttered when the ugly beast knocked him over. Many years afterward, he had discussions with his law partner at Springfield, Mr. Herndon, as to the psychological explanation of this remarkable phenomenon. One person remarked that it "was an illustration of Abe's perseverance—he always accomplished what he undertook."

The next chapter will disclose the manner in which Abraham worked and studied, growing in knowledge and popularity daily.

CHAPTER X

WORKING AND WINNING

The reader should understand the society in which Abraham mixed, in order to appreciate fully the elements of character which enabled him to work and win from fifteen to eighteen years of age. Mrs. Crawford, whom we have already quoted, in a letter to Mr. Herndon, furnishes rather a vivid picture of the social state at that time. She says:—"You wish me to tell you how the people used to go to meeting—how far they went. At that time we thought it nothing to go eight or ten miles. The old ladies did not stop for the want of a shawl, or cloak, or riding-dress, or two horses, in the winter time; but they would put on their husband's old overcoats, and wrap up their little ones, and take one or two of them up on their beasts, and their husbands would walk, and they would go to church, and stay in the neighborhood until the next day, and then go home. The old men would start out of their fields from their work, or out of the woods from hunting, with their guns on their shoulders, and go to church. Some of them dressed in deerskin pants and moccasins, hunting shirts with a rope or leather strap around them. They would come in laughing, shake hands all around, sit down and talk about their game they had killed, or some other work they had done, and smoke their pipes together with the old ladies. If in warm weather, they would kindle up a little fire out in the meeting-house yard, to light their pipes. If in the winter-time, they would hold church in some of the neighbors' houses. At such times they were always treated with the utmost kindness; a bottle of whiskey, a pitcher of water, sugar and a glass, were set out, or a basket of apples, or turnips, or some pies and cakes. Apples were scarce at that time. Sometimes potatoes were used as a treat. The first treat I ever received in old Mr. Lincoln's house (that was our President's father's house), was a plate of potatoes, washed and pared very nicely, and handed round. It was something new to me, for I had never seen a raw potato eaten before. I looked to see how they made use of them. Each took off a potato, and ate it like an apple. Thus they spent the time till preaching commenced; then they would all take their seats; the preacher would take his stand, draw off his coat, open his shirt-collar, commence service by singing and prayer; take his text and preach till the sweat would roll off in great drops. Shaking hands and singing ended the service. The people seemed to enjoy religious service more in those days than they do now. They were glad to see each other, and enjoyed themselves better than they do now." The population had increased very much at the period of which Mrs. Crawford speaks, and log meeting-houses were found here and there, at least for summer use. Some of them were too open and cold for winter use.

The people were very superstitious, as unlettered people usually are. Mr. Lamon has recorded their superstitious notions in a single paragraph, thus:—

"They firmly believed in witches and all kinds of witch-doings. They sent for wizards to cure sick cattle. They shot the image of the witch with a silver ball, to break the spell she was supposed to have laid on a human being. If a dog ran directly across a man's path whilst he was hunting, it was terrible 'luck,' unless he instantly hooked his two little fingers together, and pulled with all his might, until the dog was out of sight. There were wizards who took charmed sticks in their hands, and made them point to springs of water and all kinds of treasure beneath the earth's surface. There were 'faith doctors' who cured diseases by performing mysterious ceremonies and muttering cabalistic words. If a bird alighted in a window, one of the family would speedily die. If a horse breathed on a child, the child would have the whooping-cough. Every thing must be done at certain 'times and seasons.' They must make fence 'in the light of the moon,' otherwise the fence would sink. Potatoes and other roots were to be planted 'in the dark of the moon,' but trees and plants which bare their fruits above ground must be 'put out in the light of the moon.' The moon exerted a fearful influence, either kindly or malignant, as the good old rules were observed or not. It was even required to make soap 'in the light of the moon,' and, moreover, it must be stirred only one way, and by one person. Nothing of importance was to be begun on Friday. All enterprises inaugurated on that day went fatally amiss."

Abraham Lincoln was reared from infancy to manhood among these people. Their manners, customs, habits, and opinions, were familiar to him, and he knew no others by which to judge of them by contrast. The children of those people were his daily companions. He worked for and with their parents, heard their conversation, witnessed their want and ignorance, and nowhere found those intellectual conditions which could satisfy a mind like his. It is not strange that some of the peculiarities of the people, with whom he was reared, became his, and clung to him through life. The incidents of this chapter will serve to magnify the mental and moral qualities of Abraham, which enabled him to improve and rise higher and higher even with such unfavorable surroundings.

James Taylor, who lived at the mouth of Anderson's Creek, was anxious to secure Abraham's services.

"I will give him six dollars a month and his board," said Mr. Taylor to Mr. Lincoln; "and that is good pay for a boy sixteen years old."

"Fair pay," responded Mr. Lincoln. "You want him to run your ferry-boat?" Mr. Taylor ran a ferry-boat across both the Ohio and Anderson's Creek. "Yes, and other jobs that I want done; some farm work to take care of the horses, and chore about," was Mr. Taylor's reply. "Abe can do as well by you in such work as a man grown, though I don't expect to get a man's wages for him," added Mr. Lincoln.

"That is the reason I want him," said Mr. Taylor. "I wouldn't give many boys that price anyhow; but I know that Abe is reliable, and he knows which side his bread is buttered."

"For how many months will you pay him six dollars a month?"

"For nine months certainly and perhaps longer."

"That's satisfactory; perhaps I won't want he should stay any longer."

"Well," continued Mr. Taylor, "do I understand that he may go? I want him at once."

"He may go," answered Mr. Lincoln; "and he may begin at once if you say so."

"I say so and shall expect to see him tomorrow," added Mr. Taylor, as he turned away and drove off.

Abraham was duly installed ferryman by his employer, though he was given to understand that, at times, he would be expected to act as farmer, hostler, and house servant. He particularly enjoyed being ferryman, as it was new business for him and, like most boys, he loved boating. He was very large of his age and very strong, and could therefore handle a boat as easily and effectively as a man. He was growing rapidly still, and, at seventeen years of age, he was six feet and four inches high—both the tallest and strongest person in Spencer County.

Abraham was expected to be the first one up in the house in the morning, "build the fire," "put on the water in the kitchen," and "get things prepared for cooking," before Mrs. Taylor put in her appearance. Other things, such as bringing wood and water, he attended to with scrupulous exactness. It was not strange that the mistress of the house soon came to regard him as the most wonderful boy she ever knew. We doubt if she had ever found a man or boy, not excepting her own husband and son, who was so "wonderful" as to "chore about" as Abraham did, without protesting. He was in the truest sense a "man-of-all-work" at Taylor's, doing whatsoever his hands found to do with all his might.

Here Abraham found a History of the United States, and two or three other volumes, that engrossed his attention at night. He slept up stairs with Green Taylor, son of his employer, a young man older than himself, without any of his brightness or ambition and there he often extended his reading far into the night, much to the annoyance of his bedfellow.

"Blow out that light and come to bed, Abe," he exclaimed more than once. "I'll be bound if you shall spoil my sleep for a book."

"Let me read you a page or two," Abraham provokingly, though jocosely, answered. "A snooze is of no account in comparison with the History of the United States." And he continued to read until interrupted by another appeal out of the bedclothes.

"Abe, I say, if you don't come to bed, I'll get up and blow your light out."

"Will? Well; I would if I was in your place. Perhaps you can blow it out without getting up. Try it; there is a good amount of blow in you."

The fretted sleeper could get no satisfaction in appealing to the midnight reader. A good-natured humorous reply was all Abraham would yield to him. Once Green Taylor struck the "hired boy," in an angry mood, but Abraham did not strike back again. He was indignant enough to do it but, being a greater warrior than he who taken a city, he controlled his own spirit, and continued to read on. Years afterwards Green Taylor lived to rehearse his experience with Abraham and tell what a marvelous boy he was.

"Why, he would work hard all day, read till midnight, and then get up before anybody in the morning. I never saw such a fellow. He was like Abe Lincoln and nobody else." Referring to his act of striking him, he said, "Abe was mad, but he didn't thrash me." The language implies that Abraham could easily have avenged himself by whipping the offender, but that he forbore —his better judgment and nature controlling instead of passion.

At Taylor's, Abraham tried his hand at hog-killing for the first time. He had assisted many times in the slaughtering of hogs, but never before had played the part of butcher.

"You can try it, Abe," said Mr. Taylor, who saw that the boy could do anything he would undertake. "What do you say?"

"Just as yon say," answered Abraham; "if you'll risk the hogs I'll risk myself." Mr. Taylor, laughing at this reply, responded:—

"I'll take the risk; so you may go ahead."

In this way Abraham became a butcher, and soon grew so expert in the rough business that farmers employed him. He slaughtered hogs for John Dathan, Stephen McDaniels, John Woods, and others and Mr. Taylor received thirty-one cents a day for the boy's services in this line. He did the business well and for that reason, his labors were demanded for hog killing.

Ferryman, farmer, hostler, house-servant, butcher—all for one man and all well done. Mr. Taylor unwittingly paid him a high compliment, when he remarked to a neighbor, "Abe will do one thing about as well as another." Perhaps he did not know the reason, which was, plainly, that thoroughness was a rule with him. Whatever he did, he did as well as he could.

One year after Sarah Lincoln was married; she died, and was laid beside her mother on the knoll. This was a great sorrow to Abraham, who loved his sister tenderly and, for a time, his spirits were considerably depressed.

Some time after he served Taylor, he went to live with the storekeeper Jones, at Gentryville, only one mile and a half from his home. He was now a giant in stature—six feet and four inches tall—almost too tall to have about in log-cabins. Jones was an admirer of Abraham, and admitted him at once to his confidence.

"You can cut up pork, can't you, Abe?" Jones asked.

"Yes; I can do anything about pork, from killing and dressing to eating it." Jones bought dressed hogs, exchanging goods for them; also venison hams, corn, wheat, and corn-skins. Corn was ten cents a bushel, and wheat twenty-five cents.

"How about the store, Abe? Can you keep store?"

"I've never tried it," answered Abraham. "I'm so stylish and graceful that I might attract customers possibly." He was always jocose over his awkward and homely bearing, and so he replied to Jones in this facetious way.

"Well, I'll give you a chance to display your attractions," continued Jones. "There's a great variety of work to be done in such a place as this— teaming, cutting up and curing pork, packing and unpacking goods, measuring corn and wheat, drawing molasses and whiskey, and tending store generally."

Into this work Abraham was inducted at once, a new field of labor to him in some respects. He drove team, packed and unpacked goods drew liquids in the cellar when required, exhibited and sold crockery, and other heavy goods, to customers. Nor did he fail to render good service to Mrs. Jones, who soon discovered how "handy" he was about the house.

Mr. Jones possessed several books which Abraham had not read, among them the Life of Franklin. He, also, took a newspaper which Abraham read from beginning to end. He was quite a politician, too, a Jackson democrat, and he often discussed political questions with Abraham. In fact, he made a Jackson democrat of Abraham, and the latter continued in that faith, unshaken, until the Life of Henry Clay came into his hands, a few years later. Reading that life of the famous "Harry of the West," rather shook his confidence in Jackson's political creed. He was particularly taken with the discouraging surroundings of Clay in his boyhood and youth, when he was known as the "mill-boy of the slashes," because those surroundings were so much like those of his own boyhood. Some of his friends believe that reading the Life of Clay turned his thoughts or aims, perhaps unconsciously to himself, in the direction of a public career. It is certain that he became a "Clay Whig," and continued so until the question of liberty engaged his heart and soul in Illinois.

After Abraham ceased to serve Mr. Jones, he continued to visit his grocery often, in the evening, in company with Dennis Hanks and other companions. Here politics were discussed, stories told, jokes cracked, and general good friendship established. Abraham was the star of the group, because he was full of wit, an expert story-teller, and the only one of the number who could recite prose and poetry, and write them too.

One night, when he was returning from the grocery quite late, in company with David Turnham and others, a man was discovered lying beside a mud-puddle.

"Hallo!" exclaimed David, "what's this, Abe?" stopping, and pulling the unknown man over.

"Dead or drunk," remarked Abraham, at the same time proceeding to shake up the man. "Who is it?"

"Mor'n I know; nobody that I ever saw before," David answered. "Shake him up more and see whether there's any life in him." And they shook him thoroughly to arouse him, but in vain.

"Plenty of rum in him if there is no life," remarked Abraham, after satisfying himself that the man was dead drunk. "But his case must be attended to."

"You may attend to him if you want to, but I shan't," said Nat Grigsby. "Come, let's go home."

"So I say," added David; "it's too cold to fuss about here. If the fellow likes such a bed he may sleep it out for all me."

"He'll freeze to death before morning if we leave him here," responded Abraham.

"That's about all he's good for," chimed in Nat. By this time they had discovered that the man was a miserable drunkard who lived some miles away. "Come on, I'm going home, whether the old fellow freezes or not." And Nat started on.

"Well, I shan't go home until I make out what is going to become of this chap," said Abraham. "It would be inhuman to leave him to freeze here."

"Perhaps it would, and perhaps it wouldn't," replied David. "Nobody is any better for his living, and some folks are worse. He's a good-for-nothing fellow any way."

"That's no reason why we should let him die here like a dog or hog," retorted Abraham with some spirit. "Come, Dave, let that go, and we'll take him over to Dennis' cabin." At this time Dennis Hanks was married and lived in a cabin a half mile away.

"I think I see myself tugging the miserable wretch a half mile at this time of night," retorted David. "You may make a fool of yourself over him if you want to, but I am going home." And David started for home, hearing, as he hurried away, Abraham saying,—"Go, then, you hard-hearted fellow."

Abraham was not more than a minute in determining what to do. He put his long strong arms around the drunken man, raised him up, flung him over his shoulder as he would a bag of corn, and started for Dennis Hanks' cabin, where he safely deposited him.

"Look here, Dennis, I've brought you company," said Abraham, as he laid down his burden. "More of a job to carry him than a log."

"Where did you find that fellow, Abe?" inquired Dennis, getting out of bed.

"In the road, where he would have died before morning, if I'd left him there."

"I know him of old, not much account any way," added Dennis.

"Account enough to fix up a little," retorted Abraham. "We ought to be human beings so long as we pretend to be."

"Go ahead, then," said Dennis, acquiescing; "see how you come out." And he proceeded to assist Abraham in his merciful work. They built a fire, warmed him, and Abraham rubbed him until consciousness was restored. In fact, he remained all night with the intemperate man, and left him in the morning well satisfied with the part he had played as "good Samaritan." Afterwards, the wretched man said to John Hanks, "It was mighty clever in Abe to take me to a warm fire that cold night. Abe's strength and kindness saved my life."

CHAPTER XI

UPWARD AND ONWARD

The brief remarks made about Abraham at this time show his standing.

"He is always ready to do everything for everybody," remarked his mother.

"He is good-natured as the days are long," said Dennis Hanks.

"Always reading when he is not working," said Josiah Crawford.

"More fun in him than there is in all the rest of us put together," remarked David Turnham.

Such remarks as these were common concerning Abraham Lincoln from the time he was fourteen years of age. John Hanks, who went to live with the Lincolns, as we have said, when Abraham was fourteen, says:—

"When Abe and I returned to the house from work, he would go to the cupboard, snatch a piece of corn-bread, take down a book sit down on a chair, cross his legs as high as his head, and read. He and I worked barefooted, grubbed it, ploughed, mowed, and cradled together; ploughed corn, gathered it, and shucked corn. Abraham read constantly when he had an opportunity."

Mr. Lamon says: "Abe loved to lie under a shade tree, or up in the loft of the cabin, and read, cipher, and scribble. At night, he sat by the chimney "jamb," and ciphered, by the light of the fire, on the wooden fire-shovel. When the shovel was fairly covered, he would shave it off with Tom Lincoln's drawing-knife, and begin again. In the day time, he used boards for the same purpose, out of doors, and went through the shaving process everlastingly."

His mother says: "Abe read every book he could lay his hands on and when he came across a passage that struck him, he would write it down on boards if he had no paper, and keep it there until he did get paper. Then he would re-write it, look at it, and repeat it. He had a copy-book, a kind of scrap-book, in which he put down all things, and thus preserved them."

There is no record of how and where he obtained the scrap-book. The idea was entirely original with him, since he had never heard of any such device in his part of the country. There is no question that he possessed a scrap-book, and that it became an important agent in making him a scholar and statesman. He copied into it chiefly from the books he borrowed, thinking he would not have the opportunity to see them again. Books that he owned, as well as those belonging to his parents, he marked, that he might refer to striking passages at his leisure. Also, he frequently wrote brief compositions in that scrapbook, improving his talent for the art thereby. As an invention, at that time, the scrap-book was worthy of his genius, and, as a source of mental improvement, its value was never over-estimated.

One of the finest and most touching tributes ever paid to his memory was spoken by his mother to Mr. Herndon, and we quote it here because it had reference to his early life. She said:—

"Abe was a poor boy, and I can say what scarcely one woman— a mother — can say, in a thousand. Abe never gave me a cross word or look, and never refused, in fact or appearance, to do any thing I requested him. I never gave him a cross word in all my life. His mind and my mind—what little I had—seemed to run together, he was here after he was elected President." Here she stopped, unable to proceed any further, and after her grateful emotions had spent themselves in tears, she proceeded: "He was dutiful to me always. I think he loved me truly. I had a son, John, who was raised with Abe. Both were good boys but I must say, both being now dead, that Abe was the best boy I ever saw, or ever expect to see. I wish I had died when my husband died. I did not want Abe to run for President did not want him elected was afraid somehow—felt it in my heart and when he came down to see me, after he was elected President, I felt that something would befall him, and that I should see him no more."

Mr. Lamon relates that, when this interview closed, and Mr. Herndon was about to retire, Mrs. Lincoln took one of his hands in both of hers, and wringing it, with the tears streaming down her cheeks, as if loath to separate from one who knew her "Abe" so intimately, said: "Goodbye, my good son's friend. Farewell."

Abraham tried his father often by his persistent efforts to gain time to read and study, and by his disposition to turn night into day, that he might pore over some engrossing book, or compose a "poem" or "chronicle" upon some passing event, pleasant or otherwise. He was more tried, however, by Abraham's "preaching about" and "making "political speeches" on stumps, than anything for this interfered with business. His step-sister, Matilda Johnson, says he was remarkable for preaching and speech-making. On Monday mornings, after he had listened to a sermon, he would mount a stump, and deliver the sermon, which his memory retained with wonderful accuracy. In the field, he often amused his working companions with a speech upon some subject that was uppermost and, when he began to orate, there was an end of labor. All hands gathered about him in admiration, and cheered him on. Thomas Lincoln thought Abraham was carrying the matter too far. But he said nothing, especially authoritative, until the community was visited by a preacher of singular eccentricities. He bellowed like a bull of Bashan in the pulpit, a fearful nasal twang accompanying his cracked voice and he pounded the desk in his excitement, as if determined to reduce it to kindling wood. His performance was fun for the young people and Abraham was especially amused. His gift of imitation enabled him to reproduce the sermon, with its nasal twang and other oddities so that the eccentricities of the preacher were reproduced and re-repeated, over and over, on the stumps of the field, and at evening gatherings. When Abraham began to preach that sermon, in cabin or field, his audience could attend to nothing else until the discourse was finished. The exercise of laughing over it was well-nigh as exhaustive and violent as that of chopping. Even the old people, who thought it was not quite right to make so much merriment over a sermon, could not help laughing when Abraham became the eccentric pulpit orator. But his father felt obliged to interfere with this habit of public speaking. It became too much of an interruption to necessary work.

"You must stop it, Abe. I won't have it. You'll get to liking fun more than work; guess you do now. I've put up with it long enough,—shan't any longer. Don't let me have to speak to you about it again." So Mr. Lincoln interrupted Abraham's practice of stump speaking, in his irritation manifesting considerable feeling on the subject.

Yet there is no doubt that Mr. Lincoln was proud of the ability of his son, and, at heart, enjoyed his precocity. In his ignorance, he might have feared that his habit of speech-making would make him lazy or shiftless. Whether he did or not, Abraham evidently laid the foundation of his future greatness as an orator and debater in those remarkable days of his youth. A better practice to discipline him for public service could not have engaged his attention. The pioneer boy was unconsciously schooling himself for the highest position in the land.

Abraham worked often for William Wood, who lived one mile and a half away. Mr. Lincoln worked there, also, as a carpenter, whenever labor in his line was demanded. Abraham loved to work for Mr. Wood, for he took two papers, which the boy could read through and through. One of them was a temperance paper and its contents interested him more even than the political paper.

"I did not know that a paper like this was ever printed," he said to Mr. Wood, who was one of the most intelligent and well posted men of Spencer County. "It's true, every word of it."

"Of course it is," replied Mr. Wood. "Rum is well enough in its place, but there's no reason in men making such beasts of themselves as many do about here."

"I shouldn't care if the whole of it was at the bottom of the Ohio River, where most of my father's whiskey went," continued Abraham. "It does a great sight more evil than good any day."

"Good! It would puzzle most any one to tell what good whiskey does," responded Mr. Wood. "The evil it does is known to everybody; we can see that everywhere. It adds very much to the hardships of life in this part of the country."

Abraham became so enthusiastic over the temperance paper and the cause which it represented, that he wrote a long composition on the subject of "Temperance," and submitted it to Mr. Wood's examination.

"Did you write all this yourself, Abe?" Remarked Mr. Wood before reading it, but noticing its length.

"Every word of it; and I want you to read it over, and tell me what you think about it."

"I will read it to-night without fail," and Mr. Wood did read it. His opinion of it is learned from the fact that he remarked to a Baptist minister who called at his house:— "I have here a composition on Temperance, written by Abe Lincoln, and I think it is a wonderful production for such a boy to write. I want you should read it, and see if you do not agree with me."

"I should be glad to read it, here and now," replied the minister. "I'm glad that Abe is writing on that subject." And he applied himself to reading the composition at once.

"I agree with you entirely," said the minister, completing the reading;" it is a remarkable production for such a boy."

"I would like to see it printed in this temperance paper," continued Mr. Wood, holding the paper up.

"It is worthy of a place in it," added the minister.

"They publish articles that are not half as good," responded Mr. Wood. "You can get this composition to the editor; it is right in your way."

"Yes, I can take it there, and should be glad to do it."

"Well, you take it, and I'll make it right with Abe."

"He won't have any objection, if he is like most boys," remarked the minister. "He'll be a little proud to appear in print."

The minister took the article along with him, and, subsequently, it appeared in the columns of the paper. Mr. Wood read it over again in print, and remarked; "It excels anything there is in the paper." Abraham was both gratified and encouraged by the publication of his article. The paper was lent to the families in the neighborhood, after they heard that Abraham was a writer for its columns, and the universal verdict was, "a remarkable composition for a boy."

"Can't you write on politics, Abe?" said Mr. Wood to him, one day.

"Yes, sir; I have written some pieces on that subject."

"Well, I mean an article to be printed in some political paper."

"I can try," continued Abraham, elated with the idea of writing for a political paper. "What shall I write about?"

Mr. Wood made some suggestions about the subject and, in the course of a week, Abraham brought him the article. Mr. Wood remembers enough of it to furnish the drift of the composition:—

"That the American Government is the best form of government for an intelligent people that it ought to be sound, and preserved forever; that general education should be fostered and carried all over the country that the Constitution should be saved, the Union perpetuated, and the laws revered, respected, and enforced."

Mr. Wood was even more gratified and surprised on reading this article than he was on reading the other. We think that the composition is more remarkable now than it was then, on account of subsequent events. For it surely contained the gist of Abraham Lincoln's inaugural address when he became President. On that occasion he said:—

"I hold, that, in the contemplation of universal law and of the Constitution, the union of these States is perpetual. Perpetuity is implied, if not expressed, in the fundamental law of all national governments. Continue to execute all the express provisions of our national Constitution, and the Union will endure forever. I consider that in view of the Constitution and the laws, the Union is unbroken; and to the extent of my ability, I shall take care, as the Constitution itself expressly enjoins upon me, that the laws of the Union shall be faithfully executed."

How wonderful that the pioneer boy who wrote the aforesaid article for a political paper should become President of the United States thirty-three years thereafter, and reiterate in his inaugural address the same sentiments, when the enemies of the country were seeking to overthrow the Constitution, abrogate its laws and sever the Union!

A lawyer, by the name of Pritchard, was passing by Mr. Wood's house, when the political article in question was in his hands. Mr. Wood called him in, remarking--

"I want you should read an article I have here, and see what you think of it." He did not disclose who was the author of it.

"Your own?" inquired Pritchard.

"That's no matter; read it."

"I will, if that is your wish;" and Pritchard sat down to its perusal. As he read the last sentence, he remarked, in a very enthusiastic way—

"It can't be beat. Is it yours?"

"No; it is not mine. Tom Lincoln's son, Abe, wrote it, and I think it is wonderful for a boy."

"More than that," added Pritchard, still more interested when he learned that a boy wrote it. "Let me have it to publish in our paper," meaning the paper of his section.

"That's what it was written for, —to be published in some political paper," answered Mr. Wood. "An article of Abe's was published in my temperance paper not long ago, and it was the best thing it had. Abe is a great temperance boy."

The last remark makes it necessary to interject a paragraph here. We have undoubted testimony that Abraham was the only person in that region, at that time, who refused on all occasions to partake of intoxicating liquors. His opposition to the practice was so well known, that, at house-raisings, log-rolling, husking, and parties, it was not expected that he would touch anything which would intoxicate. It was his decided stand against intoxicants that caused his mother to say, "I think Abe carries his temperance notions to extremes."

It was arranged that Pritchard should take the article to the editor of a political paper for publication; and, in due time, it appeared, much to the satisfaction of Mr. Wood, the joy of Abraham, and the pride of the neighborhood. Abraham wrote other articles which he submitted to the examination of Mr. Wood and the exercise of writing composition became to him an excellent discipline, and did much to help him upward and onward.

A Mr. Richardson, who lived in the vicinity at that time, says:

"Abe was the best penman in the neighborhood. One day, while he was on a visit to my mother's, I asked him to write some original copies for me. He very willingly consented. He wrote several of them, but one of them I have never forgotten, although a boy at the time."

Many such "pieces," in poetry and prose, he wrote, exhibiting thought, genius, noble aspirations, and marked talents.

We have intimated that Abraham's love of books prevented his becoming a hunter. He could not spare the time. If he were not at work, he had a book in his hand. Other boys became hunters. It was necessary for them to be in order to procure food and a livelihood. Dennis Hanks says, "When we had spare time we picked up the rifle, and brought in a fine deer or turkey and in the winter-time we went coon-hunting, for coon-skins were considered legal tender, and deerskins and hams." The woods were full of rabbits, partridges, squirrels, and other game, but these were not shot much for food. Deer and turkeys were more desirable for the larder. The smaller game mentioned was so plenty, that the settlers resorted to various devices to destroy them. They devastated gardens and grain-fields, and the pioneers made war upon them as a nuisance.

Bears, wild-cats, and panthers, also, were quite numerous, and these were shot in self-defense. The scream of the latter often filled the forest with terror at night, in Abraham's early life. Yet, our hero never did much at hunting. A book, instead of a gun, captivated his heart, and he read and studied when other boys hunted and had rare sport. We do not mean that he never engaged in this pastime for he did occasionally accompany companions upon hunting excursions. But, compared with the average boy of the county, he was not a hunter.

Abraham enjoyed certain "plays" and games more than he did hunting. His social qualities and genuine humor fitted him for this sphere more than for the other. These "plays," without Abraham, were the play of Hamlet with Hamlet left out. He made things lively by his wit and geniality. Exactly what the "plays" were, we cannot affirm: we can only give their names as furnished by Dennis Hanks. "Throwing the mall," "cat," "four-corner bull-pen," "hopping and half-Hammon," and "Sister Feby," an evening game. Whatever these "plays" were, Abraham was "a bright particular star" in them, whenever and wherever his presence could be secured.

From the time Abraham was eighteen years of age, his physical strength was remarkable. Some of the stories about his strength, told by the neighbors, are almost incredible. He was not only a giant in stature, but a giant in strength. Observers looked on amazed at the exhibition. Richardson, a neighbor, declares that he could carry a load to which the strength of three ordinary men would scarcely be equal. He saw him quietly pick up and walk away with "a chicken house, made of poles pinned together, and covered, that weighed at least six hundred, if not much more." At another time, the Richardsons were building a corncrib; Abe was there; and, seeing three or four men preparing "sticks" upon which to carry some huge posts, he relieved them of all further trouble by shouldering the posts, single-handed, and walking away with them to the place where they were wanted. "He could strike with a mall," says old Mr. Wood, "a heavier blow than any man. He could sink an axe deeper into the wood than any man I ever saw." Wrestling was a common and popular sport among pioneers, and here Abraham excelled all his companions. The sequel will show how his remarkable physical strength aided him in the labors, burdens, trials, and responsibilities of his public life.

CHAPTER XII
ON THE FLAT-BOAT

On the first of March, 1828, Abraham went to work for old Mr. Gentry, the proprietor of Gentryville. Here, again, he was a "man-of-all-work," doing whatsoever his employer found for him to do. Mr. Gentry had a son by the name of Allen, with whom Abraham worked. He was a little older than Abraham, and a suitable companion for him.

"How would you like to run a flat-boat to New Orleans, Abe?" said Mr. Gentry to him, early in April. "I believe you are used to boating."

"I know something about it," Abraham replied. "I should like to go to New Orleans. How far is it?"

"About eighteen hundred miles. I'm thinking of letting Allen take a trip there if you will go with him."

"How soon?"

"Just as soon as you can get ready. I have a load of bacon and other produce on hand now. It's some work to get ready."

"Well, I'll be ready any time you say, if father don't object, and I don't think he will," added Abraham.

"He won't care if I pay you well for it," responded Mr. Gentry. "I shall give you eight dollars a month and pay your passage home on a steamer. You and Allen together can manage such a trip well."

Abraham's service of four or five weeks had satisfied Mr. Gentry that he was just the hand to send on a trading expedition to New Orleans. His tact, strength and fidelity were three essential requisites to ensure a successful expedition. Flat-boating on the Western waters, at that time, was an exciting and perilous business and some account of it here will reflect light upon

Abraham's venture.

For some years there had been a class of boatmen, fearless, hardy, athletic men, who "traversed the longest rivers, penetrated the most remote wilderness upon their watery routes, and kept up a trade and intercourse between the most distant points."

They were exposed to great perils, and were out shelterless in all kinds of weather. With no bed but the deck of their boats on which to lie at night, and no covering but a blanket, they spent months and years of their existence.

It was on such boats that the rich cargoes ascending the Mississippi were carried. By human labor they wee propelled against the strong current for nearly two thousand miles and it was a labor that required great muscular strength and remarkable powers of endurance. The result was that a class of men was trained in this business, of unusual courage, and proud only of their ability to breast storms and endure hardships.

In addition to this class, whose life-business it was to propel these Western boats, there were those who occasionally made a trip to New Orleans to sell their stores. Sometimes several farmers, or other persons, would club together and make out a cargo, and send it down to New Orleans and sometimes one alone would do the same. This was the case with Mr. Gentry, He had a quantity of stores suited to meet the wants of the sugar plantations in Louisiana, and he wanted to convert them into cash. Money was very scarce, and many families, like that of Mr. Lincoln, saw but little. What was in circulation was brought into the Western country by people moving thither from the East, or was obtained, as Mr. Gentry proposed to obtain some, by sending a boat-load of stores to New Orleans.

Abraham consulted his father, who readily consented. His mother remarked:—

"Eighteen hundred miles is rather of a long trip for a fellow who hasn't seen more of the world than you have, Abe."

"None too long, mother. I shall see some of the world now if I never have before."

"And perhaps see the bottom of the Mississippi," suggested his mother.

"I'm not afraid of that."

"But many have lost their lives in this way, and men who have been used to the business, too."

"That's no sign I shall."

"It's no sign you won't."

"But I shan't borrow any trouble about it."

"I don't ask you to do that; but it's worth while to think of these things."

"If you don't want I should go, I will give it up now." Abraham inferred from his mother's manner of speaking, that she was unwilling he should go.

"I do want you should go, I was only telling some of my thoughts. I can't help thinking."

"It may be the best thing for me that I ever did," suggested Abraham.

"Yes, if no accident happens to you, I have no doubt it will be a real good school for you. But it's a long ways to go, and a long time for you to be gone."

"But I have got to go away some time, and I may as well begin now."

"Very true; but that makes it no easier for me to have you go. But it don't do any good to talk about it now."

Preparations were made at once for the voyage. A boat was provided at Gentry's Landing, which was at Rockport, on the Ohio River, and Abraham and Allen proceeded to load the cargo. Here Abraham met with his old schoolmate, Miss Roby, whom he assisted, at Crawford's school, to spell defied correctly. She had grown into a winsome girl; at least Allen Gentry thought so for he afterwards courted and married her. At the close of one day an incident occurred that shows how Abraham was wont to pick up knowledge. He was sitting with Miss Roby on the boat, when she remarked:—

"The sun is going down."

"No; it isn't," Abraham replied naively.

"You've lost your sight, then," suggested the girl, at the same time anticipating that Abraham was indulging in some roguery.

"I can see as well as you can," responded Abraham, "and I say, honestly, the sun is not going down, and what is more, it never will go down."

"Wait and see," continued Miss Roby, laughing.

"It will seem to go down," added Abraham, in an explanatory way.

"I rather think it will," Miss Roby answered curtly.

"We go down, not the sun," Abraham continued.

"The sun stands still."

"It moves enough for me," interrupted Miss Roby.

Abraham went on to explain:—

"You see the earth turns from west to east, and the revolution of the earth carries us under, as it were; we do the sinking, as you call it. The sun does not really set; it only appears to."

"Abe! what a fool you are!" exclaimed the surprised girl, who began to think that too much learning had made her friend mad.

Forty years afterwards, Miss Roby, who became Mrs. Gentry, said:—

"Now I know that I was the fool, not Lincoln. I am now thoroughly satisfied that Abe knew the general laws of astronomy and the movements of the heavenly bodies. He was better read then than the world knows, or is likely to know exactly. No man could talk to me that night as he did unless he had known something of geography as well as astronomy. He often and often commented or talked to me about what he had read— seemed to read it out of the book as he went along—did so to others. He was the learned boy among us unlearned folks. He took great pains to explain, and could do it so simply. He was diffident then, too."

To return to the trip to New Orleans, as soon as the cargo was loaded, the two boys started upon their voyage, Abraham serving as "bow-hand, to work the front oars." It was a very important event in the life of our young friend, and his heart was greatly elated. He was floating out into the broad world now. His young eyes would behold its sights and scenes for the first time. It is not strange that he pushed out into the Ohio with a glad heart, and moved down towards the "father of waters" with such anticipation as never fired his breast before.

"I say, Abe, how many times are you going to upset before reaching the Mississippi?" asked Allen.

"I hardly think we shall do it more than once," answered Abraham, "unless you have a better faculty than I have for loading up again in the water."

"I didn't think of that; it would be a hard matter to reload at the bottom of the river."

"Yes; and we must look out for accidents, or your father will wish he had never sent us. I hope we shall make a capital thing of it."

"I hope so too, or we shall never have another such a chance. The old man never would have sent me if it hadn't been for you, Abe."

"How so?"

"Because he thinks you can do most anything that's possible, and so he was willing to risk me and all the cargo with you."

"Pshaw! You are fooling now."

"No such thing; it's the living truth. I expect he thought that you could keep me and the cargo from sinking if we did upset." "Well, my mother rather expects the opposite, I judge by her talk," replied Abraham. "She thinks it is rather of a risky piece of business to send us on such a trip." "I 'suppose 'tis," was Allen's thoughtful reply; "and it stands us in hand to do the very best we can." It must suffice to say that their trip proved to be a pleasant one. Many incidents occurred which we cannot relate here, nor is it necessary for our purpose. They lived upon the fiat-boat, of course. At night they drew it up to the bank of the river, in some favorable spot, and tied it safely; then laid down on their "running board," as a flat-boat was sometimes called, to sleep. They had no bed and nothing but a blanket to cover them. True, this was not so great a change for boys who were reared in the wilderness, as it would be for boys of this day who are used to the comforts and conveniences of affluent homes. Still it was a change, and many of their nights were extremely lonely.

Their voyage was not monotonous. The scenery was continually changing, and they frequently passed other boats with their merry crews, and held conversations with people who flocked to the banks of the river from adjacent villages. "Where are you from?" "Where are you bound?" "What are you loaded with?" were questions that they frequently had to answer. The days were not all sunshine. Heavy storms sometimes descended upon them, and they had to thought that you could keep me and the cargo from sinking if we did upset."

The days were not all sunshine. Heavy storms sometimes descended upon them, and they had to exert themselves to the utmost to keep their little craft right side up. Day after day they were drenched with rain, and still they must keep on the voyage. Violent storms sometimes raged at night, the wind blowing almost a hurricane, and the rain pouring down in torrents, and still there was no alternative—they must make their bed on their little boat and take the pelting of the storm. Those were times that tried their spirit, and yet they had no complaints to utter. Never for a moment did Abraham wish he had not undertaken the voyage. The object of his expedition had taken complete possession of his soul.

At Madame Bushane's plantation, six miles below Baton Rouge, they had an adventure that is worthy of rehearsal here. The boat was tied up, and the boys were fast asleep in the stern when footsteps on board awoke them. After listening a moment, Abraham whispered:

"Foul play, Allen! A gang of niggers come to rob us!"

Thinking to frighten them away, Allen shouted, "Bring the guns, Abe, shoot 'em."

But the negroes did not flee, and the silence was as oppressive as the darkness.

"Trouble for us," said Abraham in a low tone, as he sprung to his feet and put his hand upon a billet of wood. "We must fight for our lives. Come."

Waiting and listening again for a moment, and hearing nothing, Abraham cried out:

"Who's there?" No response.

"Who's there?" he called with more emphasis.

The voices of several negroes, in threatening tones responded.

"What are you here for, you rascals?" thundered Abraham. "Be off with yourselves, or we'll throw you into the river." And he dashed after them in the darkness, followed by Allen. The negroes stood their ground, armed with cudgels, and a fearful battle began at once.

"Kill them!" shouted Abraham to Allen. "They mean to kill us. Knock the scoundrels into the water."

And the clubs flew, and heavy blows were dealt back and forth, until the contest became so close and hot that clubs were useless, and a hand-to-hand fight was inevitable. For ten minutes or more the conflict raged, spattering the deck with blood, and threatening the saddest results. At length, however, Abraham threw one of the number into the river, when the others leaped from the boat upon the shore.

"Let's after them!" shouted Abraham, so thoroughly aroused and excited as to banish all fear. "Show them no quarter."

And the boys pursued them with their clubs for half a mile, yelling at such a rate that the negroes thought, no doubt, that a half score of boatmen were after them. They were Madame Bushane's slaves, seeking plunder on the boat, and they were thoroughly terrified. They had not counted upon such a belligerent reception. Abraham and Allen saw at once that it was a case of life and death, and therefore they fought with desperation. The negroes left some of their best blood on deck, and it was mingled with that of our two young boatmen. For they received blows well nigh as hard as those they gave, and their blood told of their wounds. Abraham received a blow over his right eye, the scar of which he carried through life.

"We must get the boat off now as quick as possible," said Allen, as they returned from the pursuit. "The scamps may come back with twice the number."

"I was just thinking of that," replied Abraham, "Jump aboard, and I will untie the boat. We must lose no time."

In a minute Allen was aboard, and scarcely another minute had passed before Abraham followed him, having loosed the boat.

"We are safe now, if the whole plantation comes," said Allen, as they shoved off into the stream.

"We shan't need to go far," added Abraham. "Only change our position, and we are safe."

"That may be, but I think I shall sleep with my eyes open the rest of the night."

"And I will keep you company," responded Abraham. "The next time I come to New Orleans, I shall coming armed. This going to war without a gun is not quite the thing."

"I wish we had been armed," said Allen. "Wouldn't we have made the feathers fly?"

"The wool, you mean," replied Abraham, jocosely. He had become as cool as if nothing had happened.

"They meant to kill us."

"Of course they did. It wouldn't have done for them to rob us, and leave us to tell the story to their master. But they might have made way with us, and robbed and sunk the boat, and nobody been any the wiser for it."

"They are no fools, if they be niggers."

"No; but after all they are not so much to blame," added Abraham. "Slavery has robbed them of everything, and so I s'pose they think it is fair play to take what they can get."

We shall only add that the voyage was continued to New Orleans, and the cargo of bacon and other produce disposed of to advantage. The boys returned to Indiana on the deck of a steamer, according to Mr. Gentry's arrangement before they started.

It is a remarkable fact, that Abraham, who fought the slaves to save his life, should become their emancipator, as we shall discover, thirty-five years thereafter.

CHAPTER XIII

SUNDRY INCIDENTS

There is very satisfactory evidence that Abraham went on a trading trip for his father before he served Mr. Gentry, and that he built a boat himself for the expedition. For Mr. Carpenter, the painter, in his "Six Months in the White House," has the following from Mr. Lincoln's lips, related to show how he came into possession of the first dollar he could call his own:—

In the Executive Chamber, one evening, there were present a number of gentlemen, among them Mr. Seward.

A point in the conversation suggesting the thought, the President said: "Seward, you never heard, did you, how I earned my first dollar?" "No," rejoined Mr. Seward. "Well," continued Mr. Lincoln, "I was about eighteen years of age. I belonged, you know to what they call down South, the ' scrubs;' people who do not own slaves are nobody there. But we had succeeded in raising, chiefly by my labor, sufficient produce, as I thought, to justify me in taking it down the river to sell.

"After much persuasion, I got the consent of mother to go, and constructed a little flat-boat, large enough to take a barrel or two of things that we had gathered, with myself and little bundle, down to New Orleans. A steamer was coming down the river. We have, you know, no wharves on the Western streams and the custom was, if passengers were at any of the landings, for them to go out in a boat, the steamer stopping and taking them on board.

"I was contemplating my new flat-boat, and wondering whether I could make it stronger or improve it in any particular, when two men came down to the shore in carriages, with trunks, and looking at the different boats, singled out mine, and asked, 'Who owns this?' I answered, somewhat modestly, 'I do.' 'Will you,' said one of them, 'take us and our trunks out to the steamer.' 'Certainly,' said I. I was very glad to have the chance of earning something. I supposed that each of them would give me two or three bits. The trunks were put on my flat-boat, the passengers seated themselves on the trunks, and I sculled them out to the steamboat.

"They got on board, and I lifted up their heavy trunks, and put them on deck. The steamer was about to put on steam again, when I called out that they had forgotten to pay me. Each of them took from his pocket a silver half-dollar, and threw it on the floor of my boat. I could scarcely believe my eyes as I picked lip the money. Gentlemen, you may think it was a very little thing, and in these days it seems to me a trifle but it was a most important incident in my life. I could scarcely credit that I, a poor boy, had earned a dollar in less than a day—that by honest work I had earned a dollar. The world seemed wider and fairer before me; I was a more hopeful and confident being from that hour."

Abraham had earned money before, considerable of it but it belonged to his father, who did not believe that a boy had any necessary use for it. The dollar received for carrying the trunks he regarded his own.

Abraham felt, after leaving Mr. Gentry that he was competent to earn more than he had done. Doubtless, also, his success in flat-boating awakened a strong desire to continue in that business. For, one day, he went to Mr. Wood's house, and stood around for some time, as if he wanted to say something he lacked courage to express.

"What is it, Abe?" inquired Mr. Wood.

"I want to get a place to work on the river."

"That so and what can I do for you?"

"I would like to have you give me a recommendation to some boat, if you will."

"But you are not of age yet, Abe. Your father has a claim on you." In that hard country, at that time, parents needed the help of their sons, and their claim upon their labor was enforced with rigor.

"I know that," continued Abraham; "but I want to get a start somewhere, and I can do more for father so than I can by staying around here."

"That may be; but that's no reason why I should interfere; you and your father must settle that."

Abraham turned away from this interview somewhat disappointed, yet disposed to make the best of it. He abandoned the idea of life on the river, and continued about home. Not long afterward, Mr. Wood saw him cutting down a large tree in the forest to whip-saw into plank.

"What's up now, Abe?" Mr. Wood inquired.

"A new house; father is talking of putting up a new house."

"Ah! And you are getting the lumber ready?"

"Yes; going to have it all ready by the time he gets ready to build."

"A better house, I suppose." said Mr. Wood, inquiringly. "I hope so; mother wants it badly."

"Well, I don't blame her," added Mr. Wood, as he turned away.

But Abraham's father did not build the house, as we shall learn in the next chapter. The lumber was prepared, but the project of removing to Illinois changed his purpose, and the lumber was sold to Josiah Crawford —the man v/ho extorted work from Abraham for the book.

David Turnham bought a copy of the "Statutes of Indiana," and Abraham heard of it, in consequence of which he called upon the neighbor.

"Can I see your copy of the Statutes of Indiana." I hear you have one," Abraham asked.

"Of course you can, Abe," answered David. "Going to study law? It wouldn't be bad business for you."

"I shan't begin today," responded Abraham; "but I want to take a look into the laws of Indiana. I don't know much about them."

"That's the case with me; and that's the reason I bought the book. I can't spare it for you to take home, for I study it every minute I have to spare."

"I can read it here, just as well," replied Abraham, as David handed him the book. "It don't make any difference where I read it."

The result was that Abraham spent much time at David Turnham's in studying the statutes of his adopted State. When David wanted the book, Abraham turned to Scott's Lessons and Sinbad the Sailor, two books which David owned. He read these books through at David's house, besides studying the laws of Indiana quite thoroughly. To him the Statutes were by no means dry, as they would have been to most of his companions; for they opened a new and wide field of research to his inquiring mind. Without doubt, the influence of that study upon his future career was marked. It began to be seen very soon; for, one day, he said to David—

"I'm going to Booneville to court; won't you go with me?"

"Going to be tried for your life?" replied David, in a vein of humor.

"Going to see how they try other folks for their lives," answered Abraham. "I never went into a courts room, and I'm going to before I'm a week older."

"How are you going, Abe?"

"Going to walk, of course; not much of a trip there."

"Well, it may not be much of a walk for your long legs, but it's a long one for mine," responded David. "I think I will be excused till you get to be a lawyer and have a case at the bar, then I'll walk fifteen miles to see and hear."

Abraham walked to Booneville, fifteen miles, to court, and was doubly paid for his trouble. The novelty and excitement of the scene captivated him so completely that he walked thither, again and again afterwards, to enjoy the treat. At one time a murder trial was on the docket, in which one of the best lawyers of the State was counsel for the defense—John Breckinridge, Esq. Abraham heard his able and eloquent plea, and would have sat a week to listen to the speaker. "If I could ever become such a speaker, I should be perfectly satisfied," he said within himself. He was so thoroughly charmed by the speech, that he forgot his usual modesty, and, at the close of the court, stepped up to Mr. Breckinridge and said—

"That was the best speech I ever heard."

The lawyer looked at the shabby boy, as if surprised at his boldness but did not deign a reply. He passed on, leaving Abraham to his own reflections. It deserves to be recorded here, that John Breckinridge met Abraham at Washington when the latter was President. Breckinridge was a resident of Texas then, and was a rebel. As he did not know who the shabby boy was who addressed him at Boonville, he did not know, of course, that it was he who had become President. But Lincoln recognized the eloquent pleader of Booneville at once, and kindly refreshed the rebel's memory. Breckinridge had applied for executive clemency, and that Booneville speech became a favorable introduction. Mr. Lincoln said to him, "It was the best speech that I ever heard up to that time. If I could, as I then thought, make as good a speech as that, my soul would be satisfied."

Through Abraham's influence a "speaking-meeting," or, as we call it now, a lycan, was started at Gentryville.

"It will be very improving," said Abraham to Nat Grigsby, "to say nothing about the fun of the thing." He was making a plea for such an institution.

"If we were all like you, Abe, there would be both improvement and fun in the thing, but we arc not," answered Nat. "I'll do what I can, though."

"And that is all any of us can do."

"What will you do at your speaking-meeting?" Nat continued.

"Speak pieces, discuss questions, and read compositions," answered Abraham. "We can have real good times."

"We might if we could all speak and write and argue as you can," responded Nat. "But most of us will have to take back seats in such a meeting, I tell you. But I go in for it."

All the young people favored the enterprise finally, and not a few of the older ones. It started with flying colors, and Abraham was in his element. The pieces he had committed to memory as a pastime now served him a good purpose, and, more than ever, the people extolled him. Old Mr. Gentry said, "Abe will make a great man sure as he lives." One of the enthusiastic women declared, "He will be President of the United States yet."

In the discussions, Abraham was logical and witty and every body was on the alert to hear him speak. Among the questions discussed were, "Which is the stronger, wind or water?" and "Which has the most right to complain, the negro or the Indian?" Abraham had picked up much information concerning wind and water, so that he was not at all limited for materials in the discussion. On the other question he had very definite views of his own, and not a little information collected from here and there. He hated Indians out of respect to his ancestors, if for no other reason; still, he considered them an abused race. But he spoke for the negro in that debate, and made his first public plea for the enslaved, at that time, on the free soil of Indiana.

That Abraham did not improve in his personal appearance, as he did in knowledge, is evident from a remark of Miss Roby, when he went to live with Mr. Gentry. She said, "Abe was then a long, thin, leggy, gawky boy, dried up and shriveled." He appeared to be much older than he was. Caring little or nothing for dress, he continued to wear apparel of the genuine pioneer pattern, which made his homeliness more homely. A remark of Dennis, on one occasion, was quite expressive: "Abe has too much legs to be handsome;" and it was true.

Still, he was the centre of attraction in all circles. Men, women and children loved to hear him talk. They would gather about him to listen, whether in house or field. He continued to improve, too, in this regard. Nat Grigsby says:—

"When he appeared in company, the boys would gather and cluster around him to hear him talk. He was figurative in his speeches, talks, and conversations. He argued much from analogy, and explained things hard for us to understand by stories, maxims, tales and figures. He would almost always point his lesson or idea by some story that was plain and near us that we might instantly see the force and bearing of what he said."

Later, Nat Grigsby and his brother were married at the same time, and brought their wives home to their father's cabin. They had a grand reception for pioneer life, but, in consequence of some pique, did not invite Abraham, who felt the slight keenly. In his chagrin, he wrote a piece of poetry, which he called "The Chronicles of Reuben," (Reuben was the name of one of the Grigsby brothers) and dropped it in the road where he was quite sure it would fall into their hands. It was a very sarcastic production, and caused quite a sensation, not only in the family, but also in the neighborhood. It was a thoughtless act of Abraham, which he regretted afterwards and the whole affair was subsequently settled on a lasting basis. Nat Grigsby wrote, after Abraham was distinguished in public life:—

"Lincoln did write what is called the 'Chronicles of Reuben'—a satire on the Grigsby and Josiah Crawford, —not the school-master, but the man who lent Lincoln 'The Life of Washington.' The satire was good, sharp, cutting; it hurt us then, but it is all over now. There is no family in the land who, after this, loved Abe so well, and who now look upon him as so great a man. We all voted for him—all that could—children and grandchildren, first, last, and always."

Dennis Hanks, who ought to know more about Abraham, from fourteen to eighteen years of age, than any of his companions, has so characteristically described his way of learning and making progress, that we quote his description here:—

"He learned by sight, scent and hearing. He heard all that was said, and talked over and over the questions heard; wore them slick, greasy and threadbare. He went to political and other speeches and gatherings; he would hear all sides and opinions, talk them over and discuss them, agreeing or disagreeing. Abe, as I said before, was originally a Democrat after the order of Jackson, so was his father, so we all were. He preached, made speeches, read for us, explained to us, etc. Abe was a cheerful boy, a witty boy, was humorous always sometimes would get sad, not very often. He would frequently make political and other speeches to the boys; he was calm, logical and clear always. He attended trials, went to court always, read the Revised Statutes of Indiana, dated 1827, heard law speeches, and listened to law trials, etc. He was always reading, scribbling, writing, ciphering, writing poetry, and the like. In Gentryville, about one mile west of Thomas Lincoln's farm, Lincoln would go and tell his jokes and stories, and was so odd, original, humorous and witty, that all the people in town would gather around him. He would keep them there till midnight. Abe was a good talker, a good reader, and was a kind of newsboy."

In consequence of the prevalence of the milk-disease, from time to time, the Lincolns discussed the subject of removal to Illinois. John Hanks had gone thither, and sent back favorable reports of the country. John returned to Kentucky after residing with the Lincolns four years, as we have said before, and afterward removed to Illinois. It was natural, therefore, when the question of escaping from the dreaded milk-disease was raised, to turn towards that State. The next chapter will furnish an account of the removal.

CHAPTER XIV
OFF TO ILLINOIS

Before the 1st of January, 1830, Mr. Lincoln decided to remove to Illinois. Dennis Hanks and Levi Hall, who had married Mrs. Lincoln's daughters, concluded to remove, also, with their families. Dennis had made a flying visit thither, after he had recovered from a severe attack of the milk-disease, and returned with marvelous stories about the country. He went to visit "Uncle John Hanks," who had settled four miles from Decatur, in Macon County. On this account, Mr. Lincoln decided to go directly to "Uncle John's."

He sold his farm to the senior Gentry, and his corn and hogs to David Turnham. He received ten cents a bushel for his corn, and sold the hogs for a "song." He took with him to Illinois "some stock-cattle, one horse, one bureau, one table, one clothes-chest, one set of chairs, working utensils, clothing, etc." The goods belonging to the three families were loaded upon Mr. Lincoln's wagon, an "ironed" wagon, which was the first one he ever owned. It was drawn by four yoke of oxen, two of them Lincoln's and the other two Hanks's; and Abraham drove the team. There were thirteen persons in all who went— men, women and children.

Abraham was twenty-one years of age on the twelfth day of February, two or three days before they started upon their journey.

"You are your own man now," said his father.

"What of that?" was Abraham's reply, suspecting what thoughts were in his mind.

"Why, you can go or stay, though I don't see how I can get along without you."

"Nor I; and I want to go to Illinois more than you do, and I shall see you safely there, and settled down, before I leave you."

"I'm glad of that," continued his father. "I won't ask you to stay at home one minute after we get settled down. You ought to be looking out for yourself, now that you are of age."

"We'll talk about that when we get there. Perhaps I shall find enough to do for a while to get you fixed up, and I can attend to that better than you can."

"Well, it's a long ways there, and I'm almost sorry that I undertook it at my time of life. It looks like a great job to get there, and begin new."

"It don't to me. We'll be there, and have a roof over our heads, in less than four weeks."

"If nothing happens, you mean."

"There will something happen, I'm thinking," answered Abraham, dryly, "or we shall never get there."

"What?"

"I expect that it will happen that we shall go there in about two weeks, by hard traveling. If that don't happen, I shall be sorry."

"We shall see," added Mr. Lincoln.

The fact was, Abraham thought too much of his father and mother to leave them to undertake such a journey alone. No money could have hired him to leave them before they were settled in Illinois. Mr. Scripps, who knows all the circumstances well, says: "He was the only son of his father, now advanced in years, and it was not in his nature to desert his aged sire at a time when all the hardships, privations, and toil of making a new home in a new country were about to be entered upon. Whatever the future may have seemed to hold in it, as a reward for effort specially directed to that end, he cheerfully put aside in obedience to his sense of duty, and engaged at once and heartily in the work before him."

The above writer, a Western man himself, describes the manner of moving in those days, as follows:—

"In those days, when people changed their residence from one State or settlement to another, they took all their movable possessions with them—their household goods, their kitchen utensils, including provisions for the journey, their farming implements, their horses and cattle. The former were loaded into wagons, drawn, for the most part, by oxen and the latter were driven by the smaller boys of the family, who were sometimes assisted by their sisters and mother. Thus arranged for a journey of weeks—not unfrequently of months, —the emigrant set out, thinking but little of the hardships before him—of bad roads, of unbridged streams, of disagreeable weather, of sleeping on the ground or in the wagon, of sickness, accidents, and sometimes death by the way—dwelling chiefly in thought upon the novelty and excitement of the trip, the rumored attractions of the new country whither he was going, and of the probable advantages likely to result from the change. By ten or fifteen miles per day, over untraveled roads, now across mountains, swamps and watercourses, and now through dense, umbrageous forests, and across broad prairies where the horizon alone bounded the vision, the caravan of wagons, men, women and children, flocks and herds, toiled onward by day, sleeping under the broad canopy of stars at night, patiently accomplishing the destined journey, sometimes of weeks', sometimes of months' duration."

In this way the Lincoln, Hanks and Hall families moved to Illinois. The distance was about two hundred miles —not much of an undertaking for the perseverance and heroism of pioneer families.

The weather proved favorable nearly all the way, though the roads were excessively muddy. For miles Abraham walked through mud a foot deep. Often, for a long distance, he waded in water up to his knees (and it is well known that his knees were not very low down). When they had performed nearly one hundred and fifty miles of the journey, they came to the Kaskaskia River, where they found the bottom lands overflowed, and the old corduroy road nearly gone.

"We're done to now," said Hanks.

"I don't know about that," answered Abraham. "Let us see about it."

"It is plain enough to see, I should think. The man who directed us back there yesterday said, if the bottom was overflowed, it would be three miles through water, and I should think it was more than that."

"I don't care if it's twice three," replied Abraham, "if it's not too deep to wade."

"We can wait some days for the water to fall, or we can go up or down the river a few miles, and possibly find a better place to cross," suggested Hanks.

"That will take too much time. The water won't fall yet awhile. It is February yet, you know, and the rivers are always high. I am for going straight ahead through thick and thin."

"That's the only way, I think," said Mr. Lincoln, who had listened to the conversation, while he was looking rather doubtfully upon the flood of water before them.

"We can't stay here for the water to fall, that's certain," continued Abraham, "and as to finding a better place to cross, I don't believe we can, if we go around twenty miles."

"And that would take time, too," suggested his father.

"Yes, and I am for going right along. I will go forward and if I go under, the rest of you may take warning." This remark was made rather in a strain of pleasantry, to inspire all hearts around him with courage. "Come, Dennis, what do you say? Will you follow me?"

"Of course; I can go where you can."

It was settled to go forward, turning neither to the right hand nor left. And for three miles Abraham drove his team through water that was up to his waist, urging his oxen along, and cheering the hearts of the company with words of encouragement. Mr. Lamon says, "In crossing the swollen and tumultuous Kaskaskia the wagon and oxen were nearly swept away." But Abraham's pluck and energy overcame the difficulty, and, on the first day of March, 1830, they arrived at John Hanks' house, four miles northwest of Decatur. What kind of a cabin Uncle John possessed, we do not know, but the advent of thirteen visitors must have fully occupied all the spare room in it. But squeezing the largest number of persons into the smallest space was incidental to pioneer life.

"I've fixed on the spot for you to settle," said Uncle John to Mr. Lincoln, "and there's a lot of logs there for a cabin, which I cut last year."

"How far away is it?" inquired Mr. Lincoln.

"Only a few miles; and it will be a short job to put up a cabin, now the logs are all ready and you are welcome to them."

"Well, that is a great lift," replied Mr. Lincoln; "with the logs all cut, Abe, Dennis, and I will make short work of building a shelter."

"And my help, too," added Uncle John; "nothing to do now but to get you fixed."

"I'm going to have a better house than we had in Indiana," chimed in Abraham, who was listening to the conversation. "Hewed logs, and less mud."

"I'll second that project," interjected his mother. "A little more labor and expense upon a habitation will increase comforts ten-fold."

The subject of a log-house was thus discussed, and the following day, Mr. Lincoln, Uncle John, Abraham and Dennis repaired to the location selected, to investigate. It was on the north side of Sangamon River about ten miles west of Decatur; and, perhaps, six miles, in a straight line, from Uncle John's cabin. All were delighted with the location, mainly because it was at the junction of the timber and prairie lands, and was well supplied with water.

Short work was made in erecting the best log-house the Lincoln family ever occupied. Abraham took charge of the work, because he was determined to have as good a house for his parents as could be built of logs. There was a good supply of material that Uncle John had prepared, from which Abraham selected the best logs, every one of which was carefully hewn, though the only tools they had to work with was a common axe, a broad-axe, a hand-saw, and a "drawer-knife."

After the cabin was built, a smoke-house and stable were erected near by. The doors and floor of the cabin were made of puncheon, and the gable-ends of the structure boarded up with plank "rived" by Abraham's hand out of oak timber. The nails used—and they were very few—were all brought from their old home in Indiana.

"You never saw such land as this," remarked John Hanks to Mr. Lincoln. "The land in Indiana can't compare with this prairie land."

"I'm convinced of that," answered Mr. Lincoln; "the half wasn't told us. And we must turn over a big piece of it this spring for corn, and fence it, too. Abe is great on splitting rails."

"He can have a chance to split 'em to his heart's content now," continued John. "It'll take a pile on 'em to fence fifteen acres, and you'll want to put in as much as that."

"And fifteen acres of such land as this will make such a corn-field as Indiana farmers are not acquainted with," added Mr. Lincoln.

"Abe and I can break it up," continued John; "and fence it into the bargain."

This was the final decision, after the Lincolns were settled in their new home—that Abraham and John should plough the fifteen acres, and then fence the field. With the four yokes of oxen, each driving two yokes, the fifteen acres were turned over within a week; and, as soon as the planting was done, the rail-splitting and fencing commenced in earnest. Abraham and John got out all the rails, and put up the fence around the fifteen acres. Those rails became historic after thirty years, and played an important part in an interesting chapter of our national career, as we shall learn hereafter.

With all his labor at home, Abraham found time to work out considerably in the neighborhood. Rev. A. Hale of Springfield, Illinois, visited the locality, after the death of Abraham Lincoln, and one Mrs. Brown related the following to him:—

"I remember Mr. Lincoln. He worked for my old man, and helped make a crap. We lived on the same farm we live on now, and he worked and made a crap, and the next winter they hauled the crap all the way to Galena, and sold it. At that time there was no public-houses, and travelers were obliged to stay at any house along the road that could take them in. One evening a right smart-looking man rode up to the fence, and asked my old man if he could get to stay over night. 'Well,' said Mr. Brown, 'we can feed your critter, and give you something to eat, but we can't lodge you unless you can sleep on the bed with the hired man.' The man hesitated, and asked, 'Where is he?' 'Well,' said Mr. Brown, 'you can come and see him.' So the man got down from his crittur, and Mr. Brown took him around to where, in the shade of the house, Abe lay his full length on the ground, with an open book before him. 'There,' said Mr. Brown, pointing to him, 'he is.' The stranger looked at him a minute, and said, 'Well, I think he'll do;' and he stayed and slept with the President of the United States."

It is claimed that Mrs. Brown was wrong in saying that Abraham worked for her husband, the fact being that he worked for one Taylor, near by, and boarded with her. It is probable, also, that he worked for him only at such times, during that first summer in Illinois, as he was not needed at home.

"Abe was the roughest looking fellow I ever saw," remarked George Cluse, who worked with him occasionally that year; "he was so tall, awkward and wrinkled!"

"Was he a good worker?"

"None better to be found; and he knew more than any man I ever saw; but his dress was comical."

"How did he dress?"

"He wore trousers made of flax and tow, cut tight at the ankles, and out at both knees. I looked bad enough myself, but compared with him, my dress was superb." At the time Thomas Lincoln left Indiana, few families in that part of the country used woolen goods. They were unknown there until about 1825.

"I split rails with him a good deal," continued Cluse. "He'd split more rails in a day than any other man. He was strong as an ox, and never got tired. He made a bargain that season with Nancy Miller, to split four hundred rails for every yard of brown jeans, dyed with white walnut bark, that would be necessary to make him a pair of trousers and that was the way he got trousers that were not out at the knees."

"What about reading? Was he fond of books?"

"When I worked with him, he'd not much chance to fool with books; but he was always talking history, and politics, and great men; and I have seen him going to his work with a book in his hand. Then, Abe walked five, six, and seven miles to his work."

It is quite evident that Abraham made himself extremely useful in Illinois in the year 1830 by his industry and hard labor. He made himself very agreeable, also, by his intelligence and social qualities. George Cluse says, "He was a welcome guest in every house in the neighborhood."

In the autumn of that year, fever and ague visited the region of Decatur, and every member of the Lincoln family were attacked by it—not severely, nevertheless with sufficient violence to make them "shake." Even Abraham's stalwart frame came under its power for a brief season; but he shook it off before it had much of a chance to shake him. The experience, however, satisfied the family that their location in Illinois was not favorable to health. And we may state here as well as anywhere that in consequence of the appearance of this disease, Mr. Lincoln removed subsequently to a more favorable locality, and finally settled in Cole's County, where he died on the 17th of January, 1851.

The first winter of the Lincolns in Illinois was a very trying one. It was the winter of the "great snow," as it was called, when, for weeks, it averaged three feet deep. Being chiefly dependent upon the rifle for meat, the severity of the winter interfered somewhat with their supplies. But for the strength, endurance, and perseverance of Abraham, their comforts would have been abridged much more. His use of the rifle during that rigorous winter well nigh disproved what one of his early associates writes to us, viz.: "Abe was not much of a hunter; we seldom went hunting together. The time spent by us boys in this amusement was improved by him in the perusal of some good book."

CHAPTER XV

ANOTHER TRIP TO NEW ORLEANS

Denton Offutt was a trader, residing at New Salem. Meeting John Hanks, one day, he said:—

"John! I want you to take a boat for me to New Orleans on a trading trip ; you understand the business." John had some reputation as a waterman.

"I can't do it; don't fancy the business."

"Fudge! you can do it if you only think so. I'll pay you extra for it. You are the only man who can do it to suit me."

"I know of a man who can do it for you," said John. "Abe Lincoln understands it; and perhaps he'll do it."

"Who's Abe Lincoln?"

"He's a relative of mine; came to Illinois from Indiana about one year ago, and settled a few miles from me."

"Well, I don't know anything about him," continued Offutt, "and I do know about you. Say you'll go."

"Maybe I'll go if Abe and John Johnston will go."

"And who's John Johnston?"

"He is Abe Lincoln's step-brother, and lives with him. He came with him from Indiana."

"And you think they are good men for the business?"

"I know they are; Abe, especially, can't be beat on a boat. He's the tallest and strongest chap in Illinois."

"Well, now, John, I'll do most any way to get you to undertake the trip," continued Offutt; "and if you'll see your two friends, and get them to go, I'll see that they'll make a good thing of it."

"How much pay will you give?"

"I'll give you—all three of you—fifty cents a day and, at the end of the trip, I will divide sixty dollars, in addition, equally between you."

"That's good pay, and no mistake," replied John, who was rather surprised at the generosity of the offer: "I think we'll be able to arrange it."

Offutt was a man of considerable property for that region, and he was generous, too, some said "too generous for his own good."

John Hanks lost no time in laying the subject before Abraham and Johnston.

"I should like the job," Abraham replied at once. "That is larger pay than I ever had, and I rather like the business."

"I can't say that I like the business," said Hanks; "but I think I'll accept this offer. Offutt is a capital fellow, and I would go on such a trip for him a little quicker than I would for anybody else."

"Agreed," was John Johnston's laconic way of saying that he would go. The fact was, Offutt had made them a very generous offer—larger pay than any one of them had ever received.

It was February, 1831, when Offutt made the offer and, early in March, the fortunate trio left home to meet Offutt at Springfield, according to arrangement. They proceeded down the Sangamon in a canoe to Jamestown (then known as Judy's Ferry) five miles east of Springfield. Thence they walked to Springfield, where they met Offutt at "Elliott's Tavern." Offutt met Abraham with a look of surprise. He was not expecting to see a giant, although Hanks told him that his relative was the tallest man in Illinois; nor was he expecting to see a man as green as he was tall. However, they were soon on the best of terms, and Offutt said:—

"I've been badly disappointed; expected a boat built by this time, at the mouth of Spring Creek, but I learned yesterday that it won't touched and now what's to be done."

"Build a boat at once," answered Abraham, with a promptness that won Offutt's heart.

"Can you build a boat?" asked Offutt.

"Of course I can," replied Abraham. "We three can put the job through in three weeks."

"We'll have the boat, then, in short order," responded Offutt. "Plenty of timber at Spring Creek, and we can raft it down to Sangamon town, and build the boat there."

They repaired to Spring Creek, and spent about two weeks there cutting timber "on Congress land," boarding a full mile from their work. While there, Abraham walked back to Judy's Ferry, ten miles distant, and brought down the canoe which they had left there. The timber was rafted down to Sangamon town, where Abraham and his two companions erected a shanty for temporary shelter. Here they boarded themselves, Abraham playing the part of "cook" to the. entire satisfaction of the two Johns. The lumber was sawed at Kilpatrick's mill, one mile and a half distant. With all these inconveniences, the boat was ready for the trip within four weeks, and a very substantial boat it was.

Offutt joined the party at Sangamon town, and was present during the construction of the boat. He soon learned that the long, tall, and green Abraham was a young man of rare talents. Offutt was a Whig, and so was Abraham now, although the latter was not willing to hear the former abuse Jackson. Offutt indulged his pique in this line, and Abraham met him squarely, and hot discussions followed, enlivening the camp and making merry times. Offutt was quite a politician, but Abraham was more than a match for him. His familiarity with the lives of a few of the great men of the country, and the habits, customs and principles of their times, gave him a decided advantage over Offutt. Abraham often contributed to the merriment of the camp by reciting "prose-like orations" and quoting poetry. He also extracted a large amount of fun out of his new occupation—that of "cook." On the whole, the two weeks at boat-building were merry ones, and they quickly sped.

While the little company was employed at Sangamon town, a juggler gave an exhibition in the upper room of John Carman's house. Another says: "Abe went to it dressed in a suit of rough blue jeans. He had on shoes, but the trousers did not reach them by about twelve inches and the naked shin, which had excited John Romine's laughter years ago in Indiana, was still exposed. Between the roundabout and the waist of the trousers there was another wide space uncovered and, considering these defects, his attire was thought to be somewhat inelegant, even in those times. His hat, however, was a great improvement on coon skins and opossum. It was woolen, broad brimmed and low-crowned. In his hat ' the showman cooked eggs.' Whilst Abe was handing it up to him, after the man had long sought for a similar favor from the rest of the audience, he remarked, 'Mister, the reason I didn't give you my hat before was out of respect to your eggs, not care for my hat."

As soon as the boat was completed, a partial cargo of barrel-pork, hogs and corn was taken on board, and the craft started down the river. Offutt went in the capacity of merchant, to make purchases along the way. Just below New Salem, of which we shall hear and see much hereafter, the boat stuck fast on Rutledge's dam through one night and part of a day —"one end of it hanging over the dam and the other sunk deep in the water behind."

"A pretty fix now," cried out Offutt; "it will take longer to get out of this scrape than it did to build the boat."

"Guess not," replied Abraham, who took in the situation at a glance. "We must unload, though."

"Into the river, I s'pose," responded Offutt.

"Borrow a boat, and transfer the cargo to it, and let us see what can be done," continued Abraham.

This was in the morning, after the boat had "stuck" through the night. Nearly all the people of New Salem had assembled on shore watching the movements.

"Your boat will sink or break in two pieces, if you are not in a hurry," cried out a looker-on. And such a result seemed inevitable. For the cargo was sliding backwards, and the peril increased with every passing minute. But, under Abraham's direction, the cargo was soon shifted to a borrowed boat, when he immediately bored a large hole in the bottom of that part of the boat extending over the dam. Then he erected "queer machinery" for tilting the part of the boat under water, and holding it in position until the water was emptied through the hole bored. Stopping up the hole after the water had run out was the work of only a few minutes, when the relieved craft was pushed over the dam, and glided into the deep pool below amidst the hurrahs of the many beholders. Offutt was particularly elated.

"That's real skill, Abe," he cried; "one in a thousand couldn't do that. Three cheers for Abe Lincoln," he shouted, swinging his hat, and leading the cheers vociferously.

It was a hearty tribute to Abraham's ingenuity in which the observers joined without reserve.

"When I get back from New Orleans," shouted Offutt, turning to the beholders on shore, "I'll build a steamboat to navigate the Sangamon River, and make Abe captain. I'll build it with runners for ice and rollers for shoals and dams, and, by thunder, it will have to go, with Abe for captain."

This funny way of putting it awoke another burst of applause from the spectators, while the tall, awkward Abraham shook his sides with laughter.

This mishap to their craft set Abraham to thinking of ways to overcome the difficulties of navigating Western rivers. It was several years, however, before his thoughts and studies thereupon took tangible shape in the form of an invention. After he was elected President, the Washington correspondent of the Boston Advertiser wrote as follows concerning it:—

"Occupying an ordinary and common-place position in one of the show cases in the large hall of the Patent Office is one little model which, in ages to come, will be prized as at once one of the most curious and one of the most sacred relics in that vast museum of unique and priceless things. This is a plain and simple model of a steamboat, roughly fashioned in wood, by the hand of Abraham Lincoln. It bears date in 1849, when the inventor was known simply as a successful lawyer and rising politician of Central Illinois. Neither his practice nor his politics took up so much of his time as to prevent him from giving much attention to contrivances which he hoped might be of benefit to the world and of profit to himself.

"The design of this invention is suggestive of one phase of Abraham Lincoln's early life, when he went up and down the Mississippi as a flat-boatman, and became familiar with some of the dangers and inconveniences attending the navigation of the Western rivers. It is an attempt to make it an easy matter to transport vessels over shoals and snags and sawyers. The main idea is that of an apparatus resembling a noiseless bellows placed on each side of the hull of the craft, just below the water-line and worked by an odd but not complicated system of ropes, valves and pulleys. When the keel of the vessel grates against the sand or obstruction, these bellows are to be filled with air and thus buoyed up the ship is expected to float lightly and gayly over the shoal which would otherwise have proved a serious interruption to her voyage.

"The model, which is about eighteen or twenty inches long, and has the air of being whittled with a knife out of a shingle and a cigar-box, is built without any elaboration or ornament, or any extra apparatus beyond that necessary to show the operation of buoying the steamer over the obstructions. Herein it differs from very many of the models which share with it the shelter of the immense halls of the Patent Office, and which are fashioned with wonderful nicety and exquisite finish, as if much of the labor and thought and affection of a lifetime had been devoted to their construction. This is a model of a different kind; carved as one might imagine a retired rail-splitter would whittle, strongly, but not smoothly, and evidently made with a view solely to convey, by the simplest possible means, to the minds of the patent authorities, an idea of the purpose and plan of the simple invention. The label on the steamer's deck informs us that the patent was obtained but we do not learn that the navigation of the Western rivers was revolutionized by this quaint conception. The modest little model has reposed here sixteen years and, since it found its resting-place here on the shelf, the shrewd inventor has found it his task to guide the Ship of State over shoals more perilous, and obstructions more obstinate, than any prophet dreamed of when Abraham Lincoln wrote his bold autograph on the prow of this miniature steamer."

When the boat was safely over the dam, in the deep pool below, it was re-loaded, and then sped on its way. At Salt Creek, Offutt stopped to make a purchase of live hogs, but the wild vicious animals were determined not to go on board and they were full of fight. Once on board, they might make fearful war upon each other, causing much trouble to the trader and his crew. After vainly trying to drive the hogs towards the river, Abraham remarked:—

"It's no use; they are too ugly to go where you want them to go."

"They wouldn't be hogs, if they did," responded Offutt. "You'll have to get up some sort of a tackling, Abe, to get them aboard, as you got the boat over the dam." The last remark was made partly in praise of Abraham, and partly in rein of humor.

"Sew up their eyes and tie their legs," exclaimed Abraham; "there's no other way to get them aboard and keep them still after they get there."

"That's it, exactly, Abe," replied Offutt; "I knew that you could find a way out of the trouble. Let's see you put your theory in practice."

Abraham seized a hog by the ears, and directed Hanks to hold him by the tail, while Offutt should tie his legs and sew up his eyelids. "If he fights, he must fight in the dark," he added.

The experiment proved successful and the hogs were loaded into a cart and drawn to the river, where Abraham took them up in his long arms, one by one, and carried them aboard.

"Rather cruel," he said, "but there's no help for it. In a battle with wild hogs we must use war-tactics."

"You're a genius, Abe," said Offutt; "ugly hogs and dams and shoals are of little account to you."

Before leaving Salt Creek, Abraham rigged up "curious-looking sails," with plank and cloth to increase their speed. The device accomplished his purpose; but it "was a sight to behold," as one reliable witness declared. When they "rushed down through Beardstown," the craft presented such a comical appearance that "the people came out and laughed at them."

"Let them laugh and take it out in laughing, so long as the thing works well," said Abraham, rather enjoying the singular exhibition because it attracted attention.

They stopped only at Memphis, Vicksburg and Natchez, after leaving Salt Creek, during the whole distance to New Orleans, where they arrived without another drawback. Offutt disposed of his goods readily, and made a very profitable trip of it. At the same time, he obtained such an insight into Abraham's character and abilities that he resolved to make the best use of him possible in future.

"Inhuman," exclaimed Abraham, one day, when they saw a gang of slaves chained together, and a merciless driver cracking his whip about their heads. "A nation that tolerates such inhumanity will have to pay for it some day."

"They are used to it," replied Offutt, "and mind no more about it than cattle."

"What if they don't?" retorted Abraham. "You can't make cattle of men without being inhuman. I tell you, the nation that does it will be cursed."

"Not in our day," remarked Offutt.

"In somebody's day, though," responded Abraham, promptly.

That Abraham's visits to New Orleans served to increase his hostility to slavery, there can be no doubt, especially his visit in 1831. For John Hanks said, thirty years afterwards, recalling the incidents of that memorable trip:—

"There it was we saw negroes chained, maltreated, whipped and scourged. Lincoln saw it, and his heart bled. It made him sad, he looked bad, felt bad, was thoughtful and abstracted. I can say, knowing it, that it was on this trip that he formed his opinions of slavery. It ran its iron into him then and there— May, 1831. I have heard him say so, often and often."

Providence was leading Abraham in a way that he knew not, disciplining him for the day when he would be forced to grapple with the system of American slavery, to overthrow it. All such incidents as these become more interesting and important in their providential connection with his future public career.

In June, Offutt, with his men, was ready to return, and he engaged passage for all on a steamer up the Mississippi to St. Louis. On the way up the river, Offutt surprised Abraham by saying:

"Abe, I think you can sell goods for me; how would you like it?"

"What kind of goods?" Abraham asked.

"Store goods, such as country stores keep," Offutt answered. "How would you like to run my store at New Salem?"

"I should like it well enough provided I could do it."

"You can do it well enough; I have no fear of that. If you'll say the word, I will put you in charge of my store at New Salem."

"I'll say the word, then," continued Abraham, "if we can agree on the terms."

They did agree upon the terms, and, before they parted company at St. Louis, it was arranged to transform Abraham into a "storekeeper." Offutt had so exalted an idea of Abraham's tact and ability that he was prepared to commit almost any trust to his keeping. Abraham was to return home, visit his parents, and then repair to New Salem to be installed over a country store.

At St. Louis, Offutt's business made it necessary for him to separate from his efficient trio; so Abraham, Hanks, and Johnston started on foot for the interior of Illinois. When they reached Edwardsville, twenty five miles from St. Louis, Hanks took the road to Springfield, and Abraham and Johnston took that to Cole's County, whither Thomas Lincoln removed after Abraham left home.

A few days after Abraham reached his father's house in Cole's County, a famous wrestler, by the name of Daniel Needham, called to see him. Needham had heard of Abraham's great strength, and that he was an expert wrestler, and he desired to see him--

"S'pose we try a hug," suggested Needham.

"No doubt you can throw me," answered Abraham. "You are in practice, and I am not."

"Then you'll not try it?" continued Needham.

"Not much sport in being laid on my back," was Abraham's evasive answer.

"It remains to be seen who will lay on his back," suggested Needham. "S'pose you make the trial."

By persistent urging Abraham finally consented to meet Needham, at a specified place and time, according to the custom that prevailed. Abraham was true to his promise, met the bully, and threw him twice with no great difficulty.

Needham was both disappointed and chagrined. His pride was greatly humbled and his wrath was not a little exercised.

"You have thrown me twice, Lincoln, but you can't whip me," he said.

"I don't want to whip you, whether I can or not," Abraham replied magnanimously; "and I don't want to get whipped;" and the closing sentence was spoken jocosely.

"Well, I stump you to whip me," Needham cried, thinking that Lincoln was unwilling to undertake it. "Throwing a man is one thing and thrashing him is another."

"You are right, my friend and I've no special desire to do either," answered Abraham.

Needham continued to press him, whereupon Lincoln said:

"Needham, are you satisfied that I can throw you." If you are not, and must be convinced through a thrashing, I will do that, too, for your sake."

This was putting the matter practically enough to open the bully's eyes, which was all Abraham hoped to accomplish. He was willing to show his strength by wrestling to please his companions and get a little sport out of it but he despised a bully like Needham, and considered such encounters for any purpose but sport as beneath his notice, Needham put the proper interpretation upon Abraham's words, and, considering "discretion the better part of valor," he withdrew as gracefully as possible.

We shall turn next to Abraham's success as a country merchant.

CHAPTER XVI
IN A PIONEER STORE

About the first of August, 1831, Abraham met Offutt at New Salem as previously arranged. His employer had collected a quantity of goods at Beardstown, awaiting transportation. Until the goods arrived, Abraham had nothing to do, but loitered about the town, then numbering only from twelve to fifteen habitations. Some of the people recognized him as the ingenious fellow who engineered the boat over Rutledge's dam a few months before; and they scraped acquaintance with him at once.

On the day of the election he was loitering about the polling place, when one of the judges remarked to Minter Graham, the schoolmaster, "We are short of a clerk; what shall we do?"

The schoolmaster replied, "Perhaps the tall stranger yonder can write and maybe he will serve in that capacity."

"Possibly," responded the judge, as he advanced towards Abraham, and said:—

"Can you write?" It must be remembered that, at that time in that region, many people could neither read nor write, so that getting a clerk was not an easy matter.

"Yes, a little," answered Abraham.

"Will you act as clerk of the election today?"

"Yes, I'll try," was Abraham's modest reply. "I will do the best I can, if you so request."

"Well, it will accommodate us very much if you will," continued the judge, conducting the stranger to the polls. As yet, Abraham had not announced to any one that he was soon to preside over the store of New Salem.

That he discharged the duties of the office acceptably on that day, we have positive evidence for Minter Graham, the schoolmaster, who was clerk also, says:—

"He performed the duties with great facility, much fairness and honesty and impartiality. This was the first official act of his life. I clerked with him on the same day, and at the same polls. The election-books are now in the city of Springfield, Illinois, where they can be seen and inspected any day."

Dr. Nelson of New Salem was about to remove to Texas, and had built a flat-boat on which to convey his goods and family thither. He was ready to start when Abraham was waiting for the arrival of Offutt's merchandize. The Sangamon river was at best a turbulent stream, and was then swollen to overflowing, so that the doctor required a pilot to Beardstown. Some one suggested to him the young fellow who took the boat over Rutledge's dam and Abraham was accordingly engaged. He piloted the flat-boat successfully to Beardstown, although he said the river over flowed its banks so unprecedentedly for that season of the year that he sometimes floated over the prairie, three miles from the channel. At Beardstown he received his pay, and left the doctor to run down the Illinois while he returned on foot to New Salem.

On the arrival of Offutt's merchandize, the inhabitants of the village understood what the tall stranger's business was in town. For Abraham proceeded at once to unpack the goods, and arrange them for exhibition in the store. There were groceries, dry goods, hardwares, stonewares, earthenwares, cups and saucers, plates, knives and forks, boots and shoes, coffee, tea, sugar, molasses, butter, gunpowder, tobacco, with other articles too numerous to mention, including the inevitable whiskey, which nearly everybody except Abraham considered indispensable.

Within a few days Abraham was well under way with Offutt's commercial enterprise. The new goods drew customers, and the new clerk attracted attention. He was "jokey," agreeable and social, "worth a dozen such fellers as Offutt's other man," as one of the citizens put it.

Offutt's business elsewhere did not allow him to remain at New Salem, though he was there long enough to risk another venture. He leased the mill of Cameron and Rutledge at the foot of the hill, and put it in charge of Abraham along with the store. At the same time he hired

William G. Green for assistant clerk in the store, that Abraham might divide his time between the two enterprises.

Offutt was a great talker, and some people said he was "rattle-brained" and "harum-scarum." But no one claimed that Abraham was like him, not even Offutt himself, for the latter was won't to magnify the abilities and fidelity of his clerk extravagantly. His confidence in him was well-nigh boundless, and he drew largely upon the dictionary for words to express his admiration of the new storekeeper. He did not hesitate to say, "Abe knows more than any man in the United States." If confronted by any one who dared to dispute his assertion, he would supplement his statement by another: "Abe will be President of the United States some time. Now remember what I say." Between engineering the boat over Rutledge's dam and the eulogiums of Offutt, Abraham was quite grandly introduced to the inhabitants of New Salem. It is not strange that he entered upon his labors there with flying colors, causing the store to become the centre of attraction in that township. New customers were multiplied, and old ones became even more reliable patrons.

Then, in Illinois, the merchant of the town was second to no citizen in importance. Abraham stepped at once into this position of notoriety and then, in addition, his knowledge, affability, and uprightness, contributed to make him a still more important personage.

"The best feller we've had in the store yet," remarked Jason Duncan to a companion named Carman; "and he knows a thing or two."

"Not so much as Offutt thinks he does," replied Carman; "but it's fun to hear him talk."

"And he is so accommodating and honest;" continued Duncan. "Mother says she'd trust him with anything because he's so honest. She paid him a few cents too much, and he brought it back to her."

"Not many on 'em who'd do that," replied Carman. "Every body says that he gives Scripture weight and measure."

"And he is none of your high-fly gentry," added Duncan, "if he does keep store. He knows more in half an hour than Offutt's other man did in a week."

"Yes, and he's drawing customers that haven't traded there before, just because he does the thing that is right. Everybody knows that he won't He nor cheat and they believe just what he says, and they like to trade with him on that account."

"Offutt was a fortunate man to get him to keep his store," continued Duncan. "It will be money in his pocket."

"And he seems to attend to the business just as closely as he would if it was his own," said Carman; "he is there early and late, and he is always reading when he has nothing else to do."

"That's because he is honest," replied William; "a dishonest clerk wouldn't care whether the business prospered or not, nor whether people were pleased or not. Offutt is off so much that he would not know whether a clerk was faithful or not, and it's lucky for him that he hit upon Abe as he did."

"And it's about as lucky for us. I tell you how 'tis: that store is now just about the best place to go to that there is anywhere about, Abe is the greatest fellow on stories that I ever heard, and many of them are real facts of history. You ought to hear him tell about Washington and Franklin and Clay, as he did the other day. He knows a heap more about such things than any body about here."

Two or three incidents in this place will show what reason existed for such discussions as the foregoing concerning Abraham.

One day he sold a bill of goods to Mrs. Duncan, amounting to two dollars and six cents. On running over his account again in the evening, he found that Mrs. Duncan paid him six cents too much. Immediately on closing the store and locking the door for the night, he started for Mrs. Duncan's house, more than two miles away, to carry the six cents to her. He slept better that night for the walk and honesty.

On another occasion a woman came into the store late in the evening, just as he was closing, for half a pound of tea. The tea was weighed and delivered, and he left for the night. On returning in the morning he noticed a four-ounce weight was on the scales, instead of an eight-ounce and he knew at once that he had given the customer a quarter of a pound of tea, instead of a half pound. He weighed another quarter of a pound, closed the store, and delivered the tea to the woman, before commencing the labors of the day. Such acts of uprightness won universal confidence and they formed the subject of conversation in many social gatherings.

One day a bully entered the store when Abraham was waiting upon two or three female customers. He belched out profanity and vulgarity, regardless of the presence of ladies. Abraham leaned over the counter, and whispered, "Shut up; don't talk so in the presence of ladies."

The fellow was too full of whiskey to be suppressed in that way, and he became more profane and vulgar than before.

"I'd like to see the man who'll stop me from saying what I'm a mind to. I've wanted to thrash you for a long time."

Abraham simply replied, "Wait until these ladies have gone, and I'll satisfy you."

The bully was raving and the ladies soon retired. "Now," exclaimed Abraham, springing over the counter, "we'll see whether you'll talk such stuff in this store before ladies."

"Come on, long-legs," the bully shouted.

"If you must be whipped, I may as well do it as any other man," continued Abraham, as he collared the fellow, and put him out of doors. The bully grappled with him, whereupon Abraham threw him upon his back, and, snatching a handful of smart-weed, rubbed it into his face until the fellow bellowed with pain, and promised to behave. Then Abraham allowed him to get up and showed his real kindness of heart by getting water and washing his face, to relieve him of his distress. The outcome of this affair was that the bully was a better man himself from that time, and became a fast friend of Abraham, who was as much of a stickler for politeness to ladies as he was for honesty to all.

Minter Graham, the schoolmaster, was very intimate with Abraham. He was in the store one day when Abraham said to him:

"I want to study English grammar; I never did."

"You've not much time for it, I judge," replied Graham. "Between mill and store, your time is pretty well occupied."

"Well, I have some leisure moments on some days, and can always find time at night when folks are in bed."

"You propose to turn night into day?" Responded Graham, inquiringly. "Too much of such business will wear you out?"

"I'll risk it if I can get a grammar," replied Abraham. "The trouble is to find a grammar about here."

"I know where there is one," said Graham.

"Where?"

"Six miles from here, at Vaner's, is a copy of Kirkham's Grammar."

"I'll buy or borrow it before I'm much older," remarked Abraham. "The time may come when I may want to use it."

"If you ever expect to go before the public in any capacity, it will be a good thing for you," responded Graham. At this time, Graham had inferred from certain remarks of Abraham that he was looking forward to a more public career.

The result of this interview was, that, Abraham walked six miles and borrowed the grammar, the study of which he commenced at once, improving leisure moments in the store, and sitting up late at night to pursue his task.

The grammar rather interfered with the good time young men had with Abraham in the store. Instead of spending leisure moments in entertaining the company, Kirkham's Grammar entertained him. Lamon says, "Sometimes when business was not particularly brisk, he would lie under a shade-tree in front of the store, and pore over the book at other times, a customer would find him stretched on the counter intently engaged the same way. But the store was a bad place for study and he was often seen quietly slipping out of the village, as if he wished to avoid observation, when, if successful in getting off alone, he would spend hours in the woods, 'mastering a book or in a state of profound abstraction. He kept up his old habit of sitting up late at night but as lights were as necessary to his purpose as they were expensive, the village cooper permitted him to sit in his shop, where he burnt the shavings, and kept a blazing fire to read by, when every one else was in bed. The Greens lent him books; the schoolmaster gave him instructions in the store, on the road, or in the meadows; every visitor to New Salem who made the least pretensions to scholarship was waylaid by Abe, and required to explain something which he could not understand. The result of it all was, that the village and the surrounding country wondered at his growth in knowledge, and he soon became as famous for the goodness of his understanding as for the muscular power of his body, and the unfailing humor of his talk."

Kirkham's Grammar appears to have given him a new impulse after knowledge; and his companions felt that they lost considerable enjoyment in consequence. Some of them had a poor opinion of Kirkham.

"Studying grammar, yet," remarked Alley in a contemptuous way.

"Yes; I want to know something about it. I never did."

"Nor I, and that ain't the worst don't;" and Alley laughed as he said it.

"Well, I intend to know a little of it," added Abraham. "It is rather dry, but I am determined to master it, if I can. I want, at least, to discover whether I am a common noun or not."

"You're an luiconunon noun, Abe," said Alley, meaning to compliment his friend at the same time that he got off a pun.

"Your word for it."

"Of course, my word for it. But I am quite sure that if there is anything in that book, you will get it out."

"But really. Alley, this is a very important study, and I think that every one ought to understand it, if they can."

"Not many know anything about it."

"And that does not prove that it is useless. There are a great many things of importance that many people know nothing about."

"That's so but most people have got along without it. My father and mother never studied it in their lives, and I never did, and we've got along well enough so far without it."

"Perhaps you would have got along better with it. I've learned enough already to be of great service to me, and I intend to know more yet."

"But it is only a little time that you get here," suggested Alley. "Just as you get at it somebody comes. I don't think much of that."

"We don't all think alike," responded Abraham.

"That's a fact; I'm pretty sure that if you thought as I do, you wouldn't be troubling your brains over that grammar."

"Perhaps nobody else would, and the 'King's English' would be shockingly murdered. We should have another Babel almost."

"How's that? For the life of me, I can't see any particular good that comes of studying grammar."

"That is because you do not know even the definition of it," replied Abraham. "Grammar is the art of speaking and writing the English language with propriety. And that shows what good it does."

"Perhaps it does."

"Of course it does, whether you can see it or not and I am willing to study for it by day and night."

"I should think it was about enough to study by day, and let the nights go," said Alley, demurely.

"There is where we don't think alike again. It would take me a long time to master this grammar, if I should study only by leisure moments in the daytime. I have used up from two to three hours over it every night."

"Just like you, Abe."

"Just like every poor fellow like me, who must do so, or know little or nothing. Dr.

Franklin carried a book in his pocket, to study when he could, and he kept one by his side in the printing-office to read every minute he had to spare."

"How do you know that? Were you there?" "and Alley's roguishness appeared in his expressive eye.

"Probably," answered Abraham, in the same vein of remark.

"But did you ever read the Life of Dr. Franklin?"

"Certainly, several years ago; and if he had not done just what you think is quite foolish, he would have made candles all his life."

"And that would be shedding on the world, I'm sure," said Alley, with an attempt at punning. "Lucky that somebody was willing to make candles."

But no bantering or pleas for sport could separate Abraham from his grammar. Kirkham was his boon companion in a more important sense than Green, Duncan, Alley, Carman, Herndon, and all the rest of the New Salem associates.

It became customary for the citizens to take their visitors over to Offutt's store to introduce them to Abraham, of whom the whole villages were proud. Richard Yates came to town to visit friends, and they took him over to the store to make Abraham's acquaintance. This was the Richard Yates, who, subsequently, became famous as a public man. He became Governor of Illinois when Abraham became President of the United States, and did noble service for the country in conquering the "Southern Rebellion." Abraham was soon engaged in close conversation upon various subjects, and while they were talking. Alley and Yates' friend left.

The dinner-time arrived before they were aware that nearly an hour had passed since they were introduced to each other. Abraham invited his new acquaintance to dine with him, and they proceeded to the house where he boarded—a low, rough, log house.

"Aunt Lizzie," said Abraham, "I have brought some company home to dinner."

"I'm glad of it, Abe, if you'll take me as you find me," replied the old lady, addressing her remark partly to Abraham, and partly to the visitor.

"No apologies are necessary," said Yates.

"No, none at all," added Abraham.

The dinner was on the table, and it was a very plain one. There was plenty of bread, and milk enough for the company, and the addition of another bowl and spoon provided a dinner for visitor and all.

There were quite a number of members of the family, boarders and children, and the aged matron waited upon the table, pouring the milk, and passing a brimming bowl to each. When Abraham was waited upon, by some mishap, his bowl slipped and rolled over upon the floor, dashing it to pieces, and covering the floor with its contents.

"O dear me!" exclaimed the old lady, in great trouble; "that was all my fault."

"Perhaps not," said Abraham.

"It surely was," she answered. "I am so careless."

"Well, Aunt Lizzie, we'll not discuss whose fault it is," continued Abraham; "only if it don't trouble you, it don't trouble me."

"That's you, Abe, sure," replied Aunt Lizzie. "You're ready to comfort a body."

"A very good trait," said Yates, who was both amused and enlightened by the accident.

"Never mind, Aunt Lizzie," continued Abraham, "you have the worst of it but I am really sorry that your bowl is broken. I don't care so much for the milk, as there is plenty more where that came from. Much worse things happen sometimes."

By this time Aunt Lizzie had another bowl filled for Abraham, and the company proceeded to eat their dinner, while the old lady gathered up the fragments of the broken bowl, and wiped up the floor.

Here Abraham exhibited a trait of character for which he was distinguished from boyhood. He disliked to make trouble for any one, and wanted to see all persons at ease. Hence he was accommodating, never disposed to find fault, inclined to overlook the mistakes and foibles of others. Also, his readiness to assist the needy, and comfort the distressed and unfortunate, proceeded in part from this quality. It was made up of gentlemanly bearing, affability, generosity, and a true regard for the welfare and happiness of others. A rare character is this, though it is always needed, and is popular wherever it is appreciated.

We were absorbed in the discussion of Abraham and Alley about the grammar, and were interrupted by the arrival of Yates in consequence of which the conversation was broken off. We will only add that Abraham became a very good grammarian by dint of perseverance. He did not cast aside the old grammar until he had mastered it, and it was all accomplished while he was the most faithful clerk that the store at New Salem ever had. He found time enough at odd moments during the day, and took enough out of his sleeping hours at night, within the space of a few months, to acquire all the knowledge of grammar that he ever possessed.

We should say, however, that his companion, William Green, rendered him assistance in this study. William had some knowledge of grammar, and he cheerfully aided Abraham all that he could. The latter always said that William taught him grammar, although William still affirms "that he seemed to master it, as it were, by intuition."

It is probable that Kirkham's Grammar laid the foundation, in part, of Abraham's future character. It taught him the rudiments of his native language, and thus opened the golden gate of knowledge. There is much in his experience at this point to remind us of that of Alexander Murray, the world renowned linguist. His father was too poor to send him to school, or to provide him with books. The Bible, and a catechism containing the alphabet, was all the volumes in the family, and the latter Alexander was not allowed to see except on the Sabbath. During the week his father would draw the letters on the back of an old wool-card "with the black end of an extinguished heather-stem or root, snatched from the fire." In this way he learned the alphabet, and became a reader. At twelve years of age a friend presented him with a copy of Salmon's Grammar, which he mastered in an incredibly short period and here commenced his progress in earnest. He borrowed a Latin grammar and mastered it. Then a French grammar was studied with success. Then the Greek was taken in hand, and thus on till all the Oriental and Northern languages were familiar to him. And the study of Salmon's Grammar laid the foundation for all this. That was the key to the vast treasures of knowledge that were opened before him. By making himself master of that, he unlocked the temple of wisdom.

And so the grammar that Abraham studied exerted a great influence upon his character and destiny.

CHAPTER XVII

STILL A CLERK

There was a "gang" of young and middle aged men in New Salem, called the "Clary Grove Boys," who had become a terror to the people. They were never more flourishing than they were when Abraham became a citizen of the town. They prided themselves upon their strength and courage, and had an established custom of "initiating" new comers of the male sex by giving them a flogging. Perhaps they were no more malicious than a class of college students who perform similar operations upon Freshmen though they were rougher and more immoral. Such "gangs" existed in different parts of the West at that time, a coalition of ignorance, rowdyism and brute force. One writer says of the "Clary Grove Boys":—

"Although there never was under the sun a more generous parcel of ruffians, a stranger's introduction was likely to be the most unpleasant part of his acquaintance with them. In fact, one of the objects of their association was to initiate or naturalize newcomers as they termed the amiable proceedings which they took by way of welcoming any one ambitious of admittance to the society of New Salem. They first bantered the gentleman to run a foot-race, jump, pitch the mall, or wrestle and if none of these propositions seemed agreeable to him, they would request to know what he would do in case another gentleman should pull his nose or squirt tobacco-juice in his face. If he did not seem entirely decided in his views as to what should properly be done in such a contingency, perhaps he would be nailed in a hogshead and rolled down New Salem hill; perhaps his ideas would be brightened by a brief ducking in the Sangamon or perhaps he would be scoffed, kicked and cuffed by a number of persons in concert, until he reached the confines of the village, and then turned adrift as being unfit company for the people of that settlement. If, however, the stranger consented to engage in a tussle with one of his persecutors, it was usually arranged that there should be 'foul play,' with nameless impositions and insults, which would inevitably change the affair into a fight ; and then if the subject of all these practices proved to be a man of mettle, he would be promptly received into their society, and in all probability would never have better friends on earth than the roistering fellows who had contrived his torments."

These "ruffians" had not "initiated" Abraham for some reason. Perhaps a wholesome recollection of his strength, courage and tact in engineering the boat over Rutledge's dam, or the extravagant statements of Offutt concerning his marvelous achievements, had restrained them. At any rate they did not molest him, until one day, when Bill Clary had a dispute with Offutt in his store, and both became exasperated. Bill exclaimed:

"Jack Armstrong can lick Abe easy as a boy knows his father." Jack was the strongest man of the "gang," and perhaps the most ignorant.

"You don't know what you are talking about. Bill," retorted Offutt; "he could duck the whole Clary Grove crew in the Sangamon, before Jack Armstrong could get up after he'd laid him on his back."

"I'll bet ten dollars on that," shouted Bill. "The fact is, Abe wouldn't dare to risk a fight with Jack."

"The whole of you are blowers and cowards," responded Offutt, angrily. "There's more in Abe's little finger than the whole of you have got in your soul and body."

The knowledge of this hot interview spread like wildfire, and the "Clary Grove boys" would not consent to peace any longer. "Jack Armstrong must wrestle with Abe," and settle the vital question with "ruffians." They proposed all sorts of bets, staking money, whiskey and what not upon the issue.

Soon the proposition from the "Clary Grove Boys" came direct to Abraham, and he answered:

"I must decline such a trial with Jack."

"Then you are not the man to live in New Salem longer," shouted one.

"Perhaps not," replied Abraham, with a quizzical look, as if he meant to say, "that is none of your business."

"We'll duck you in the Sangamon," exclaimed another.

"Whether you do or not," answered Abe, "I tell you that I never tussle and scuttle, and I will not, I don't like this wooling and pulling."

"Don't, hey!" shouted one of the number, at the same time pulling Abe's nose.

"Be careful; not too familiar," said Abraham in a warning manner.

Thus the provocations were multiplied until Abraham, seeing that the only way of settling the difficulty was to lay Jack upon his back, consented to wrestling. They took side holds, and presently Abraham, having the advantage by reason of his long legs and arms, lifted Jack completely from the ground, and, swinging him about, thought to lay him on his back, but Jack came down upon his feet squarely and firmly.

"Now, Jack," said Abraham, "let's quit; I can't throw you, and you can't throw me."

"No, Jack, don't give up," shouted Bill Clary; "Abe's begging for quarter now." Bill supposed that Abraham's courage was failing him, or else it was the plan of the gang to play foul. Be this as it may, Jack at once broke his hold and adopted the unfair method of "legging," whereupon Abraham seized him by the throat, and lifting him from the ground, and holding him at arm's length, shook him like a child. The astonished ruffians saw that their champion was worsted, and they cried:—

"Fight, Jack, fight!"

No doubt all of them would have attacked Abraham had Jack led off. But the latter saw little encouragement in continuing a contest with a man who could hold him out at arm's length by the throat and the moment Abraham relinquished his hold. Jack grasped his hand in friendship, and declared that "Abe was the best feller that ever broke into their settlement." Their friendship became almost like that of David and Jonathan; and from that moment the sway of the "Clary Grove Boys" was broken in New Sale. Abraham did not hesitate to denounce their acts publicly and others soon joined him in open hostility to such ruffianism. The result was that the gang gradually faded out, and quite a number of them became respectable citizens. Abraham's great strength and kindness of heart did more to reform the scoundrels than a missionary from New England could have done.

Everybody now became as enthusiastic over Abraham as Offutt was.

"I told you so," said the latter, "I've seen something of the world, and, I tell you, his like I never saw."

There was no one to dispute Offutt now. There was an end to all riotous proceedings for Abraham declared that such ruffianly conduct should be stopped, and some of the citizens were bold enough to back him. Even Jack Armstrong promised him assistance. Abraham's influence became regnant in New Salem. He was even appealed to by neighbors to settle difficulties, so that he wore the honors of "peacemaker" in Illinois as he did in Indiana.

It was in New Salem that Abraham won the soubriquet "Honest Abe," which he carried through life. The public confidence in his integrity and fair mindedness was such that he was usually chosen for umpire in all games and trials where two sides enlisted. And finally, he became in so great demand in this line, that both sides, in those friendly contests, made him judge.

An incident illustrates how strong a friend Jack Armstrong became to Abraham. A stranger came into town, and he proved to be a kind of bully, and got into a difficulty with Jack.

"You are a coward and a liar," said Jack.

"You'll find out whether I am or not," exclaimed the stranger.

"You're a coward and a liar, I say," shouted Jack, more loudly and defiantly, while the stranger backed towards a wood-pile as Jack advanced.

Before Jack perceived the purpose of the stranger, the latter seized a stick of wood, and struck him such a blow as to bring him to the ground. Jack recovered himself in a moment, and was about to leap upon his antagonist, when Abraham, who was near, interfered, saying—

"I wouldn't. Jack; it won't do you any good."

"I'll thrash the rascal," retorted Jack with wrath.

"No, Jack; we've done with that kind of business in New Salem, you know," Abraham continued.

"But he insulted me."

"And what did you say to him?" inquired Abraham. The question mollified Jack's wrath somewhat, for he began to get his eyes open.

"I called him a coward and a liar," replied Jack.

"Well, suppose you were a stranger, in a strange place, and a man should call you a coward and a liar, what would you do?"

"Thrash him terribly," answered Jack.

"Then this man has done no more to you than you would have done to him," suggested Abraham.

"That's so," responded Jack, as if he saw the point clearly. "It's all right, Abe." And turning to the stranger, he added, "Give us your hand;" and suiting the action to his words, he took the hand of the stranger, and declared himself a friend, supplementing his pledge of friendship with an invitation to "take a drink," according to the custom of the "Clary Grove Boys."

Offutt came into the store one afternoon perplexed as to the disposition of a large drove of hogs he had purchased. He had no pen large enough to contain them.

"Build one," said Abraham promptly.

"Too much work; take too long," replied Offutt.

"It's more work to be without a pen when you need a larger one," was Abraham's suggestive answer.

"Can't get anybody to build it," continued Offutt.

"I can build it myself," said Abraham.

"What can't you do?" answered Offutt.

"There are a great many things I can't do; but I can build a pig-pen," Abraham replied with a smile.

"Well, go at it, then, and I'll help William about the store and look after the mill," was Offutt's quick decision.

Abraham went into the woods and cut down the trees and split rails enough to make a pen sufficiently large to hold a thousand hogs.

During the time that Abraham served Offutt, he attended a debating club. Dr. Holland says:—

"During this year he was also much engaged with debating clubs, often walking six or seven miles to attend them. One of these clubs held its meetings at an old store-house in New Salem. He used to call these exercises practicing polemics. As these clubs were composed principally of men of no education whatever, some of their 'polemics' are remembered as the most laughable of farces. His favorite newspaper, at this time, was the Louisville, a paper which he received regularly by mail, and paid for during a number of years when he had not money enough to dress decently. He liked its politics, and was particularly delighted with its wit and humor, of which he had the keenest appreciation. When out of the store he was always busy in the pursuit of knowledge. One gentleman, who met him during this period, says that the first time he saw him he was lying on a trundle-bed, covered with books and papers, and rocking a cradle with his foot. Of the amount of uncovered space between the extremities of his trousers and the top of his socks which this informant observed, there shall be no mention. The whole scene, however, was entirely characteristic—Lincoln reading and studying, and at the same time helping his landlady by quieting her child."

The question whether the Sangamon river was navigable or not had been under discussion several years, and reached the crisis while Abraham was in the employ of Offutt, or just after he closed his labors for him.

"The 'Talisman' is chartered for the experiment," said a citizen of New Salem to Abraham; "and you ought to be her captain."

"It will take a man of more experience than I have had to run her up the river," was Abraham's modest answer.

"Well, there's nobody here that understands the business better than you do," continued the citizen. "Will you undertake if you are wanted?"

"I'll try, and do the best I can," was Abraham's characteristic reply. "I have tried this river considerably with a flat-boat."

"That is what I thought, and for that reason you ought to pilot the 'Talisman'; and I think that is the general opinion."

"I am willing to undertake it if it is thought best," Abraham added.

The result was that he was sent, with others, to meet the steamer at Beardstown, and pilot her up. There was great excitement over the experiment, and the inhabitants came from far and near to witness the trial from the banks of the river, Abraham took his place at the helm, and piloted her with comparative ease and safety as far as the New Salem dam, the people gathered upon the banks of the river frequently cheering at the top of their voices. Here it was necessary to remove a part of the dam to let the steamer through. She ran up to Rogue's mill, when the rapidly falling water admonished the successful captain that she must be turned down stream or be left there for the season. No time was lost in beginning the return trip, which was accomplished at the slow rate of three or four miles a day, "on account of the high wind from the prairie." J. R. Herndon was sent for, and he says: "I was sent for, being an old boatman and I met her some twelve or thirteen miles above New Salem. We got to Salem the second day after I went on board. When we struck the dam she hung. We then backed off, and threw the anchor over the dam, and tore away part of the dam; then, raising steam ran her over the first trial. As soon as she was over, the company that chartered her was done with her. I think the captain gave Lincoln forty dollars to run her down to Beardstown. I am sure I got forty dollars to continue on her until we landed at Beardstown. We that went with her walked back to New Salem."

While Abraham was in the employ of Offutt, the latter made some unprofitable ventures, by reason of which he became peculiarly embarrassed. His mill enterprise did not prove as successful as he anticipated, and other speculations left him considerably out of pocket. Fortune ceased to smile upon any of his enterprises, and his difficulties multiplied from week to week, until he failed, closed his store, shut down his mill, and left Abraham without employment. It was, however, a period of very great advancement to Abraham. He had acquired much knowledge of mercantile business, had become familiar with grammar, had read many books, made many friends, and improved himself generally. Dr. Holland says, that, when he terminated his labors for Offutt, "every one trusted him. He was judge, arbitrator, referee, umpire, authority in all disputes, games and matches of man-flesh and horse-flesh; a pacificator in all quarrels; everybody's friend; the best-natured, the most sensible, the best-informed, the most modest and unassuming, the kindest, gentlest, roughest, strongest, best young fellow in all New Salem and the region round about."

CHAPTER XVIII

ON THE WAR PATH

The Black Hawk War was causing great excitement in Illinois and other Western states when Abraham closed his labors with Offutt. Not long afterward, the Governor of Illinois called for four regiments of volunteers.

"I shall enlist," said Abraham to his intimate friend and companion, William Green, as soon as the news reached New Salem.

"I shall if you do," responded William.

"Well, I shall do it, honest. Nothing else on hand now. Besides, Black Hawk is one of the most treacherous Indians on the footstool, and he ought to be shot. It is not more than a year ago, and hardly that, that he entered into a treaty and he was to keep his people on the other side of the Mississippi, and now he has crossed to make war on the whites."

"Real Indian, that is," continued William; "the only way to deal with an Indian is to shoot him."

"I don't know about that; it's the only way to treat Black Hawk, though, —a cunning, artful warrior, who is in his element when he can massacre the whites," added Abraham.

"They expect to make short work of it, or the governor would have called for volunteers for more than thirty days," suggested William.

"They may call for them again after the expiration of thirty days, and the same volunteers may re-enlist. I shall enlist for the war, whether it is thirty days or thirty months." Abraham meant just what he said, as the sequel will show.

"Clary Grove Boys" were now the fast friends of Abraham, and all were eager to enlist with him. Other young men, and older men, also, were ready for the war. In consequence of the general interest awakened, Abraham said:—

"We can raise a company in New Salem."

"True as you live," answered Herndon.

"We must be about it in a hurry if we are going to do it," remarked Green.

The whole town became fired with military ardor, in consequence of Abraham's leadership, and the result was that a recruiting office was opened in New Salem. Within a few days the company was full, Abraham being the first to enlist and the choice of officers became the exciting topic. However, the officers were not elected at New Salem; but the volunteers marched to Bushville, in Schuyler County, where the election took place.

There were only two candidates for captain, Abraham and Fitzpatrick, the owner of the saw-mill at Spring Creek. He sawed the lumber for Abraham when he built the boat for Offutt, and treated his customer rudely. Fitzpatrick was a popular man, but there was a small show for him in a race with Abraham.

The method of electing captain was peculiar; perhaps the best method for that place, under the circumstances. The two candidates were required to take their positions opposite each other, at a suitable distance; and, at a given signal, each volunteer went to the one whom he desired for his captain. Three fourths of the whole number at once took their stand with Abraham; and, when those who first went to Fitzpatrick saw the overwhelming majority for

Abraham, one by one they left the former and joined the latter, until but one or two stood with Fitzpatrick.

"I felt bad for Fitzpatrick," said Green; "he was the most lonesome-looking fellow I ever saw."

"He might have known that we shouldn't vote for him when Abe is about," remarked Herndon. "He was too anxious to serve his country."

These, and kindred remarks, were bandied about after the company had indulged in vociferous cheering, that Black Hawk might have heard if he had been within a reasonable distance.

"A speech from the captain," was the imperative call from the company and Abraham promptly accommodated them to one of his best efforts, in which he thanked them for the honor conferred, maintained that their choice might have fallen upon one much better qualified for the position than himself, and promised that he would do the best he could to prove himself worthy of their confidence.

"Captain Lincoln!" exclaimed William Greene, addressing Abraham facetiously, and tipping his hat; and, henceforth, "Captain Lincoln" was alone the soubriquet by which he was known.

One incident occurred before the organization of this company, which should be rehearsed. It illustrates his temperance principles, at the same time that it shows his marvelous strength. Green said to a stranger, who happened to be in New Salem—

"Abe Lincoln is the strongest man in Illinois."

"I deny it," answered the stranger, immediately naming a stronger party.

"How much can he lift," asked Green.

"He'll lift a barrel of flour as easily as I can a peck of potatoes."

"Abe can lift two barrels if he could get hold of them."

"Ha! ha! ha!" laughed the man. "You can tell a greater story than I can."

"Great story or not, I will bet that Abe will lift a barrel of whiskey, and drink out of the bunghole."

"Worse yet," replied the man. "I'll bet he can't do any such thing."

"What will you bet?"

"I'll bet a good hat; and we'll have him try right off, if he will."

"Agreed," said Green. The truth was he had seen Abraham do this very thing, minus the drinking part, so that he knew he should win.

Without delay they sought Abraham, and proceeded to the store, where the whiskey was found.

"I don't think much of the betting part," said Abraham, "but I guess I'll help William out of the scrape, though he won't have much chance to wear the hat yet awhile, if he is going to war with me."

"Well, if you can do what he says you can, I want to see it," said the man.

"You shall have the privilege," answered Abraham.

At once he proceeded to perform the feat, and accomplished it with seeming ease. The barrel was raised, and a quantity of liquor taken from the bunghole.

"There it is!" exclaimed Green. "But that is the first dram I ever saw you drink in my life, Abe," he added, turning to Abraham.

The words had scarcely escaped his lips, before Abraham set down the barrel, and spirited the whiskey that was in his mouth upon the floor, at the same time replying, "And I haven't drank that, you see.

Green burst into a hearty laugh at this turn of the affair, and added, "You are bound to let whiskey alone, Abe."

And this same Green writes to us: "That was the only drink of intoxicating liquor I ever saw him take, and that he spirited on the floor."

The stranger was satisfied, as well as astonished. He had never seen the like before, and he doubted whether he ever should again. He did not know that the whole life-discipline through which Abraham had passed was suited to develop muscular strength. Probably he did not care, since there was the actual deed.

We are interested in it mostly for the determination it showed to reject whiskey. The act was in keeping with all his previous temperance habits.

On the evening after this affair, Abraham was alone with his friend William Green, who won the aforesaid hat, and he said to him, "William, are you in the habit of betting?"

"No; I never bet before in my life, never."

"Well, I never would again, if I were you. It is what unprincipled men will do, and I would set my face against it."

"I didn't see anything very bad in that bet," said William.

"All bets are alike," answered Abraham, "though you may not have any bad motives in doing it."

"I only wanted to convince the man that you could lift the barrel."

"I know it; but I want you should promise me that you will never bet again. It is a species of gambling, and nothing is meaner than that."

"I don't suppose I shall ever do it again."

"I want you should promise me that you won't," continued Abraham, with increased emphasis. "It will please your mother to know of so good a resolution."

"I will promise you, Abe," answered William, grasping his hand, while tears glistened in his eyes. And there was true seriousness in this transaction, more than might appear to the reader at first view. The one who thus pledged himself to Abraham writes to us now, in his riper years: "On that night, when alone, I wept over his lecture to me, and I have so far kept that solemn pledge."

The New Salem company went into camp at Beardstown, from whence, in a few days, they marched to the expected scene of conflict. When the thirty days of their enlistment had expired, however, they had not seen the enemy. They were disbanded at Ottawa, and most of the volunteers returned. But a new levy being called for, Abraham re-enlisted as a private. Another thirty days expired, and the war was not over. His regiment was disbanded, and again, the third time, he volunteered. He was determined to serve his country as long as the war lasted. Before the third term of is enlistment had expired, the battle of Bad Axe was fought, which put an end to the war.

He returned home. "Having lost his horse, near where the town of Janesville, Wisconsin, now stands, he went down Rock River to Dixon in a canoe. Thence he crossed the country on foot to Peoria, where he again took a canoe to a point on the Illinois River, within forty miles of home. The latter distance he accomplished on foot."

Several incidents transpired during his connection with the army, which are so expressive of certain elements of his character, that we record them here. One day an old Indian found his way into camp, professing to be friendly to the whites, and casting himself upon the mercy of Lincoln's soldiers.

"We came to fight Indians," shouted one of the "boys," "and we'll give you cold lead instead of mercy."

"Shoot him! shoot him!" cried several voices.

"A spy! a spy!" shouted others.

The demonstration terrified the Indian, and, in his distress, he flung down a crumpled paper that he bad been holding in his hand, and begged them to read it. Captain Lincoln took it up, and found that it was a certificate of character and safe-conduct from General Cass, endorsing the Indian as a faithful man who had done good for him.

"A forged document!" was the cry raised at once.

"The old savage can't run it on us like that," cried Bill Clary, raising his gun in a threatening manner.

"Kill him! show him no quarter!" cried another of the "Clary Grove Boys," several of whom had made considerable trouble for their captain by their unruly conduct.

The "boys" were bound to kill the red-skin, and were actually rushing upon him when Captain Lincoln sprang before him, confronting the assailants, and commanding them to desist.

"You shall not shoot the Indian," he cried. "General Cass's order must be respected."

"We WILL shoot him," yelled a Clary Grove ruffian.

"Not unless you shoot me," fiercely cried Captain Lincoln, towering up to his full height, and covering the Indian by his bodily presence.

His determined manner, resolute and invincible spirit, and terrible earnestness, evinced by every motion of his body, cowed the "boys," so that they fell back sullenly, and desisted from firing the fatal shot. Some of them, however, still muttered vengeance in a low tone, and finally, one, more defiant than the rest, exclaimed:

"This is cowardly on your part, Lincoln."

Aroused to the highest pitch of determination by this insolent and unreasonable charge, Captain Lincoln shouted:

"If any of you think I am a coward, let him test it, here and now."

"You are larger and heavier than we are, Lincoln," replied one.

"You can guard against this; choose your own weapons," Captain Lincoln retorted, the unconquerable spirit within him manifesting itself through every lineament of his face and every gesture. "He never appeared so powerful and fearless before," says one who was present. Even the most rebellious of the "Clary Grove Boys" dared not lift his finger against the Indian; and never more did they associate the term "coward" with Lincoln's name.

In this affair Captain Lincoln's life was in as great peril as that of the Indian. One of his biographers says: "He often declared that his life and character were both at stake, and would probably have been lost, had he not at that supremely critical moment forgotten the officer and asserted the man. To have ordered the offenders under arrest would have created a formidable mutiny; to have tried and punished them would have been impossible. They could scarcely be called soldiers; they were merely armed citizens, with a nominal military organization. They were but recently enlisted, and their term of service was about to expire. Had he preferred charges against them, and offered to submit their differences to a court of any sort, it would have been regarded as an act of personal pusillanimity, and his efficiency would have been gone forever."

Wrestling, jumping, and lifting was a pastime in camp, and Captain Lincoln excelled every man in the regiment in these feats. His company declared that there was not a man in the whole army who was his equal as a wrestler and they boastfully pitted him against the "whole field." This challenge brought out a man from another regiment, by the name of Thompson, who offered to wrestle with Lincoln. The latter's company at once staked money, weapons, and outfit, believing that their captain would lay the "great Western wrestler," as he was called, on his back.

Captain Lincoln had tussled with Thompson but a few minutes when he remarked to his friends—

"This is the most powerful man I ever had hold of. He will throw me, and you will lose."

The company urged him on, believing he was more than a match for Thompson; but they were sadly disappointed when the latter threw their champion flat on his back. As, according to the custom, it required two out of three falls to settle the contest, they were soon struggling again, when both of them came to the ground, Thompson on top. In their great disappointment, Lincoln's men claimed that Thompson was thrown as really as their captain, the second time, and refused to give up their property staked. This brought on a collision with Thompson's friends, and they were about to proceed to blows, when Captain Lincoln magnanimously stepped in and prevented further trouble. Addressing his men, he said—

"Boys, Thompson actually threw me once fair, broadly so and the second time he threw me fairly, though not apparently so." And he counseled them to be honest and accept the inevitable. This was a very remarkable example of magnanimity, and served to exalt Lincoln still higher, if possible, in the estimation of all.

Another incident we will give in the language of William Green: "One other word in reference to Lincoln's care for the health and welfare of his men, and justice to them. Some officers of the United States had claimed that the regular army had a preference in the rations and pay. Captain Lincoln was ordered to do some act which he deemed unauthorized. He, however, obeyed, but went to the officer and said to him, 'Sir, you forget that we are not under the rules and regulations of the War Department at Washington are only volunteers under the orders and regulations of Illinois. Keep in your own sphere, and there will be no difficulty but resistance will hereafter be made to your unjust orders and, further, my men must be equal in all particulars, in rations, arms, camps, etc., to the regular army.' The man saw that Lincoln was right, and determined to have justice done. Afterwards we were treated equally well, and just as the regular army was in every particular. This brave, just, and humane act in behalf of the volunteers at once attached officers and rank to him, as with hooks of steel."

Mr. Irwin pays the following deserved tribute to Lincoln in the army: "During the campaign Lincoln himself was always ready for an emergency. He endured hardships like a good soldier; he never complained, nor did he fear danger. When fighting was expected, or danger apprehended, Lincoln was the first to say 'Let's go.' He had the confidence of every man of his company, and they obeyed his orders at a word. His company was mostly young men, and full of sport."

The Black Hawk war was not much of a war after all, and our hero did not engage directly with the enemy face to face. Yet two officers in that war, Colonel Zachary Taylor and Captain Abraham Lincoln, subsequently became Presidents of the United States.

One of the most humorous speeches Abraham Lincoln ever made in Congress had reference to this war. General Cass was the Democratic candidate for President, and certain congressional orators made capital out of the General's connection with the Black Hawk war.

Lincoln rose in his seat, and said, among other things, " By the way, Mr. Speaker, do you know that I am a military hero, "Yes, sir, in the days of the Black Hawk war, I fought, bled, and came away. Speaking of General Cass's career reminds me of my own. I was not at Stillman's defeat, but I was about as near it as Cass to Hull's surrender and like him I saw the place very soon afterward. It is quite certain that I did not break my sword, for I had none to break; but I bent my musket pretty badly on one occasion. If General Cass went in advance of me in picking whortleberries, I guess I surpassed him in charges upon the wild onions. If he saw any live, fighting Indians, it was more than I did, but I had a good many bloody struggles with the mosquitoes and, although I never fainted from loss of blood, I can truly say I was often very hungry. If I should ever turn Democrat, and be taken up as a candidate for the Presidency by the Democratic party, I hope they will not make fun of me by attempting to make me out a military hero."

CHAPTER XIX
UNSOUGHT HONORS

On his return from the Black Hawk war, Lincoln took up his abode in the family of J. R. Herndon. The people of New Salem gave him a hearty welcome, and delighted to call him "Captain Lincoln." The Herndon family was soon more strongly attached to him than ever, "He had one of Herndon's children around with him nearly all the time," says an eye-witness. "He was at home wherever he went, and made himself wonderfully agreeable to the people he lived with, or happened to be visiting," says Mr. Herndon. That his kind and benevolent disposition did not suffer by his service in the army is quite evident from a remark of Mr. Herndon, "He was kind to the widow and orphan, and chopped their wood."

He was casting about for some employment, whereby to earn a livelihood. For some reason, to us unknown, the blacksmith's trade attracted his attention.

"What do you think of my learning the blacksmith's trade?" he said to his friend, William Green, one day.

"A blacksmith!" exclaimed William with much surprise. "That would be quite a descent from Captain Lincoln to smithy Lincoln. You are joking, Cap'n."

"Never was more serious in my life, William. A blacksmith is of more practical use to the community than a captain in an Indian war."

"But less than in it," replied Green. "You don't seem to understand that war makes heroes, and heroes get into political life. Why, Abe, we're going to send you to the legislature."

"None of your bantering, William," Lincoln answered, supposing that his friend was joking. "I'm talking business."

"So am I. Haven't you heard, Abe, that the Clay men are going to run you for the legislature?"

"No, nor you. Yesterday I heard the names of John T. Stuart, Colonel Taylor and Peter Cartwright, named as Jackson candidates and nobody would think of running me against such men."

"All that may be, and there may be a half-dozen other candidates; but we are going to run you against the whole batch, unless you positively decline."

"You are crazy, William, and all the rest of you who entertain such a thought. What! run me, nothing but a strapping boy, against such men of experience and wisdom! Come, now, no more of your ganimon."

"Then you won't believe me?"

"I didn't say so."

"Well, believe it or not, you will be waited upon by older persons than I am, to get your consent."

And, sure enough, he was waited upon by several the most influential citizens of New Salem, within twenty-four hours thereafter, to ask his consent to run as a candidate for the legislature.

"It will only subject me to ridicule," he said.

"Why so?" inquired one of the number.

"For the folly of running against such men as Stuart and Cartwright."

"Not if you beat them."

"That is impossible. I should not expect to be elected, if I should consent to be a candidate."

"I don't know about that," answered one; "we expect to elect you."

"But I have lived in the county only a few months, and am known only in New Salem, while the other candidates are known in every part of the county. Besides, it is only ten days before the election, and there is little time to carry your measures."

"Very true; but there is a principle involved in your nomination, and we shall sustain that, whether you are elected or not."

Here was a point of importance. There were no distinct political parties then in the State, as there are now. But there were "Jackson men and Clay men" not to mention others. Abraham was a "Clay man," while the majority votes of the county, at the previous presidential election, was cast for Jackson. In these circumstances there was little prospect that the young candidate would be elected.

Suffice to say that Abraham at last yielded very reluctantly, and became a candidate. He was not elected but his popularity may be learned from the fact that he stood next to the successful candidate, and only a few votes behind him. "His own precinct, New Salem, gave him 277 votes in a poll of 284,"—all but seven. No one was more surprised than Abraham himself. Although he was not elected, yet the result, in the circumstances, was a signal triumph.

Mr. R. B. Rutledge was the citizen who really secured Lincoln's consent to be a candidate. He had heard him make a speech before the "New Salem Literary Society," on one occasion, which impressed him so much that he did not hesitate to say, "Abe will make a great man." Of that speech he says: "As he rose to speak, his tall form towered above the little assembly. Both hands were thrust down deep in the pockets of his pantaloons. A perceptible smile at once lit up the faces of the audience, for all anticipated the relation of some humorous story. But he opened up the discussion in splendid style, to the astonishment of his friends. As he warmed with his subject, his hands forsook his pockets and enforced his noble thoughts with awkward gestures. He pursued the question with reason and argument so pithy that all were amazed." The president, at his fireside, after the meeting, remarked to his wife, "There is more in Abe's head than wit and fun. He is already a fine speaker, and all that is needed is culture, to enable him to reach the high place which I believe is in store for him."

While Mr. Rutledge admitted to Abraham that there was little or no chance of his election, he assured him that the canvass would bring his name prominently before the voters of the county for future use. His arguments prevailed with Lincoln.

Candidates for State offices were obliged to take the stump, and declare their sentiments and vindicate them. Abraham followed the custom, and made several speeches, with the expressed condition, however, that "his friends should not laugh at him." His first speech was made at Pappsville about eleven miles west of Springfield. It was as follows:—

"Gentlemen and fellow-citizens, I presume you all know who I am. I am humble Abraham Lincoln. I have been solicited by many friends to become a candidate for the Legislature. My politics are short and sweet: I am in favor of a national bank; I am in favor of the internal improvement system and a high protective tariff. These are my sentiments and political principles. If elected, I shall be thankful; if not, it will be all the same."

The brevity of his speech was the fruit of his modesty, which did not fail to captivate his hearers. He made several other speeches, and issued an address also, of considerable length and real merit, to the voters of the county. In closing that address, he said:—

"Considering the great degree of modesty that should always attend youth, it is probable that I have been more presuming than becomes me. However, upon the subjects of which I have treated, I have spoken as I have thought. Every man is said to have his peculiar ambition. Whether it be true or not, I can say, for one, that I have no other so great as that of being truly esteemed of my fellow-men, by rendering myself worthy of their esteem."

His opponents made fun of his appearance wherever he spoke; and it must be confessed that there was some occasion for it, judging from the description of his dress furnished by his friend, Mr. A. B. Ellis, who accompanied him during a part of the campaign. He says: "He wore a mixed jeans coat, claw-hammer style, short in the sleeves, and bobtail—in fact, it was so short in the tail he could not sit on it—flax and tow linen pantaloons, and a straw hat. I think he wore a vest, but do not remember how it looked. He then wore pot-metal boots."

Thoughtful, substantial citizens regarded Abraham's mode of dress rather complimentary. It denoted the absence of pride and vanity to them more than an absence of taste. "Abe's no dandy," remarked one of his most enthusiastic admirers, designing to pay him a high compliment.

When the labor and excitement of the campaign were over, Abraham's pocket was empty. He was, therefore, under the necessity of finding "something to do." The vote of New Salem convinced him that he had plenty of friends there. A citizen remarked, referring to his poverty, "Abe has nothing except plenty of friends." But he must have work, also.

"You must stay here," said his friend Green, very earnestly.

"There is no must about it, if there's no work for me," answered Lincoln.

"There'll be enough that you can do, only take time for it; the world wasn't made in a minute."

"No; I suppose it took about six days, and if I can find employment in that time, I shall be satisfied."

"I'll tell you what to do, Abe,— study law. you're just the man for it."

"Whew! I should laugh to see myself trying to make a lawyer."

"Why not be one, I should like to know?"

"For the very good reason, that I haven't brains enough."

"Just what I thought you would say. You are altogether too sparing of good opinions of yourself. You've more brains than half the lawyers in Illinois."

"Perhaps that isn't saying much," replied Abraham, laughing; "although it is a pretty handsome compliment on your part. Much obliged."

"Well, compliment or not, I have heard a good many people say that you ought to be a lawyer."

"And I have heard one propose that I be a blacksmith, as I told you; and I suppose I could swing a sledge-hammer equal to any of them."

"And throw away your talents? Any fool could be a blacksmith."

"By no means. No man can be successful at anything unless he is industrious, and has common sense, and a good share of perseverance."

"That's so, I s'pose; but a blacksmith is the last thing I would be if I were in your place. I would like to know who ever suggested such an idea to you."

"My father several years ago and less than five years ago I came within an ace of putting his advice into practice. I almost decided to go at it for life."

"Ha! ha! ha!" laughed his friend, heartily. "Wouldn't you cut a dash donning a leather apron and blowing the blacksmith's bellows, like another Jack Smuttyface, as they used to call Jake Tower."

"An honest calling," answered Lincoln; "and that is the main thing. A lawyer can look a little more spruce than a son of Vulcan, to be sure; but a black smith can be just as upright, if not a little more so."

"And what do you mean by 'a little more so?" asked Green.

"Why, don't you know that nearly everybody suspects lawyers of trickery,—doing anything for a fee, blowing hot or cold for the sake of a case,—shielding the meanest culprits as readily as they do the best men—and all that sort of thing."

"Not quite so bad as that, Abe. I know that lawyers are not over particular, and that is true of a good many folks who are not lawyers. If you won't follow a calling because there are scapegraces in it, you will not choose one right away."

"Perhaps so; but no man has any more right to defend the wrong because he is a lawyer than he has because he is a blacksmith, in my way of thinking."

"I give it up, Abe; you've got the case already, and I am more convinced than ever that you ought to study law."

"That is, if you are judge and jury," responded Lincoln. "But I don't understand why it is that people are determined I shall be a lawyer. As many as ten months ago, two or three people gave me the same advice, though I thought they were half in joke."

"Well, Abe, perhaps you'll get your eyes open, if you live long enough, to see what you ought to be," said Green, in a strain of pleasantry. "Not many folks live that have to go to their neighbors to find out what they are. By the time you are seven feet high, perhaps you will understand."

"I should think I was pretty near that now, by what people say," archly replied Lincoln.

"I think you are in a fair way to be, if you keep on."

"And I shall be a lawyer by that time, and not before." And here they parted.

Lincoln had no intention of being a lawyer, after all that his friends had suggested. He had no confidence in his abilities for that profession. Indeed, he could not see how a young man reared as he was could expect to enter upon such a calling. Yet he longed for some permanent pursuit, —a life-vocation. He did not like this going from one thing to another, and he only did it from sheer necessity. He believed that a young man should choose a calling, and stick to it with unwearied devotion, if he would make anything in the world. He wanted to do this but what should he choose? He was perplexed, troubled, and the more so, because admiring friends advised him to do what he really supposed was beyond his ability. He underrated his talents, (a very good failing), and all the time thought that others were overrating them. Few youth and young men suffer in this way. They are more apt to injure themselves by too exalted views of their talents. Some of the very simpletons esteem themselves as the wisest and greatest men. Ignorance is more likely to be vain and proud than ripe talents and learning. True knowledge is humble. Great talents are marked by humility. And so young Lincoln did not stand so high in his own estimation as he did in the estimation of others. This was the case with Sir Humphrey Davy, Nathaniel Bowditch, Arkwright, Franklin, Washington, and many others. From their youth they were devoid of that vain self confidence which many shallow-brained people possess.

Instead of becoming a blacksmith, however, Abraham became a merchant. Mr. Herndon, with whom he boarded, was running a grocery with one Berry, and he sold out his interest to Lincoln. Soon afterwards William Green bought out Radford, and immediately sold his stock of groceries to Lincoln for a bonus of one hundred and fifty dollars, taking Lincoln's note. The name of the firm was "Lincoln & Berry." Berry turned out to be an intemperate, worthless fellow, embarrassed the business, cheated his partner, "cleared out," and left Lincoln with all the debts to pay. The settlement left him penniless, without a copper to pay his note to Green. "All right," said Green; "don't trouble yourself about me. When you are able to pay it you can ; but if you don't, it's all the same.'

Abraham facetiously called it "the national debt," and declared that he "should never rest until it was paid." And he did not. Green removed to Tennessee before the note was paid, and scarcely expected that his friend would ever be able to redeem it. But, in 1840, after Abraham had entered the legal profession, the last dollar was paid.

Being through with his store Abraham was again without employment. To add to his disappointment, Mr. Herndon, with whom he boarded, removed from town, obliging him to take up his quarters at the village "tavern" — a log house with four rooms. While waiting for some opening, he devoted himself to mental improvement with more earnestness than ever. He read Rollin's Ancient History. Gibbon's Decline and Fall of the Roman Empire, and similar works, borrowed of William Green, Minter Graham, Bowlin Greene, and other parties. Copies of the works of the poets. Burns and Shakespeare were lent him, and Kirkham's Grammar was reviewed, also. He was so won by Burns and Shakespeare that he committed many of their best productions to memory and through life, these poets were his favorite reading.

He wrote a careful synopsis of all the books he read, in order to treasure the contents in his memory. This habit was of inestimable value to him. To it is to be traced, in part at least, that clearness of expression, and that fund of illustrations and facts, for which the public addresses of his ripe manhood were distinguished.

Citizens of New Salem claim, also, that he began to study law at this time. There is no reliable evidence, however, that he began the study of law, with the expectation of ever entering the profession, at that time. He purchased an old copy of Blackstone, or some other law book, at an auction in Springfield and there is no doubt that he studied it as thoroughly as he did other works, but with no settled determination to become a lawyer.

Mr. Henry says of him, at this time, "He used to read law, barefooted, seated in the shade of a tree, and would grind around with the shade, just opposite Berry's grocery store, a few feet south of the door. He occasionally varied the attitude by lying flat on his back, and putting his feet up the tree. Another says that "he studied, also Natural Philosophy, Chemistry, Astronomy, etc. He had no regular teacher, but perhaps received more assistance from Minter Graham than from any other person."

Mr. Ellis, of whom we have spoken, opened a store in New Salem, and boarded at the "tavern" when Abraham did. He says of him:—

"He used to assist me in the store on busy days, but he always disliked wait on the ladies; he preferred trading with the men and boys, as he used to say. I also remember that he used to sleep in the store, on the counter, when they had too much company at the tavern."

"I well remember how he was dressed; he wore flax and tow linen pantaloons—I thought about five inches too short in the legs—and frequently he had but one suspender, no vest or coat. He wore a calico shirt, such as he had in the Black Hawk War: coarse brogans, tan color; blue yarn socks, and straw hat, old style, and without a band."

"He was very shy of ladies. On one occasion, while we boarded at this tavern, there came a family, containing an old lady and her son, and three stylish daughters, from the State of Virginia, and stopped there for two or three weeks ; and, during their stay, I do not remember of Lincoln ever eating at the same table when they did. I then thought it was on account of his awkward appearance and his wearing apparel."

Mr. Lamon says of him, at this time: "He read with avidity all the newspapers that came to New Salem, — chiefly 'The Sangamon Journal,' 'The Missouri Republican' and the 'Louisville Journal' The latter was his favorite; its wit and anecdotes, were after his own heart." He also read "The Cincinnati Gazette" and other papers.

His quarters at the "tavern" subjected him to many interruptions. People enjoyed his conversation so much that they paid little regard to his time for study. In consequence, he was obliged to seek quiet elsewhere. "Sometimes he went to James Short's on the Sand Ridge; sometimes to Minter Graham's; sometimes to Bowlin Greene's; sometimes to Jack Armstrong's, and as often, perhaps, to Abel's or Ben Herndon's. All of these men served him faithfully and signally at one time and another, and to all of them he was sincerely attached."

Lincoln found work after a time. Unexpectedly he met John Calhoun of Springfield, — the Calhoun who subsequently became notorious for his efforts to enslave Kansas. He became President of the Lecompton Constitutional Convention, and disgraced himself, by plans and tricks, to force slavery upon Kansas. But when he met Abraham, he was engaged in a more legitimate and honorable business; he was "Surveyor for Sangamon County."

"Try your hand at surveying," said Calhoun.

"I know nothing about it," answered Abraham.

"Learn, then."

"How can I do that?"

"Easy enough if you want to do it."

"I do want to do it. I think I should like the business, if I could qualify myself for it."

"You can, and in a few weeks, too. I will lend you Flint and Gibson, the authors you will want to study and you can provide yourself with a compass and chain, and I will render you any assistance I can."

"You are very kind, Mr. Calhoun, and I will do the best I can. Your generous offer shall not come to nothing for want of my trying."

"You'll make a good surveyor, I'm sure of that, and find plenty of business. And, what is more, I will depute to you that portion of my field contiguous to New Salem."

"It is more than I could expect of you," said Lincoln. "I could not ask so great a favor."

"Take it without asking," said Calhoun, in a jolly way. "I have much more than I can do, and I am glad to give you a portion of the county. The great influx of immigrants, and the consequent entry of government lands, has given me more than my hands full."

"I shall be glad to accept your offer as soon as I am qualified for the business."

"The bargain is closed, then, and in six weeks you can be surveying, if you're a mind to," said Calhoun.

"I shall have a mind to, if that is all," replied Lincoln; "and with a thousand thanks, too, for your assistance. It is worth all the more to me now, because I am thrown out of business."

"Well, this will make business enough for you, and it needs a long-legged, tough, wiry fellow like you to do it well. This is a great country for surveyors."

"But shall I not need to take some lessons of you in the field when I get through the study."

"It will be a capital idea, and you are welcome to all I can aid you any time you will come where I am. It will give you a sweat to keep up with me."

"Perhaps so," replied Lincoln, looking very much as if he did not believe it. The actual experiment proved that the sweat was given to the other party.

Lincoln took Flint and Gibson, and went to Minter Graham's, the schoolmaster, out of the village, and spent six weeks in close study. Then after a few lessons in the field with Calhoun, he set up as surveyor, and soon found plenty of business, and good pay; and his friend Green concluded that the chance of his making a lawyer was lost, "The accuracy of his surveys was seldom, if ever, questioned. Disputes regarding 'corners' and 'lines' were frequently submitted to his arbitration and the decision was invariably accepted as final."

When Abraham had leisure time, at this period of his life, he made himself very useful. His sympathy for the unfortunate, needy and suffering grew stronger from year to year. That tumultuous element of society that prevailed so alarmingly when he first went to New Salem, he denounced more and more. When troubles arose between two or more parties, he would Start up and say. "Let's go and stop it." Jack Armstrong had not lost altogether his love of cruel sport, such as he indulged in when the "Clary Grove Boys" were in power and he bargained with a drunken fellow, by the name of Jordan, to allow Jack to put him into a hogshead and roll him down New Salem hill, as once the "Boys" did with Scanlon and Solomon Spears. Jack was to give the fellow a gallon of whiskey, expecting to get more than the value of several gallons of the vile stuff in fun out of the operation. When Jack had the hogshead ready at the top of the hill, and his victim was waiting to be headed up within, Abraham, who had heard of the affair, came rushing to the scene of action.

"Jack!" he shouted at the top of his voice, "stop that game forthwith. No more such rascally tricks in New Salem."

Jack cowered and looked cheap. "You'll send Jordan into eternity before he gets to the foot of the hill," Abraham continued, "You must stop such cruelty, or you'll feel my long arms around you."

"Only a little fun," answered Jack.

"Fun!" exclaimed Abraham. "There'll be no more such fun in New Salem so long as I live here." And there was not. Jack was not cruel, and he was one of Abraham's close friends; and so was his wife, Hannah. She said, a few years ago: "Abe would come out to our house, about three miles, drink milk, eat mush, corn-bread and butter, bring the children candy, and rock the cradle while I got him something to eat. He would tend babies and do any thing to accommodate anybody."

On a cold winter day he saw Ab Trent cutting up an old house for Mr. Hill into firewood. Ab was barefooted, and shivered with the cold.

"What do you get for that job?" Abraham inquired.

"One dollar," replied Ab; "I want a pair of shoes," and he pointed to his almost frozen feet.

"Well, give me your axe," continued Abraham, seizing it, "and you clear to the house where it is warm."

Ab "cleared," glad to put his bare feet to a fire, and Abraham cut up the "house" so quickly, that "Ab and the owner were both amazed when they saw it done."

About this time, Henry McHenry had a horse-race and he applied to Abraham to act judge.

"No; I've done with that," replied Abraham.

"But you must," urged McHenry.

"I must not, and I will not," responded Abraham, with more emphasis. "This horse-racing business is all wrong."

"Just this once; never'll ask you again," said McHenry.

"Well, remember, 'just this once' it is," was Abraham's conclusion. He acted as judge, and decided correctly. The judge for the other side said, "Lincoln is the fairest man I ever had to deal with; if Lincoln is in this county when I die, I want him to be my administrator, for he is the only man I ever met with that was wholly and unselfishly honest." This is another of the incidents that show how he came to be known as "Honest Abe."

James Short, who lived four miles from New Salem, says that Abraham often came to his house, and, if it was a very busy time on the farm, "Abe would pull off his roundabout and go to work with more energy than any man I could hire. He was the best man at husking corn on the stock I ever saw. I used to consider myself very good, but he would gather two loads to my one."

In 1833, President Jackson appointed him postmaster of New Salem, because he was better qualified for the position than any man in the town. The post office was kept in Mr. Hill's store, the proprietor taking charge of it when Lincoln was engaged in surveying or other business. When he was in the office, he made himself useful by reading letters for parties who could not read. He read all the newspapers received at the office, and frequently read them aloud to an ignorant assembly in front of the store.

A story which fastened itself to him in manhood was that, when he was Postmaster in New Salem, he "carried the office in his hat." Of course mail-matter at such an office was light. Few letters were received; and, sometimes, when Lincoln was going out, he would put the letters in his hat, that he might deliver them to the parties addressed, should he meet them or go near their residences. This novel arrangement discloses both his kindness of heart and fidelity to trusts.

CHAPTER XX

LAURELS WON

Members of the Legislature served two years in Illinois, so that the next election occurred in 1834. Lincoln was a candidate. There was a Whig party then, and he was a member of it. Yet many Democrats supported him in the contest, so that he was elected by a larger majority than any other man on the ticket.

"Who is this man Lincoln I hear talked about for the Legislature?" inquired one Dr. Barrett, who was a stranger to the candidate, but a friend of Herndon. The question was put to the latter.

"Go to Berlin tomorrow, and you will learn who he is; he is going to speak there," Herndon replied.

Dr. Barrett was there promptly, and when the tall, awkward, homely candidate was pointed out by Herndon, he said—

"Can't the party raise any better material than that!"

"Wait," answered Herndon, "until you hear his speech before you pass judgment. He is our candidate and good material enough for us."

"Well, if that fellow is qualified to go to the Legislature, then his looks belie him; that's all," continued Dr. Barrett.

He soon heard his speech, however; and, at the conclusion of it, Herndon inquired—

"Doctor, what do you think now?"

"I give it up now. Why, sir, he is a perfect take in—he knows more than all of them put together."

Lincoln received 1,376 votes, and was elected, causing great joy among his friends. Many who did not vote for him were perfectly satisfied with his election. Nor did he resort to the dishonorable means of getting votes which some candidates employed, such as furnishing a grog-shop for their use on election day and paying the bills. He utterly refused to promote his own election by proffering the intoxicating cup, although such was the custom.

The time between the election and the assembling of the Legislature, Lincoln spent in very close study, that he might be better qualified to discharge his duties in the State House.

One thing was indispensable if he would make a respectable appearance in the Legislature; he must have a new suit of clothes and some money for expenses—much more than he possessed. His wants, in this respect, were supplied in the following providential manner.

When he had charge of Offutt's store, in 1832, a stranger entered one morning, and introduced himself as Mr. Smoot. Lincoln jumped over the counter and grasped the stranger's hand in his cordial way, saying:—

"Glad to see you, Mr. Smoot. I have heard of you often, but never had the pleasure of meeting you before."

"And I am equally glad to meet you, Abe Lincoln," rejoined Mr. Smoot; "I've heard so much about you that I feel acquainted already."

Lincoln stood surveying him from head to foot, looking for all the world as if the humor within him would burst out, and finally remarked:—

"Smoot, I am very much disappointed in you; I expected to see a scaly specimen of humanity."

Smoot, equal to the occasion, replied: "Yes; and I am equally disappointed, for I expected to see a good-looking man when I saw you."

This laid the foundation of lasting friendship between the two men; and, when Lincoln was elected to the Legislature, and needed clothes and money, he knew that Smoot would loan him the amount. Taking Hugh Armstrong with him, he went to his friend and said:—

"Smoot, did you vote for me?"

"Vote for you? Of course I did."

"Well, do you want I should make a decent appearance in the Legislature?" added Lincoln.

"Certainly; I don't expect you'll make any other appearance, though you are not as handsome as I am," responded Smoot, humorously.

"Then you will have to lend me some money; I must buy some decent clothes."

"That I can do without any trouble at all a nice suit of clothes may make a handsome man of you," answered Smoot. "How much money do you want?"

"Two hundred dollars, and will pay you at the close of the session."

Smoot lent him two hundred dollars upon his word of honor, and he says, "Lincoln returned the amount to me according to promise."

About this time, Lincoln was exposed to peculiar temptations to infidelity, through associates and books. Several of his boon companions were infidels and they made light of religion and the Bible. At the same time Paine's "Age of Reason," and Volney's "Ruins," came into his hands, and he read them with avidity. In these circumstances, his belief in the Scriptures began to waver. He expressed his doubts freely to others. He discussed the matter with intimate friends and finally, he wrote an essay in which his doubts of the divine authenticity of the Bible were plainly expressed.

However, this proved but a freak of humanity, such as often appears in the lives of smart young men; for his essay was soon cast aside forever; and his early familiarity with, and confidence in, the Scriptures, asserted themselves, as the sequel will show. It is not our purpose to tell what "Acts and Resolves" occupied Lincoln's attention, in the Legislature, during the session. Other things, bearing upon his future career, demand the brief space we can give this period. We may say, however, that he was comparatively a silent member, observing and learning, though he was faithful and efficient on committees.

It was during the sitting of the Legislature that Lincoln decided to study law, without waiting to become seven feet high. It was on this wise.

He was thrown much into the society of Hon. John T. Stuart, an eminent lawyer, from Springfield. This gentleman was a close observer, and he soon discovered that young Lincoln possessed unusual talents. He had no doubt that he would make his mark, if he could have the opportunity; so he embraced a favorable time to advise him about studying law.

"Have you ever thought of studying law?" Mr. Stuart inquired, in a delicate manner.

"Never, though the subject has been named to me by others," replied Lincoln.

"And why have you not entertained the suggestion favorably?"

"Because I have not talents enough to warrant such a decision; and then I have no means, even if I had the talents."

"Perhaps you have too exalted views of the abilities required. Let us see. Is there anything in the law so intricate as to demand superior talents? Does it require more ability than medicine or theology? No, I think you will say. And then, if it did, perhaps the future will reveal that you possess the talents for it."

"But then, a poor fellow like me, with no friends to aid, can hardly think of going through a long course of study."

"It is not very long after all, and there need not be much expense about it, except for your board and clothes."

"How can that be?"

"You can read law by yourself, working at your business of surveyor enough to board and clothe yourself, and in less than three years be admitted to the bar."

"But books are expensive, especially law-books."

"Very true; but that difficulty is easily remedied. You shall be welcome to my library. Come as often as you please, and carry away as many books as you please, and keep them as long as you please."

"You are very generous, indeed. I could never repay you for such generosity."

"I don't ask any pay, my dear sir," responded Mr. Stuart, shaking his sides with laughter. "And if I did, it would be pay enough to see you pleading at the bar."

"I am almost frightened at the thought of appearing there," added Lincoln.

"You'd soon get over your fright, I reckon, and bless your stars that you followed the advice of John T. Stuart."

"I dare say."

"Only think of it," continued Mr. Stuart; "a brighter prospect is before you than hundreds of distinguished men enjoyed in early life, on account of the advantages offered to you. You are a 'Clay man,' and you now have the offer of better opportunities to rise than he had when he left his mother's log cabin. All the schooling he ever enjoyed was in his boyhood, when he went to school to Peter Deacon, in a log school-house without a window or floor. All the learning he acquired after that was by industry and perseverance, improving every leisure moment, and extending his studies far into the night."

"I don't see but he had as good advantages in his early life as I did," interrupted Lincoln.

"That is so; and there is much in your history that reminds me of his. I suppose that is what suggested the comparison to me. You have a right to be a 'Clay man.' One would scarcely have thought, when he was seen riding his mother's old horse, without a saddle, and with a rope for a bridle, on his way to mill with a grist on the horse's back, that he—'The Mill Boy of the Slashes,' as he was called—would become one of the most renowned men of the land."

"That is so; and I admire the man for his noble efforts to rise in the world. He made himself just what he became," said Lincoln.

"And that is what you, and every other young man, will do, if you ever make a mark. 'Self-made, or never made,' is the adage. It is of little consequence what advantages a youth possesses, unless he is disposed to improve them; and I am almost of the opinion that it matters but little how few the privileges a young man enjoys, if he only possesses the energy and industry to make the most of them."

"And the ability, you might add," suggested Lincoln.

"Perhaps so, if you choose. But the history of our country abounds with examples of these self-made men, as poor and unknown as Henry Clay was. But now I must go; remember my counsel, and decide rightly."

"Many thanks for your interest," answered Lincoln. "I shall ponder the subject, and feel grateful to you, whether I decide as you recommend or not."

Lincoln decided to study law. He concluded that he must possess some ability for the legal profession when such a man as Mr. Stuart advised him to enter it. More than any other influence, the counsel of Mr. Stuart determined him to become a lawyer.

There was much joy among Lincoln's friends in New Salem when they learned of his wise decision. All were ready to render him any assistance possible. His own familiar associates soon found that his studies would interfere constantly with that social intercourse which they had enjoyed so much. To pursue his studies, while earning a livelihood by surveying, would require an amount of industry, perseverance and self denial of which they understood but little.

"I am as fond of society as either of you," remarked Lincoln to several of his companions who were discussing the question together at one time; "but I must deny myself this enjoyment, if I would succeed in my plans. It is pretty clear that I must do two things: I must practice economy of time and money, and be as industrious as possible."

"A solemn view of the future," remarked Alley, in a playful way.

"And a correct one, too, I guess," said Green.

"Correct or not," responded Lincoln, "it is the course I have mapped out for myself, and I must not depart from it."

This decision was in response to an appeal to engage in a definite pastime that would interrupt his studies for a whole evening.

"I shall walk to Springfield and back tomorrow," he continued. "Esquire Stuart has offered to loan me law-books, and I shall go for some tomorrow."

Here is an illustration of his self-denial, and the decision with which he adhered to his purpose. He canvassed the whole subject in the beginning, and he resolved to spend no evenings in social entertainments. He saw that he must do it from sheer necessity, as he would be obliged to use up the night hours much more economically than the laws of health would permit. And now he was inflexible. His purpose was fixed, and no allurements or promises of pleasure could make him swerve a hair's breadth therefrom.

Springfield was twenty-two miles from New Salem, and yet Lincoln walked there and back on the day proposed. He made a long day of it, and a wearisome one, too. On the following evening Green called upon him, to learn how he succeeded.

"What?" he exclaimed. "Did you bring all these books home in your arms?" They were Blackstone's Commentaries, in four volumes.

"Yes; and read forty pages of the first volume on the way," Lincoln replied. "Come, now, just examine me on the first volume."

He had a faculty of perusing a volume when he was walking, and he often did it. He gained time thereby.

"I don't see what you are made of to endure so," continued Green. "It would use me all up to carry such a load a quarter part of that distance."

"I am used to it, you know, and that makes the difference. But, come, just see what I know about the first part of that volume." And he passed the first volume to him.

"If you pass muster, you'll want I should admit you to the bar, I suppose," responded Green. "That I shall be glad to do."

So he proceeded to examine Lincoln on the first volume and he found, to his surprise, that he was well posted on the forty pages read. By his close attention, and the ability to concentrate his thoughts, he readily made what he read his own.

Thus Lincoln began and continued the study of law, alternating his time between surveying and study, going to Springfield for books as often as it was necessary, and often pursuing his reading of law far into the night.

With such devotion did he employ his time in study and manual labor, denying himself much that young men generally consider essential, that he might have said, as Cicero said of himself: "What others give to public shows and entertainments, to festivity, to amusements, nay, even to mental and bodily rest, give to study and philosophy." Even when he was engaged in the fields surveying, his thoughts were upon his books, so that much which he learned at night was fastened in his mind by day. He might have adopted the language of Cicero concerning himself: "Even my leisure hours have their occupation."

Sometimes he was engaged days and weeks together in surveying, having only his nights in which to study; and then, again, he had both day and night to give to his books for a time. Nor did his interest abate in the least; it rather increased than otherwise. The longer he studied, the more deeply absorbed he became in his books. His robust physical constitution enabled him to endure hard toil both of body and mind, otherwise he would have broken down.

He served his constituents so faithfully in the Legislature, that he was re-nominated for the position in 1836. He had grown so rapidly in mental power, that, in this campaign, his speeches were of high order. R. L. Wilson, who was a Representative elect with Lincoln, says:—

"The Saturday evening preceding the election, the candidates were addressing the people in the Court House at Springfield. Dr. Early, one of the candidates on the Democratic side, made some charge that N. W. Edwards, one of the candidates on the Whig side, deemed untrue. Edwards climbed on a table, so as to be seen by Early and by every one in the house, and at the top of his voice told Early that the charge was false. The excitement that followed was intense, —so much so, that fighting men thought a duel must settle the difficulty. Mr. Lincoln, by the programme, followed Early. He took up the subject in dispute, and handled it fairly, and with such ability, that every one was astonished and pleased. So that difficulty ended there. Then for the first time, developed by the excitement of the occasion, he spoke in that tenor intonation of voice, that ultimately settled down into a clear, shrill, monotonous style of speaking, that enabled his audience, however large, to hear distinctly the lowest sound of his voice."

Lincoln was followed in that meeting by George Forquer, who was a prominent Whig member of the Legislature in 1834, but left his party for the sake of getting the berth of Register of the Land Office at Springfield. He was a wily politician, ready to change front at any time, and to resort to political tricks for the sake of office. Forquer assailed Lincoln bitterly, and began his speech by saying, "the young man must be taken down." Lincoln stood by and listened to every word. As soon as Forquer closed his tirade, Lincoln mounted the platform, and replied "with great dignity and force," closing his speech thus:—

"The gentleman says 'this young man must be taken down.' It is for you, not for me, to say whether I am up or down. The gentleman has alluded to my being a young man; I am older in years than I am in the tricks and trades of politicians. I desire to live, and I desire place and distinction as a politician; but I would rather die now, than, like the gentleman, live to see the day that I would have to erect a lightning rod to protect a guilty conscience from an offended God." This termination of his speech convulsed the audience, and they roared with laughter, and cheered, at Forquer's expense.

In the Legislature of 1836-37, Lincoln found himself associated with many men who became great in public life thereafter—Stephen A. Douglas, James Shields, John A, McClernand, Dan Stone, Edward D. Baker, John J. Hardin, and a dozen others of equal ability.

There were nine Representatives from Sangamon County, and not one of them was less than six feet high. Lincoln was the tallest of the number. Members of the Legislature dubbed them "The Long King;" and they said, "Lincoln is the longest."

Lincoln's second term in the Legislature brought him face to face with the Slavery question. The "Abolitionists" had been busily at work, scattering anti-slavery literature North and South, lecturing in the Free States upon the sin and curse of Slavery, and agitating the subject in every possible way. The State governments, even at the North, were bent on suppressing these "agitators," as they were called. Even the governors of Massachusetts and New York denounced them, as if they were more dangerous than horse-thieves. The bitterest feeling prevailed against them in Illinois and one of their leaders. Rev. E. P. Lovejoy, who published an anti-slavery paper at Alton, in that State, was shot while defending his printing-office against the attacks of a pro-slavery mob.

In these circumstances, the Democratic party of Illinois, largely in the majority in the Legislature, waxed bold and violent. In the great excitement they introduced a series of resolutions against "abolitionists," and in favor of Slavery, that would have been a disgrace to any Slave State. They sought to intimidate and lash the Whigs into the support of the infamous measures and they succeeded with most of them except Abraham Lincoln. He denounced the resolutions and the party which introduced them. He spoke against them, and voted against them and he drew one Whig to his side— Dan Stone—who stood with him fearlessly to the end. And when the House finally adopted them, these two members presented a carefully prepared protest against the measure, as "injustice" and "bad policy," and asked to have it entered, in their name, upon the journal of the House. His good fight for Freedom in the House, from 1836 to 1838, put him before the State and the country as a fearless and powerful opponent of the slave system.

It was during this legislative term that an act was passed, removing the capital from Vandalia to Springfield and the prime mover in it was Lincoln. To him was credited the success of the measure, which proved of great value to the State.

Lincoln was admitted to the bar in 1837, and, soon after, removed to Springfield, and became the partner of John T. Stuart, his benefactor, in the practice of law, and he boarded with Hon. William Butler, In New Salem, for two years before, "he wrote deeds, contracts, notes, and other legal papers for his neighbors; and 'pettifogged' before the justice of the peace; but in all this he was only trying himself, and never charged a penny for his services."

In 1838, he was elected, for a third term, to the House of Representatives, by a larger majority than ever. He was candidate for Speaker at this term; but the Democrats being largely in the ascendancy elected their candidate. An incident is related by Mr. Wilson, connected with the campaign that preceded the election of 1838, illustrative of Lincoln's decided temperance principles. Mr. Wilson accompanied him in his stumping tours, and he says: "At that time it was the universal custom to keep some whiskey in the house, for private use and to treat friends. The subject was always mentioned as a matter of etiquette, but with the remark to Mr. Lincoln: 'You never drink, but may be your friend would like to take a little.' I never saw Mr. Lincoln drink. He often told me that he never drank; had no desire to drink, nor for the companionship of drinking men."

During that campaign, a dinner was tendered to the "Long Nine," at Athens; where, in response to the toast, "Abraham Lincoln, one of Nature's noblemen," he delivered one of his ablest speeches. It was universally agreed that the toast was a deserved compliment.

Before Lincoln removed to Springfield, he was invited by the "Young Men's Lyceum" of that town, to deliver a literary lecture before them. The invitation shows that he had won a wide reputation, although he was only twenty-eight years of age, and only six years removed from the log-cabin that he built for his father in Macon County. His subject, on that occasion, was: "The Perpetuation of Our Free Institutions." He handled it in a manner that showed the familiarity of a statesman with the genius and history of Republican institutions.

Lincoln was re-elected once more to the House of Representatives in 1840. The campaign was a very hot one, the Democrats in several localities making violent demonstrations. Colonel E. D. Baker was making a speech to a promiscuous assembly in the court-room at Springfield, when the Democrats proposed to "pull him off the stage." A riot was impending, when Lincoln threw himself between his friend and the audience, exclaiming:—

"Gentlemen! let us not disgrace the age and country in which we live. This is a land where freedom of speech is guaranteed. Mr. Baker has a right to speak, and ought to be permitted to do so. I am here to protect him, and no man shall take him from this stand, if I can prevent it." Mr. Baker proceeded without interruption thereafter."

There was a very troublesome member in that Legislature from Wabash County. He was frequently upon his feet opposing measures on the ground of "unconstitutionality." His stereotyped cry against this and that measure was "unconstitutional." Lincoln was deputed to silence him; and he soon enjoyed the opportunity. A measure was introduced, in which Lincoln's constituents were specially interested. The member from Wabash immediately arose, and expended his utmost energies upon its "unconstitutional" features, although others could not discover them. Mr. Lincoln arose and said:—

"Mr. Speaker, the attack of the member from Wabash upon the unconstitutionality of this measure reminds me of an old friend of mine. He is a peculiar-looking old fellow, with shaggy, overhanging eyebrows, and a pair of spectacles under them. (Here every member turned to the man from Wabash, and recognized a personal description) One morning, just after the old man got up, he imagined he saw a squirrel on a tree near his house. So he took down his rifle, and fired at the squirrel, but the squirrel paid no attention to the shot. He loaded and fired again and again, until, at the thirteenth shot, he set down his gun impatiently, and said to his boy, who was looking on, "Boy, there's something wrong about this rifle. "Rifle's all right, I know 'this,' responded the boy, 'but where's your squirrel?' 'Don't you see him, humped up about half-way up the tree? inquired the old man, peering over his spectacles, and getting mystified. 'No, I don't,' responded the boy; and then turning and looking into his father's face, he exclaimed, 'I see your squirrel. You've been firing at a louse on your eyebrow!'"

The House was convulsed with laughter, and the member from Wabash dropped his "unconstitutional" dodge.

Mr. Lincoln grew rapidly in public favor as a lawyer, and within ten years after he left his log-cabin home, in Macon County, citizens of Springfield would point him out to strangers on the street, and say: "One of the ablest lawyers in Illinois."

His partnership with Mr. Stuart terminated in 1840, and he soon after associated himself with Judge S. T. Logan. He married Miss Mary Todd, daughter of Honorable Robert S. Todd of Lexington, Kentucky, in 1842, when he was thirty-three years of age. The fruits of this marriage were four sons, viz. Robert, Edwards, William, and Thomas. Edwards died in infancy; William died at the age of twelve years in Washington; Thomas died in Illinois at the age of twenty; and Robert is now our honored secretary of war at Washington.

Soon after his marriage he wrote two letters, which so reveal his strong friendships as well as his simplicity of character, that we quote a brief extract from each. The first he wrote to his old friend, J. F. Speed of Louisville, Kentucky, and in addition to the characteristics of the man which it reveals, it discloses somewhat his humble mode of living. "We are not keeping house, but boarding at the Globe Tavern, which is very well kept now by a widow by the name of Beck. Boarding only costs four dollars a week. I most heartily wish you and your Fanny will not fail to come. Just let us know the time a week in advance, and we will have a room prepared for you, and we'll be merry together for a while."

The other letter was penned to newly married friends in another State, about a month after his own marriage. "I have no way of telling you how much happiness I wish you both, though I believe you both can conceive it. I feel somewhat jealous of both of you now, for you will be so exclusively concerned for one another, that I shall be forgotten entirely. I regret to learn that you have resolved not to return to Illinois: I shall be very lonesome without you. How miserably things seem to be arranged in this world! If we have no friends we have no pleasure, and if we have them, we are sure to lose them, and be doubly pained by the loss. I did hope she and you would make your home here, yet I own I have no right to insist. You owe obligations to her ten thousand times more sacred than any you can owe to others and in that light let them be respected and observed. It is natural that she should desire to remain with her relatives and friends. As to friends, she could not need them anywhere:—she would have them in abundance here. Write me often, and believe me, yours forever, Lincoln." His heart was in his pen, as it usually was in his hand.

CHAPTER XXI
A SUCCESSFUL LAWYER

When Lincoln commenced the practice of law he was too poor to own a horse and saddlebags. He was obliged to borrow this outfit of a friend, until he scraped together enough money to purchase one.

"But why did he need a horse and saddle-bags?" the reader will ask.

At that time, the Court went to the clients instead of the clients going to the Court. That is, Court business was laid out in Circuits; and the Court traveled from place to place, holding sessions, and transacting such business as the locality brought to it. Lincoln was in the "Eighth Judicial Circuit" of Illinois; and for several years traveled over it on horseback, with no other outfit than the contents of his saddle-bags and a cotton umbrella. A longer or shorter period was occupied in completing the "Circuit," according to the amount of business brought to the Court. Lincoln was sometimes absent three months from home on the Circuit. During one of these long absences, his wife had a second story and new roof put upon their house, as a surprise to him. It was nicely finished when he returned. Coming in front of his old home, he sat upon his horse surveying the changed habitation, and pretending not to recognize it, he called to a man across the street:—

"Stranger, can you tell me where Lincoln lives? He used to live here."

When he got a little more of this world's goods, he set up a one-horse buggy,—a very sorry and shabby looking affair, which he generally used when the weather promised to be bad. But the lawyers were always glad to see him, and the landlords hailed his coming with pleasure.

Honesty, kindness, generosity, fairness, justice, and kindred qualities, distinguished him in the practice of law. A whole volume of incidents might be related, illustrating these qualities of the man, but a few only can be given.

A stranger called to secure his services.

"State your case," said Mr. Lincoln. The man stated it at considerable length, when Lincoln surprised him by saying:—

"I cannot serve you; for you are wrong and the other party is right."

"That is none of your business, if I hire and pay you for taking the case," retorted the man.

"Not my business!" exclaimed Lincoln. "My business is never to defend wrong if I am a lawyer. I never take a case that is manifestly wrong."

"Well, you can make trouble for the fellow," added the applicant.

"Yes," responded Lincoln, "there is no reasonable doubt but that I can gain the case for you. I can set a whole neighborhood at loggerheads; I can distress a widowed mother and her six fatherless children, and thereby get for you six hundred dollars, which rightfully belongs as much to the woman and her children as it does to you. But I won't do it."

"Not for any amount of pay?" inquired the man.

"Not for all you are worth," replied Lincoln. "You must remember that some things which are legally right are not morally right. I shall not take your case."

"I don't care a snap whether you do or not," angrily replied the man, starting to go; "there are other lawyers in the State."

"I'll give you a piece of advice without charge," added Lincoln. "You seem to be a sprightly, energetic man. I would advise you to try your hand at making six hundred dollars some other way."

One afternoon an old colored woman came into the office of Lincoln and Herndon to tell her sad story. She was once the slave of one Hinkle in Kentucky, who brought herself and children into Illinois, and made them free. Her son had gone down to New Orleans on a steamer, and very imprudently went ashore, when the police arrested him, under a State law that authorized the seizure and sale of free negroes from other States and he would be sold back into slavery unless immediately redeemed. Lincoln's sympathetic nature was deeply stirred, and his indignation was also aroused.

"Run over to the State House and ask Governor Bissell if something cannot be done to obtain possession of the negro," he said to Mr. Herndon.

The inquiry was soon made, and Herndon returned to say: "The governor says that he has no legal or constitutional right to do anything in the premises."

Lincoln was thoroughly aroused by this feature of inhumanity which the legal status disclosed, and starting to his feet, and raising his long, right arm heavenward he exclaimed:—

"By the Almighty's help, I'll have the negro back soon, or I'll have a twenty years' agitation in Illinois, until the governor does have a legal and constitutional right to do something in the premises."

He and his partner immediately sent money of their own to a New Orleans correspondent, who procured the negro and returned him to his mother.

A person applied to Colonel E. D. Baker, who afterwards became United States Senator from Oregon, for aid in behalf of a fugitive slave.

"I'm sorry that I cannot serve you," Colonel Baker replied; "I should be glad to help the fugitive, but, as a political man, I cannot afford it."

The applicant then sought the advice of an ardent anti-slavery friend, who said:—

"Go to Lincoln; he's not afraid of an unpopular case. When I go for a lawyer to defend an arrested fugitive slave, other lawyers will refuse me, but if Mr. Lincoln is at home, he will always take my case."

Judge Treat furnishes the following:—

"A case being called for hearing in the court, Mr. Lincoln stated that he appeared for the appellant, and was ready to proceed with the argument. He then said: "This is the first case I have ever had in this court, [it was just after he was admitted to practice in the Circuit Court of the United States, Dec. 3, 1839] and I have therefore examined it with great care. As the court will perceive, by looking at the abstract of the record, the only question in the case is one of authority. I have not been able to find any authority to sustain any side of the case, but I have found several cases directly in point on the other side. I will now give these cases, and then submit the case."

One lawyer, who could not understand that the true purpose of a court is to "establish justice," remarked, "The fellow is crazy."

Once, in a closely-contested civil suit, he found himself upon the wrong side of the case. His client had misrepresented the case, being "a slippery fellow." Lincoln succeeded in proving an account for his client, when the opposing attorney then "proved a receipt covering the entire cause of action." By the time he was through, Lincoln had disappeared from the courtroom. The court sent to the hotel for him. "Tell the Judge," said Lincoln, "that I can't come: my hands are dirty, and I came over to clean them."

In the celebrated Patterson trial, a case of murder, Lincoln and Swett were counsel for the accused. After hearing the testimony, Lincoln was satisfied that the accused was guilty, and calling his colleague into another room, he said:—

"Swett, the man is guilty."

"No doubt about that," Swett replied.

"And you must defend him; I can't."

Swett promised to do it, and he did it so well that he saved the guilty man from justice. They received a thousand dollars for services; but Lincoln declined to take a cent of it.

At another time, he was defending a man indicted for larceny; and, being satisfied by the evidence that the accused was guilty, he called aside his colleagues, Parks and Young, and said: "He is guilty. If you can say anything for him, do it; I can't. If I attempt, the jury will see that I think he is guilty, and convict him, of course."

He conducted a suit against a railroad company, and damages were awarded to him. The railroad company proved, and the court allowed, a certain offset; and when the court was footing the amount, Lincoln arose and stated that his opponents had not proved all that was justly due them in offset, and proceeded to prove and allow a further offset against his client. His purpose was to establish "exact justice." Sometimes, however, his sympathy for a poor fellow who was in danger of the penitentiary or gallows, caused him to overlook "exact justice," as we have seen.

A woman called upon him to secure his services to prosecute a real-estate claim and she put a check for two hundred and fifty dollars into his hand as a retaining fee,

"I will look the case over, and see what can be done," said Mr. Lincoln, "You may call tomorrow."

The woman called as requested on the next day, "I am obliged to say that there is not a peg on which to hang your claim," Mr. Lincoln said to her.

"How so?" she inquired, with not a little disappointment.

He explained the case to her satisfaction, and she started to go.

"Wait a minute," he urged, fumbling in his pocket; "here is the check you left with me."

"But, Mr. Lincoln, that belongs to you; you have earned it," she answered.

"No, no, no," responded Mr. Lincoln; "that would not be right. I can't take pay for doing my duty." And he insisted that she should take the check.

The testimony of his legal associates, at this point, is interesting. Mr. Gillespie says: "Mr. Lincoln's love of justice and fair play was his predominating trait. I have often listened to him when I thought he would state his case out of court. It was not in his nature to assume, or to attempt to bolster up, a false position. He would abandon his case first. He did so in the case of Buckmaster for the use of Denham vs. Beenes and Arthur, in our Supreme Court, in which I happened to be opposed to him. Another gentleman, less fastidious, took Mr. Lincoln's place, and gained the case."

S. C. Parks, Esq., says: "I have often said, that, for a man who was for a quarter of a century both a lawyer and politician, he was the most honest man I ever knew. He was not only morally honest, but intellectually so. He could not reason falsely; if he attempted it, he failed. In politics he never would try to mislead. At the bar, when he found he was wrong, he was the weakest lawyer I ever saw."

His old friend, Jack Armstrong, of New Salem, whose kind, good wife darned his stockings, made his shirts, and "got him something to eat while he rocked the baby," died not long after Lincoln settled in Springfield. The baby whom he rocked had grown into a stout but profligate young man of twenty-two years—William D. Armstrong—and he was arrested for murder. The circumstances were as follows:—At a camp meeting in Mason County, several fast young men became intoxicated, and then engaged in a "free fight," in which one Metzgar was killed. Armstrong and James H. Norris were charged with the murder. Norris was "tried in Mason County, convicted of manslaughter, and sentenced to the penitentiary for the term of eight years."

"Aunt Hannah," as Lincoln used to call his old benefactress, was plunged into terrible sorrow for her misguided son. She scarcely knew what to do. But, in her great grief, she recalled one who would come to her aid if possible — "the noble, good Abe," who rocked her Billy when he was a baby in the cradle. She sat down and wrote to Lincoln, telling him of her anguish, and beseeching him to help her boy if possible. The appeal brought tears to Lincoln's eyes, and enlisted his whole soul to save the accused for the sake of his mother. Now was the time for him to requite the many kindnesses "Aunt Hannah" showed him under her humble roof. He sat down and wrote to her an affirmative answer, at the same time encouraging her to hope for the best, and asking her to come to Springfield at once. He pledged his services, also, gratuitously.

Lincoln's letter was like a promise from the skies to "Aunt Hannah." Her almost broken' heart took courage, and away she hastened to Springfield, the benefactress seeking a benefactor in the once poor boy she helped in her humble abode.

"Aunt Hannah" believed that her boy was not guilty of murder—that the fatal blow was not struck by him, but by another— that others sought to fasten the crime upon him because of his bad reputation. At the close of the interview, Lincoln was of the same opinion; or, at least, thought there was no positive evidence that her son was the murderer. His heart was so thoroughly moved for the old lady that he resolved to save her boy from the gallows if possible. The excitement was intense, and everybody seemed willing to believe that Armstrong killed Metzgar. Lincoln saw that it would be well-nigh impossible to secure an impartial jury in these circumstances, and he said to Mrs. Armstrong:—

"We must have the case put off if possible, until the excitement dies away."

"And let my son lie in prison all the while," Mrs. Armstrong answered, as if horrified by the thought that he should be incarcerated so long.

"There is no other alternative. Better that than to be condemned and executed in advance," Lincoln rejoined calmly.

"True, very true; but I'm impatient to see him free again."

"That is not strange at all, but I am satisfied that the case cannot be conducted so favorably for him now, when the public mind is so excited."

"I understand you exactly," responded Mrs. Armstrong, "and shall agree to any decision you make. The case is in your hands, and you will conduct it as you think best."

"Another thing too," added Lincoln, "I need more time to unravel the affair. I want to produce evidence that shall vindicate William, to the satisfaction of every reasonable man."

Lincoln secured the postponement of the trial until the following spring and he spent much time, in the interval, in tracing evidence, laboring as assiduously to pay his old debt of gratitude as he would have done under the offer of a fee of five thousand dollars.

The time for the trial arrived, and it drew together a crowd of interested people, nor were they under so much excitement as they were when the case was postponed. The "sober second thought" had moderated their feelings, and they were in a better frame of mind to judge impartially.

The witnesses for the State were introduced; some to testify of Armstrong's previous vicious character, and others to relate what they saw of the affair on the night of the murder. His accuser testified in the most positive manner that he saw him make the dreadful thrust that felled his victim.

"Could there be no mistake in regard to the person who struck the blow?" asked the counsel for the defense.

"None at all: I am confident of that," replied the witness.

"What time in the evening was it?"

"Between ten and eleven o'clock."

"Well, about how far between? Was it quarter past ten or half-past ten o'clock, or still later? Be more exact, if you please."

"I should think it might have been about half-past ten o'clock," answered the witness.

"And you are confident that you saw the prisoner at the bar give the blow? Be particular in your testimony, and remember that you are under oath."

"I am; there can be no mistake about it."

"Was it not dark?"

"Yes; but the moon was shining brightly."

"Then it was not very dark, as there was a moon?"

"No; the moon made it light enough for me to see the whole affair."

"Be particular on this point. Do I understand you to say that the murder was committed about half-past ten o'clock, and that the moon was shining brightly at the time?"

"Yes, that is what I testify."

"Very well; that is all."

His principal accuser was thus positive in his testimony and the sagacious attorney saw enough therein to destroy his evidence.

After the witnesses for the State had been called, the defense introduced a few, to show that young Armstrong had borne a better character than some of the witnesses gave him, and also that his accuser had been his personal enemy, while the murdered young man was his personal friend.

The counsel for the Commonwealth considered that the evidence was too strong against Armstrong to admit of a reasonable doubt of his guilt; therefore, his plea was short and formal.

All eyes were now turned to Lincoln. What could he say for the accused, in the face of such testimony? Few saw any possible chance for Armstrong to escape his condemnation was sure.

Mr. Lincoln rose, while a deeply impressive stillness reigned throughout the court-room. The prisoner sat with a worried, despairing look, such as he had worn ever since his arrest. When he was led into the courtroom, a most melancholy expression sat upon his brow as if he were forsaken by every friend, and the evidence presented was not suited to produce a change for the better.

His counsel proceeded to review the testimony, and called attention particularly to the discrepancies in the statements of the principal witness. What had seemed to the multitude as plain, truthful statements he showed to be wholly inconsistent with other parts of the testimony, indicating a plot against an innocent man. Then, raising his clear, full voice to a higher key, and lifting his long, wiry right arm above his head, as if about to annihilate his client's accuser, he exclaimed: "And he testifies that the moon was shining brightly when the deed was perpetrated, between the hours of ten and eleven o'clock, when the moon did not appear on that night, as your Honor's almanac will show, until an hour or more later, and consequently the whole story is a fabrication."

The audience was carried by this sudden overthrow of the accuser's testimony, and they were now as bitter against the principal witness as they were before against the accused.

Lincoln continued in a strain of singular eloquence, portraying the loneliness and sorrow of the widowed mother, whose husband, long since gathered to his fathers, and his good companion with the silver locks, welcomed a strange and penniless boy to their humble abode, dividing their scanty store with him, and, pausing, and exhibiting much emotion— "that boy stands before you now pleading for the life of his benefactor's son—the staff of the widow's declining years." The effect was electric; and eyes unused to weep shed tears as rain. With unmistakable expressions of honest sympathy around him, Lincoln closed his remarkable plea with the words, "If justice is done, as I believe it will be, before the sun sets, it will shine upon my client a free man."

The jury returned to the court-room, after thirty minutes of retirement, with the verdict of "Not Guilty." Turning to his client, Lincoln said, "It is not sundown, and you are free!"

A shout of joy went up from the crowded assembly; and the aged mother, who had retired when the case was given to the jury, was brought in with tears of gratitude streaming down her cheeks, to receive her acquitted boy, and thank her noble benefactor for his successful effort.

"Where is Mr. Lincoln?" she asked. And from her saved boy, she pressed her way through the crowd to him, and, seizing his hand convulsively, attempted to express her gratitude, but utterance was impossible. Tears only told how full her heart was. Lincoln answered only with tears for a few moments. At length, however, controlling his feelings, he said:—

"Aunt Hannah, what did I tell you? I pray to God that William may be a good boy hereafter—that this lesson may prove in the end a good lesson to him and to all."

Subsequently, Lincoln went to see her at her home, when she pressed him to take pay for his services.

"Why, Aunt Hannah, I shan't take a cent of yours—never. Anything I can do for you, I will do willingly and without any charge."

Months after this, Lincoln heard that some men were trying to defraud her of land, and he wrote to her:—

"Aunt Hannah, they can't have your land. Let them try it in the Circuit Court, and then you appeal it; bring it to the Supreme Court, and Herndon and I will attend to it for nothing."

This William Armstrong, whom Lincoln saved from the gallows, enlisted in the Union army, in response to Abraham Lincoln's first call for seventy-five thousand volunteers. Two years later, his mother wrote to President Lincoln that she wanted her boy. She did not speak of any disability, only said that she wanted him. But that was enough for Mr. Lincoln, who had not yet fully paid his old debt of gratitude to his early benefactress, as he thought. He ordered the discharge of her son, and wrote the following brief epistle to her with his own hand:—

September, 1863.

Mrs. Hannah Armstrong—I have just ordered the discharge of your boy William, as you say, now at Louisville, Ky.

A lawyer was associated with Lincoln in this case, Mr. Walker, and he says of his plea:—

"At first he spoke slowly, and carefully reviewed the whole testimony, —picked it all to pieces, and showed that the man had not received his wounds at the place or time named by the witnesses, bid often towards, and at the house of some one else. He skillfully untied here and there a knot, and loosened here and there a peg, until fairly getting warmed up, he raised himself in his full power, and shook the arguments of his opponents from him as if they were cobwebs. The last fifteen minutes of his speech was as eloquent as I ever heard; and such the power and earnestness with which he spoke to that jury, that all sat as if entranced, and when he was through, found relief in a gush of tears." Even one of the prosecutors said, "He took the jury by storm. There were tears in Mr. Lincoln's eyes while he spoke, but they were genuine. His sympathies were fully enlisted for the young man, and his terrible sincerity could not help but arouse the same passion in the jury. I have said a hundred times that it was Lincoln's speech that saved Armstrong from the gallows."

By this time, old Mrs. Armstrong must have realized the full, deep significance of the divine promise, "Cast thy bread upon the waters, for thou shalt find it after many days."

In his circuit practice, Lincoln devoted himself to self-improvement, by taking books with him—reading books, his grammar, arithmetic and Shakespeare. He read and studied much when riding. The finest passages of Shakespeare were committed in these travels and he would sometimes stop by the way, and recite them to strangers whom he met. Out of court, during his absence on circuit business he found considerable time to pore over his books, so that little of his time was lost.

Soon after he began the practice of law, he continued to remit money to his poor parents. There was a mortgage of two hundred dollars on his father's little farm, and he paid it. His foster-brother, John Johnston, was poor and needy, and he assisted him, also. John was shiftless and lazy, and Lincoln once wrote to him, "I now promise you, that for every dollar you will, between this and the first of next May, get for your own labor, either in money or as your own indebtedness, I will then give you one other dollar. By this, if you hire yourself at ten dollars a month, from me you will get ten more, making twenty dollars a month for your work." He visited his parents, also, as often as was consistent with his growing business and many cares.

In his early law practice, he received five hundred dollars for conducting a criminal case successfully. A legal friend called upon him the next morning, and found him counting his money.

"Look here, judge," he said; "more money out of this case than I ever had in my life. If I had two hundred and fifty dollars more, I would go directly and purchase a quarter-section of land, and settle it upon my old stepmother."

"I will loan you the required amount," answered the judge.

"Agreed," rejoined Mr. Lincoln, and proceeded to write a note at once.

"I would not use the money just as you have indicated," then added the judge.

"Why not?"

"Your stepmother is getting old, and will not live many years. I would settle the property upon her for her use during -her lifetime, to revert to you upon her death."

"I shall do no such thing," answered Lincoln, decidedly. "It is a poor return, at the best, for the good woman's devotion and fidelity to me, and there is not going to be any half way business about it."

As soon as he could, he purchased the quarter section, and settled it upon his stepmother.

On hearing of his father's serious illness in January, 1851, at a time when pressing business and the sickness of his own wife rendered it impossible for him to leave her, he wrote a very touching filial letter, addressing it to Johnston. The letter has the following paragraph:—

"You already know I desire that neither father or mother shall be in want of any comfort, either in health or sickness, while they live; and I feel sure that you have not failed to use my name, if necessary, to procure a doctor or any thing else for father in his present sickness. I sincerely hope father may yet recover his health; but, at all events, tell him to remember and call upon and confide in our great and good and merciful Maker, who will not turn away from him in any extremity. He notes the fall of a sparrow, and numbers the hairs of our heads; and he will not forget the dying man who puts his trust in him. Say to him, that, if we could meet now, it is doubtful whether it would not be more painful than pleasant; but that, if it be his lot to go now, he will soon have a joyous meeting with loved ones gone before, and where the rest of us, through the help of God, hope ere long to join them."

That the reader may know we have not spoken with partiality of Mr. Lincoln as a lawyer, the following tribute of two of the most distinguished jurists of his day, spoken after his tragic death, will prove.

Judge David Davis said: "In all the elements that constitute the great lawyer he had few equals. The framework of his mental and moral being was honesty. He never took from a client, even when the cause was gained, more than he thought the service was worth and the client could reasonably afford to pay. He was loved by his brethren of the bar."

Judge Drummond said: "With a probity of character known to all, with an intuitive insight into the human heart, with a clearness of statement which was in itself an argument, with uncommon power and felicity of illustration,—often, it is true, of a plain and homely kind, —and with that sincerity and earnestness of manner, which carried conviction, he was one of the most successful lawyers in the State."

CHAPTER XXII
THE RISING STATESMAN

Mr. Lincoln was elected to Congress in 1846. He was brought forward in a meeting to nominate delegates to a Congressional Convention in 1844, but Col. Baker received the endorsement of the convention. Mr. Lincoln, however, was chosen one of the delegates to the district convention, whereupon he wrote to his old friend Speed, in a vein of humor, "The meeting appointed me one of the delegates, so that in getting Baker the nomination I shall be 'fixed' a good deal like the fellow who is made groomsman to the man who has 'cut him out,' and is marrying his own dear gal."

Henry Clay, his favorite statesman, was the Whig candidate for President that year and Mr. Lincoln entered into the canvass with all his heart, making numerous speeches, and winning golden opinions. He was chosen a presidential elector, a merited honor.

One day he was coming down the steps of the State House, when he met an old client, whose note for services he held.

"Hallo, Cogdal!" Lincoln exclaimed, heartily extending his hand: "you have been very unfortunate, I hear." Cogdal had been blown up by an accidental discharge of powder, and lost one hand by the calamity.

"Yes, rather unfortunate; but it might have been worse," answered Cogdal.

"Well, that is a philosophical way of looking at it, certainly," continued Lincoln. "But how are you getting along in your business?"

"Badly enough. I am not only broken up in my business, but crippled for life also."

"I am sorry for you, very sorry indeed," replied Lincoln with profound sympathy.

"I have been thinking about that note of yours," Cogdal added, in a despairing tone.

"Well," responded Lincoln, in a half-laughing way, "you need not think any more about it," at the same time taking the note from his pocket-book and handing it to him.

Cogdal protested against taking the note, and expressed the hope that some day he might be able to pay it. But Lincoln insisted, adding, "If you had the money I would not take it," and he hurried away.

We said that he was elected to Congress in 1846. He was elected too, by a surprisingly large majority. Henry Clay received but nine hundred and fourteen majority in the district in 1844 but Lincoln's majority was one thousand five hundred and eleven. Many voted for him who were not Whigs, his honesty and peculiar fitness for the office winning their votes. He took his seat in the National House of Representatives, Dec. 6, 1847 and the fact that he was the only Whig member from Illinois contributed somewhat to his popularity. At the same session Stephen A. Douglas took his seat in the United States Senate—Democratic senator from Illinois. He was "the youngest and shortest member of the senate," while Lincoln was the "youngest and longest member of the house;" so a waggish associate claimed.

The country was thoroughly excited, at that time, upon the questions of "the Mexican war" and the "admission of Texas as a slave State." The war with Mexico was unjustly waged in the interests of slavery, and the South was looking to Texas for the extension of their inhuman institution. Lincoln at once arrayed himself against these unrighteous measures, and he delivered a speech which was acknowledged to be the best that was delivered against them during the session.

The anti-slavery conflict in Congress was hot and bitter during the two years he served in the House. Those mighty champions of Liberty, John Quincy Adams of Massachusetts, and Joshua R, Giddings, of Ohio, were members and Lincoln found himself fighting for his principles by their side. He assailed slavery as "unjust and cruel;" and did not hesitate to declare that God would visit the land in terrible retribution, if the American people continued to legislate and govern in the interests of human bondage. He voted forty two times, in one way and another, for that famous anti-slavery measure—"The Wilmot Proviso."

He became popular with both Whigs and Democrats, by reason of his genial spirit, fairness, and sincerity in debate, his quick-witted ability in controversy, and his transparency and uprightness of character man of strength was its enemy and that he intended to blast it if he could by strong and manly efforts. He was most successful; and the house approved the glorious triumph of truth by loud and long-continued huzzas. Women waved their white handkerchiefs in token of their silent but heartfelt consent. Every man felt that the speech was unanswerable—that no human power could overthrow it, or trample it under foot.

Mr. Lincoln followed Douglas to Peoria and other places, and was equally triumphant in his replies to the advocate of slavery. The result was a complete political revolution in the state. The Democrats had been in power in Illinois, ever since their party was organized. But now their power was broken, and a Whig legislature was elected, Lincoln being among its members. A press of business, however, compelled him to resign before taking his seat. Many Democrats voted with the Whigs, because they were opposed to forcing slavery upon Kansas and Nebraska.

This new Whig Legislature had to elect a United States Senator and Mr. Lincoln was the Whig candidate; Lyman Trumbull the anti-Kansas-Nebraska Democratic candidate; and General James Shields, the Douglas party candidate. After several indecisive ballots, the Democrats dropped Gen. Shields and took up Governor Matheson, who had not committed himself to either side of the great question; and Matheson came within three votes of an election. At this juncture, an effort was made to unite the friends of Lincoln and Trumbull upon one of them. Here the remarkable magnanimity of Lincoln's nature came to the rescue, showing how much more he cared for the principle at issue than he did for himself.

"Withdraw my name and support Trumbull," urged Lincoln; "we shall be whipped if you don't."

"Never; never," protested one and another.

"Four votes only will make Matheson senator, and we must not risk another ballot," urged Lincoln, with still more earnestness.

"Impossible," answered one. "We cannot do it," said another.

Lincoln grew determined over the danger of losing in the contest, and straightening himself up to his full height, as he was wont under great emotion:—

"It MUST be done," he shouted.

The Whigs yielded, though several of them wept at the necessity and the united effort made Trumbull senator. But, to the Whigs of Illinois, Lincoln never appeared so truly great, as he did after that act of superior magnanimity. No man in the State or country rejoiced more heartily over the triumph than Mr. Lincoln.

In 1856, the Republican party of Illinois was organized at Bloomington, and the foremost man in its organization was Abraham Lincoln. With one of his ablest speeches, on that occasion, he fired all hearts. Mr. Scripps says: "Never was an audience more completely electrified by human eloquence. Again and again during the progress of its delivery, they sprang to their feet and upon the benches, and testified by long continued shouts and the waving of hats, how deeply the speaker had wrought upon their minds and hearts."

From the organization of the Republican party, Mr. Lincoln was not only the first Republican in Illinois, but also in all the Western States and a month later, at the National Republican convention to nominate a candidate for President, his name was brought forward for the Vice-Presidency. On the informal ballot he received one hundred and ten votes, and Mr. Dayton two hundred and fifty-nine. This complimentary vote was secured without Mr. Lincoln's knowledge. He was attending court at Urbana in his own State. The newspaper report that reached Urbana said, "Lincoln received one hundred and ten votes."

"Is that Mr. Lincoln?" inquired one of the lawyers.

"Of course, it is," replied another. And turning to Mr. Lincoln, who made his appearance just then, he remarked:—

"I congratulate you upon so handsome a vote for Vice-President."

"Me!" exclaimed Lincoln, who had already read the paper. "Have you any idea that means me?"

"Certainly, I have no idea that it means anybody else."

"Well, you were never more mistaken in your life," protested Mr. Lincoln; "it can't mean me. It must be the great Lincoln from Massachusetts."

He utterly refused to believe the newspaper report until he read a full account of the proceedings of the convention. The humble estimate he put upon his own abilities and influence, and the fact that he had indulged no aspirations for the office, is sufficient explanation of the affair.

He took part in the campaign that followed for Fremont and Dayton, striking some telling blows for liberty. The opposition found a powerful antagonist in him, and sometimes resorted to mean expedients to show their hostility. At a meeting at Charleston, Coles County, a Democrat interrupted him by saying, "Mr. Lincoln, is it true that you entered this State barefooted, driving a yoke of oxen?"

Mr. Lincoln paused a few moments, and then answered, "I think I can prove the fact by at least a dozen men in the crowd, any one of whom is more respectable than my questioner."

Then he branched off upon the helps of a free government to a poor boy, and "the curse of Slavery to the white man, wherever it existed," speaking, in a strain of thrilling eloquence, and closing his response with the following inspiring sentence, that thoroughly aroused the assembly:—

"Yes, we will speak for freedom and against slavery, as long as the Constitution of our country guarantees free speech, until everywhere on this wide land, the sun shall shine and the rain shall fall and the wind shall blow upon no man who goes forth to unrequited toil."

Mr. Lincoln had prophesied not only bloodshed in Kansas, but also a bloody contest between the North and South, in consequence of the repeal of the Missouri Compromise, and the Kansas-Nebraska outrage. Already the first prophecy was fulfilled, and "Border Ruffians" were burning houses, shooting Free-State men, and sacking villages, to frighten freedom out of Kansas. Douglas saw that political death awaited him in Illinois if he pursued his Kansas-Nebraska measure and, all at once he changed front, and voted with the Republicans in Congress against the very measure his own political recklessness inaugurated. His senatorial term was drawing to a close, and now he sought a re-election by appealing to Republicans for support. Those of Illinois were too familiar with his duplicity to believe he was honest, and refused to support him. In other States, where his political character was not so well understood, there were prominent Republicans who asked their brethren of Illinois to return him to the United States Senate.

Mr. Lincoln was never bolder, more earnest and stronger, than he was in this campaign. The Republican State convention met at Springfield on the sixteenth day of June and it was scarcely organized when a banner was borne into the hall, on which was inscribed, "Cook County for Abraham Lincoln." The sight of it seemed to craze the whole assembly. They sprang to their feet, jumped upon the benches, swung their hats, shouted, cheered and gave themselves up to demonstrations of delight for several minutes. Mr. Lincoln was unanimously nominated and, in the evening, delivered before the convention his famous speech, known in history as "The House divided against itself Speech." This title was derived from a single paragraph at the opening of the speech, as follows:—

"A house divided against itself cannot stand. I believe this government cannot endure permanently, half slave and half free. I do not expect the Union to be dissolved, —I do not expect the house to fall but I do expect it will cease to be divided. It will become all one thing, or all the other." Late in the afternoon of that day, Mr. Lincoln went over to his office, with his carefully prepared speech in his pocket and, locking the door behind him, he said to his partner, Mr. Herndon:—

"Let me read you a paragraph of my speech." He read the foregoing extract, which was a part of the first paragraph.

"How do you like it?" inquired Mr. Lincoln, before Herndon had time to express his surprise. "What do you think of it?"

"I think it is true," replied Mr. Herndon, "but is it entirely politic to read or speak it just as it is written?"

"That makes no difference," answered Mr. Lincoln. Mr. Herndon was still more surprised. "Radical" as he was, Lincoln was in advance of him.

"That expression is a truth of all human experience—a house divided against itself cannot stand," added Mr. Lincoln with emphasis. "The proposition is indisputably true, and has been true for more than six thousand years and— I will deliver it as written I would rather be defeated with this expression in the speech, than be victorious without it.

An hour before the address was to be delivered in the Representatives' Hall, a dozen of his friends assembled in the library room, and Mr. Lincoln read to them several paragraphs of his speech, including the extract rooted.

"What do you think of it?" he asked.

"Fifty years in advance of public opinion," answered one leader almost angrily.

"Very unwise," replied another.

"It will kill the Republican party," said a third.

"And you too, Lincoln," said a fourth.

"Nothing could be more unwise; it will certainly defeat your election;" added a fifth.

And so the criticisms fell fast from nearly every tongue. Every one, except Mr. Herndon, condemned the extract in question. He sprang to his feet after all had delivered themselves freely, and said:— "Lincoln, deliver it just as it reads."

Mr. Lincoln sat in silence for a moment, then, rising from his seat, he walked backwards and forwards a few moments longer. Suddenly stopping and facing the company, he said:—

"Friends, I have thought about this matter a great deal, have weighed the question well from all corners, and am thoroughly convinced the time has come when it should be uttered and if it must be that I must go down because of this speech, then let me go down linked to—die in the advocacy of what is right and just."

He delivered the speech just as he had prepared it, and great, indeed, was the excitement occasioned thereby. Many of his warmest friends were provoked by his "unwisdom."

"A fool's speech," cried one.

"Wholly inappropriate!" cried another.

"That foolish speech of yours will kill you, Lincoln," remarked Dr. Loring. "I wish it was wiped out of existence; don't you wish so now?"

"Well, doctor," replied Mr. Lincoln, "if I had to draw a pen across, and erase my whole life from existence, and had one poor gift or choice left, as to what I should save from the wreck, I should choose that speech, and leave it to the world un-erased."

More than a year afterwards, he was dining with a party of friends at Bloomington, when that speech became the theme of discussion, and every person present declared it was "a great mistake."

"Gentlemen," replied Mr. Lincoln, "you may think that speech was a mistake; but I never have believed it was, and you will see the day when you will consider it the wisest thing I ever said."

His prophecy was completely fulfilled. The fact was, Mr. Lincoln was led "in a way that he knew not." A higher intelligence than mere human sagacity guided him in the right. That speech was one of the most marvelous productions in American annals, and it not only gave the keynote to his great senatorial contest with Mr. Douglas, but it settled the character and issue of the next presidential election and finally sealed the doom of slavery in this country.

After the delivery of this speech, Mr. Lincoln challenged Mr. Douglas to joint debates throughout the canvas. The latter accepted the challenge so far as to arrange for debates with the former in seven important places of the state. Mr. Douglas conducted his part of the affair with great pomp and noise proceeding to his appointments on a chartered train accompanied with a band of music, and artillery to fire salutes, at a cost of fifty thousand dollars. On the other hand, Mr. Lincoln pursued his usual quiet, unostentatious and honest way; yet he won the victory every time. "To say that he was the victor, morally and intellectually, is simply to record the judgment of the world." "In this canvass he earned a reputation as a popular debater second to that of no man in America—certainly not second to that of his famous antagonist." At the close of one of his debates with Mr. Douglas, even after the latter had occupied thirty minutes in closing the discussion, the assembly was so thoroughly "enthused" by Mr. Lincoln's victorious effort, that they seized him, in their exuberance of joy, and bore him out of the hall to the hotel upon their shoulders, amidst cheers and shouts that made the welkin ring. In the popular vote he received a majority of four thousand and eighty-five over Mr. Douglas; but owing to the unfair apportionment of the legislative districts, Mr. Douglas was returned to the United States Senate.

In one of these debates he paid one of the most eloquent tributes to the "Declaration of Independence" (after having enunciated its principles) that ever fell from human lips and he closed with these memorable words:

"You may do anything with me you choose, if you will but heed these sacred principles. You may not only defeat me for the senate, but you may take me and put me to death. While pretending no indifference to earthly honors, I do claim to be actuated in this contest by something higher than an anxiety for office. I charge you to drop every paltry and insignificant thought for any man's success. It is nothing; I am nothing; Judge Douglas is nothing. But do not destroy that IMMORTAL EMBLEM OF HUMANITY, THE DECLARATION OF American Independence."

CHAPTER XXIII

GOING UP HIGHER

The Republican State Convention of Illinois met at Decatur, May 9, 1860, in a "Wigwam" erected for the purpose. Directly after the convention was organized, Governor Oglesby, the chairman, arose, and said, "I am informed that a distinguished citizen of Illinois, and one whom Illinois will ever delight to honor, is present, and I wish to move that this body invite him to a seat on the stand." After a pause, as if to awaken curiosity, he called out the name in a much louder voice, Abraham Lincoln. Such a round of applause, cheer upon cheer, followed the announcement, as shook every board and joist of the wigwam. A rush, too, was made for the gentleman, who stood near the door, and he was actually taken up and borne through the dense crowd to the platform. The cheering was like the roar of the sea. Hats were thrown up by the Chicago delegation, as if hats were no longer useful.

The convention proceeded to business, and was fairly under way, when the chairman interrupted by saying:

"There is an old Democrat outside, I understand, who has something to present to this convention."

"Receive it! receive it!" responded several.

"What is it? what is it?" cried out others.

"Let us have it," shouted another.

The convention voted to receive the Democrat, and in walked Mr. Lincoln's old friend, John Hanks, who helped him to split the rails for his father's fifteen acre lot; the same Hanks who went with him to New Orleans for Offutt, and enlisted with him in the Black Hawk War. John bore on his shoulders two rails, from the lot he and Abe split, surmounted with a banner with this inscription:— "Two Rails From a Lot Made by Abraham Lincoln and John Hanks, in the Sangamon Bottom, in the Year 1830."

Wild, tumultuous applause greeted the rails, and the scene became simply tempestuous and bewildering. The tumult subsided only to make way for another.

"A speech!" "Let's hear the rail-splitter!" "A speech!" "Old Abe must show his hand!" These and other demands were made in one incessant noisy clamor, lasting several minutes, until Mr. Lincoln arose, confused, blushing, yet smiling, and remarked—

"Gentlemen, I suppose you want to know something about those things (pointing to the rails). Well, the truth is, John Hanks and I did make rails in the Sangamon Bottom. I don't know whether we made those rails or not; the fact is, I don't think they are a credit to the makers. But I do know this: I made rails then, and I think I could make better ones than these now."

Another storm of applause shook the wigwam for several minutes and was followed by a resolution declaring "Abraham Lincoln to be the first choice of the Republican party of Illinois for the Presidency." The resolution was carried unanimously, amidst the wildest demonstrations.

Five thousand people attended this convention, among them many Democrats who were friends of Lincoln. Other Democrats were there, who were not a little provoked at the course of John Hanks and others of their party. One of them accosted Mr. Lincoln, after the adjournment:—

"And so you're Abe Lincoln?"

"That's my name, sir," answered Mr. Lincoln.

"They say you're a self-made man."

"Well, yes; what there is of me is self-made," replied Mr. Lincoln.

"Wall," added the Democrat, after surveying him from head to foot, "all I've got to say is, that it was a very bad job."

It should be said that, after Mr. Lincoln's senatorial contest with Mr. Douglas, particularly in 1859, he spoke by invitation in Kansas, Ohio, New York, and several of the New England States. His speeches were pronounced masterly. Cooper Institute was thronged to hear him in New York city and he was introduced by the poet Bryant. The next morning, the Tribune said, "No man ever before made such an impression on his first appeal to a New York audience."

While in New York, two incidents transpired, which show much of the man. He met an old acquaintance from Illinois in a mercantile establishment. "How have you fared since you left Illinois?" inquired Mr. Lincoln.

"I have made a hundred thousand dollars, and lost it all. And how is it with you, Mr. Lincoln?"

"Oh, very well," Mr. Lincoln replied; "I have the cottage at Springfield, and about eight thousand dollars in money. If they make me vice-president with Seward, as some say they will, I hope I shall be able to increase it to twenty thousand; and that is as much as any man ought to want."

He stopped in New York over Sunday, and strolled alone into the Sabbath School of the Five Points Mission, interested to learn what could be done for the street children of the city. The superintendent was impressed by the appearance of the visitor, and invited him to address the girls and boys. Without hesitation, he consented, and immediately began a little speech that completely captivated his young listeners. Several times he essayed to stop, but his listeners cried out, "Go on, go on, sir." "Do go on." It was an unusual address, and charmed both teacher and pupil alike. When he was about to depart, the superintendent said:

"Pardon me; may I have the pleasure of knowing who my visitor is ."

"Abraham Lincoln of Illinois," he replied.

He spoke at Norwich, Conn., and subsequently Dr. Gulliver published the following instructive and interesting account of his interview with him, on the next morning after listening to him:—

"The next morning I met him at the railroad station, where he was conversing with our Mayor, every few minutes looking up the track and inquiring, half impatiently and half quizzically, 'Where 's that "wagon" of yours? Why don't the "wagon" come along?' On being introduced to him, he fixed his eyes upon me, and said: "I have seen you before, sir!"' 'I think not,' I replied: "you must mistake me for some other person.' 'No, I don't; I saw you at the Town Hall, last evening.' 'Is it possible, Mr. Lincoln, that you could observe individuals so closely in such a crowd.' 'Oh, yes' he replied, laughing; 'that is my way. I don't forget faces. Were you not there?' 'I was, sir, and I was well paid for going; 'adding, somewhat in the vein of pleasantry he had started, "I consider it one of the most extraordinary speeches I ever heard.'

"As we entered the cars, he beckoned me to take a seat with him, and said, in a most agreeably frank way, "Were you sincere in what you said about my speech just now?"

"I meant every word of it, Mr. Lincoln. Why, an old dyed-in-the-wool Democrat, who sat near me, applauded you repeatedly and when rallied upon his conversion to sound principles, answered: "I don't believe a word he says, but I can't help clapping him, he 's so pat." That I call the triumph of oratory.'

"When you convince a man against his will, Though he is of the same opinion still."

"Indeed, sir, I learned more of the art of public speaking last evening than I could from a whole course of lectures on Rhetoric."

"'Ah! that reminds me,' said he, "of a most extraordinary circumstance which occurred in New Haven the other day. They told me that the Professor of Rhetoric in Yale College, —a very learned man, isn't he?"

"Yes, sir, and a fine critic too."

"Well, I suppose so; he ought to be, at any rate, —they told me that he came to hear me, and took notes of my speech, and gave a lecture on it to his class the next day; and, not satisfied with that, he followed me up to Meriden the next evening, and heard me again for the same purpose. Now, if this is so, it is to my mind very extraordinary. I should like very much to know what it was in my speech you thought so remarkable and what you suppose interested my friend, the professor, so much."

"The clearness of your statements, Mr. Lincoln; the unanswerable style of your reasoning, and especially your illustrations, which were romance and pathos, and fun and logic all welded together. That story about the snakes, for example, which set the hands and feet of your Democratic hearers in such vigorous motion was at once queer and comical, and tragic and argumentative. It broke through all the barriers of a man's previous opinions and prejudices at a crash, and blew up the very citadel of his false theories before he could know what had hurt him."

"Can you remember any other illustrations,' said he 'of this peculiarity of my style.'

"I gave him others of the same sort, occupying some half-hour in the critique, when he said: 'I am much obliged to you for this. I have been wishing for a long time to find some one who would make this analysis for me. It throws light on a subject which has been dark to me. I hope you have not been too flattering in your estimate. Certainly, I have had a most wonderful success, for a man of my limited education.'

"'That suggests, Mr. Lincoln, an inquiry which has several times been upon my lips during this conversation. I want very much to know how you got this unusual power of "putting things." It must have been a matter of education. No man has it by nature alone. What has your education been?'

"Well, as to education, the newspapers are correct; I never went to school more than six months in my life. But, as you say, this must be a product of culture in some form. I have been putting the question you ask me to myself, while you have been talking. I can say this, that among my earliest recollections I remember how, when a mere child, I used to get irritated when any body talked to me in a way I could not understand. I don't think I ever got angry at anything else in my life. But that always disturbs my temper, and has ever since. I can remember going to my little bed-room, after hearing the neighbors talk of an evening with my father, and spending no small part of the night walking up and down, and trying to make out what was the exact meaning of some of their, to me, dark sayings. I could not sleep, though I often tried to, when I got on such a hunt after an idea, until I had caught it and when I thought I had got it, I was not satisfied until I had repeated it over and over, until I had put it in language plain enough, as I thought, for any boy I knew to comprehend. This was a kind of passion with me, and it has stuck by me; for I am never easy now, when I am handling a thought, till I have bounded it North, and bounded it South, and bounded it East, and bounded it West. Perhaps that accounts for the characteristic you observe in my speeches, though I never put the two things together before.'"

"Mr. Lincoln, I thank you for this. It is the most splendid educational fact I ever happened upon. But, let me ask, did you prepare for your profession."

"'Oh, yes! I "read law," as the phrase is; that is, I became a lawyer's clerk in Springfield, and copied tedious documents, and picked up what I could of law in the intervals of other work. But your question reminds me of a bit of education I had, which I am bound in honesty to mention. In the course of my law-reading, I constantly came upon the word demonstrate. I thought at first that I understood its meaning, but soon became satisfied that I did not. I said to myself, "What do I mean when I demonstrate more than when I reason or prove? How does demonstration differ from any other proof?" I consulted Webster's Dictionary. That told of "certain proof," "proof beyond the possibility of doubt;" but I could form no idea what sort of proof that was. I thought a great many things were proved beyond a possibility of doubt, without recourse to any such extraordinary process of reasoning as I understood "demonstration" to be. I consulted all the dictionaries and books of reference I could find, but with no better results. You might as well have defined blue to a blind man. At last I said, "Lincoln, you can never make a lawyer if you do not understand what demonstrate means; "and I left my situation in Springfield, went home to my father's house, and stayed there till I could give any proposition in the six books of Euclid at sight. I then found out what "demonstrate" means, and went back to my law-studies.'

"I could not refrain from saying, in my admiration at such a development of character and genius combined: "Mr. Lincoln, your success is no longer a marvel. It is the legitimate result of adequate causes. You deserve it all, and a great deal more. If you will permit me, I would like to use this fact publicly. It will be most valuable in inciting our young men to that patient classical and mathematical culture which most minds absolutely require. No man can talk well unless he is able first of all to define to himself what he is talking about. Euclid, well studied, would free the world of half its calamities, by banishing half the nonsense which now deludes and curses it. I have often thought that Euclid would be one of the best books to put on the catalogue of the Tract Society, if they could only get people to read it. It would be a means of grace."

"'I think so,' said he, laughing; "I vote for Euclid."

"As we neared the end of our journey, Mr. Lincoln turned to me very pleasantly, and said:

'I want to thank you for this conversation. I have enjoyed it very much.' I replied, referring to some stalwart denunciations he had just been uttering of the demoralizing influence of Washington upon Northern politicians in respect to the slavery question, "Mr. Lincoln, may I say one thing to you before we separate?"

"Certainly, anything you please."

"'You have just spoken of the tendency of political life in Washington to debase the moral convictions of our representatives there by the admixture of considerations of mere political expediency. You have become, by the controversy with Mr. Douglas, one of our leaders in this great struggle with slavery, which is undoubtedly the struggle of the nation and the age. What I would like to say is this, and I say it with a full heart. Be trite to your principles and we will be true to you, and God will be true to us all! 'His homely face lighted up instantly with a beaming expression, and taking my hand warmly in both of his, he said: "I say Amen to that—Amen to that!'

The National Republican Convention assembled in Chicago on the sixteenth day of June, 1860. A mammoth "Wigwam" was erected to accommodate the delegates and crowd of spectators It was estimated that twenty-five thousand men attended that convention. Fifteen hundred of them slept under the roof of a single hotel.

The candidates for President were William H. Seward, Salmon P. Chase, Edward Bates, Judge McLean, William L. Dayton, Simon Cameron, Abraham Lincoln and Benjamin F. Wade. It must be conceded, however, that Mr. Seward was by far the most prominent, and his nomination was generally expected by Republicans in the East, if not in the West. Indeed, Mr. Lincoln was not known to the rank and file of the Republican party outside of the western States. Mr. Chase and Judge Bates were better known to the people of the whole country than he. But the balloting proved that Mr. Seward was not so strong a candidate as many anticipated. Mr. Chase had forty nine votes, and Judge Bates forty-eight, in the informal ballot, while Mr. Lincoln had one hundred and two. It was evident that Mr. Seward could not be nominated. There were not a sufficient number to leave their favorite candidates for him, to secure his nomination. But as the result proved, there were enough who would leave the men of their choice and vote for Mr. Lincoln, to elect him. To them Mr. Lincoln was a compromise candidate, whom they preferred, if they could not have the man of their choice. Mr. Lincoln was nominated on the third ballot. The scene that followed the announcement beggars description. Not a storm, but a hurricane of uncontrollable enthusiasm burst from the vast assembly, augmented by the multitude waiting outside, who in response to the cry of a messenger stationed upon the roof of the "Wigwam," "Fire the salute! Abe Lincoln is nominated" rent the air with their deafening shouts, while the thundering roar of cannon, peal on peal, swelled the din into fearful proportions.

The news was flashed over the wires to Springfield and, when it was received at the office of the Journal, where Mr. Lincoln and a few of his neighbors were gathered, the excitement of Chicago was repeated on a smaller scale, and the nominee was overwhelmed with congratulations. Taking the telegram up, Mr. Lincoln remarked:— "Well, gentlemen, there is a little woman at our house who is probably more interested in this dispatch than I am; and if you will excuse me, I will take it up and let her see it."

The committee of the Chicago Convention officially notified Mr. Lincoln of his nomination, at his home on the following day. A few citizens, desiring that their distinguished townsman should conform to an old political custom, on so important an occasion, purchased a quantity of the choicest liquors they could find, and sent them to his house. Mr. Lincoln promptly returned them, with the characteristic message:—

"You know that we never do any such thing at our house."

The correspondent of the "Portland Press," who was present, says that, after the official ceremonies and formal introductions ended, a servant brought in a waiter, containing a large pitcher and several glass tumblers, when "Mr. Lincoln arose, and gravely addressing the company, said: 'Gentlemen, we must pledge our mutual health in the most healthy beverage which God has given to man —it is the only beverage I have ever used or allowed in my family, and I cannot conscientiously depart from it on the present occasion—it is pure Adam's ale, from the spring;' and, taking a tumbler, he touched it to his lips, and pledged them his highest respects in a cup of cold water. Of course all his guests were constrained to admire his consistency and to join in his example."

His neighbors supposed that he would yield his temperance principles to the demands of the august occasion but he was not the man to do that. The statesman who dared to oppose his own best friends, and say to the world, "a house divided against itself cannot stand," would not sacrifice his principles now for a glass of wine.

He received the honored guests with the simplicity and informality for which he was famed, and, after assuring them that he had nothing stronger than "Adam's ale" in his house, he drank their health in the "sparkling beverage." He never performed a more independent, consistent, and worthy act than that. He stood by his temperance principles just as he did by his anti-slavery principles.

His nomination created the most intense excitement and bitterness in the slave States. Threats of secession and rebellion came from them with every wind that blew. His election in the following November was the signal for the southern leaders to prepare for civil war and the dissolution of the Union. Before Inauguration Day arrived seven of the southern States had seceded and organized a southern Confederacy. Mutterings of the coming storm were heard. The war-cloud was gathering, dark and ominous. The thunder of arms was heard in the distance. Beaten with the ballot, the champions of slavery resolved to conquer with the bullet. War seemed inevitable.

Mr. Lincoln was overwhelmed with visitors from the day of his nomination, until he removed to the White House. All classes, high and low rich and poor, great and little, flocked to see the "tall man eloquent," and shake his hand. Some curious incidents occurred, which exhibit the noble qualities of the presidential candidate far better than words. Two young men entered the Executive chamber of the State House, where he received his friends, and lingered near the door. Observing them, Mr. Lincoln approached them, saying:—

"How do you do, my good fellows? What can I do for you." Will you sit down?"

"We do not care to sit," replied the shorter of the two.

"I am at your service," continued Mr. Lincoln in his familiar way, aiming to make the different young men feel at home.

"I had some talk with my friend here," continued the young man, "about your height, Mr. Lincoln. He thinks he is just as tall as you are."

"Ah!" responded Mr. Lincoln with a broad smile, at the same time scanning the "tall companion," "he is long certainly. Let us see about that." He went for his cane and returning, said:

"Here, young man, we'll see who is the longest." Placing the end of the cane upon the wall, he said:

Come under here, young man. We can settle that question in a minute."

The young man stepped under the cane, and when it was carefully adjusted, Mr. Lincoln continued: "Now step out and hold the cane while I go under."

No quicker said than done.

"He is just my height exactly," he remarked to the shorter visitor; "he guessed with remarkable accuracy." Then taking each of them by the hand with words of encouragement, he bade them good by.

He saw that the two young men were well meaning, but verdant, unacquainted with the proprieties of the occasion but, sooner than have them feel that they had insulted his dignity he would measure "height" with them a dozen times over.

An old woman came in to see him "because he used to dine at her house when he was on the Circuit." Mr. Lincoln could not remember her, until she had called his attention, definitely to certain incidents.

"Oh, yes; I remember now," he said, shaking her hand heartily; "I hope it is well with you, my dear woman."

"Do you remember that scanty dinner I gave you one day?"

"No, I am sure I do not remember anything scant at your house."

"Well, you did have a scanty dinner one day," she added. "You came along just as we were through dinner, and every thing was eaten up; so that I had nothing to give you but a bowl of bread and milk, and you ate it, and when you got up, and I apologized for having nothing better, you replied, ' Why, that is quite good enough for the President of the United States.'"

Mr. Lincoln laughed and invoked a blessing on her head, fully appreciating the well-meant friendship that brought her eight miles on purpose to remind him of the "scanty dinner."

Among his callers was Hannah Armstrong, widow of Jack and mother of William; and a more sincere and worshipful visitor he did not have. "He talked to me just as he did when Jack was alive," she said afterwards. "I talked to him some time, and was about to bid him good-by. I had told him that it was the last time I should ever see him; something told me I should never see him again; they would kill him. He smiled and said, 'Hannah, if they do kill me, I shall never die another death.' Then I bade him good.

A grand reception was tendered him in Chicago. He observed a little girl approaching very timidly. Beckoning to her kindly, he said: "Little girl, what will you have."

"I want your name," she hesitatingly replied. Just then Mr. Lincoln observed several other little girls approaching, and he responded:

"But here are several other little girls—they would feel badly if I should give my name only to you."

"There are eight of us in all," she answered, "and all of us want your name."

"Then get me eight sheets of paper, with pen and ink, and I will see what can be done for you."

The paper was brought, and Mr. Lincoln sat down at a table, in the crowded room, and wrote a line upon each sheet, appending his name thereto.

A little boy of about three years came into the room with his father. As soon as he entered, he swung his hat, and cried out, "Hurrah for Lincoln!" The people laughed, and Mr. Lincoln, joining them, caught up the little fellow and gave him a toss towards the ceiling, exclaiming, "Hurrah for you!"

These were pleasant episodes to a man of so much simplicity and real kindness as Mr. Lincoln possessed, in the general reception of dignitaries—governors, statesmen, senators, judges, divines, etc.

On the sixth of November, Mr. Lincoln was elected President by the popular vote of 1,857,610—491,634 votes more than were cast for Mr. Douglas. In the Electoral College he received 180 votes, and Mr. Douglas only 12; the others being divided between Breckinridge and Bell.

A few days before the election, the Republicans of Springfield placed the result of a canvass of Springfield in Mr. Lincoln's hand. He called into the Executive Chamber Mr. Newton Bateman, Superintendent of Public Instruction for the State of Illinois, whose office was in the building. Having locked the door, he said:—

"I have called you in to assist me in looking over this canvass of Springfield; I desire to know how the ministers and some good people will vote."

Mr. Bateman assented to his proposition, and proceeded to examine the book. Mr. Lincoln frequently inquired if such and such a person was not a minister or member of the church, to which Mr. Bateman replied according to the best of his knowledge. With pencil in hand, Mr. Lincoln kept a memorandum. When the examination was completed, he sat in silence and with a face full of sadness for several minutes. Then, turning to Mr. Bateman, he remarked:—

"I don't understand it. Here are several ministers, of different denominations, against me, and here are prominent members of the churches against me. Mr. Bateman, I am not a Christian—God knows, I would be one—but I have carefully read the Bible, and I do not so understand this book," drawing a copy of the New Testament from his pocket. After a brief pause, he continued:—

"These men well know that I am for freedom in the Territories, freedom everywhere as far as the Constitution and laws will permit, and that my opponents are for slavery. They know this, and yet, with this book in their hands, in the light of which human bondage cannot live a moment, they are going to vote against me. I do not understand it at all."

Mr. Lincoln was on his feet, evidently filled with emotion over the grave and perilous condition of the country. In silence he walked up and down the room, going back and forth several times, with deep sadness depicted on his face, as if a mighty burden were resting on his heart. At length, suddenly stopping in the centre of the hall, and lifting his right arm heavenward, while tears were on his cheek, he exclaimed:—

"I know there is a God, and that he hates injustice and slavery. I see the storm coming, and I know that His hand is in it. If He has a place and work for me, I am ready. I am nothing, but truth is everything. I know I am right, because I know that liberty is right. I have told them that a house divided against itself cannot stand, and Christ and reason say the same; and they will find it so. Douglas don't care whether slavery is voted up or voted down; but God cares, and humanity cares, and I care; and with God's help, I shall not fail. I may not see the end; but it will come and I shall be vindicated; and these men will find that they have not read their Bibles aright."

He spoke much of this as if soliloquizing, and then, turning to Mr. Bateman, he added:—

"Does it not appear strange that men can ignore the moral aspects of the contest? A revelation could not make it plainer to me that slavery or the government must be destroyed. The future would be something awful, as I look at it, but for this rock on which I stand, especially with the knowledge of how some of these ministers are going to vote. It seems as if God had borne with slavery until the very teachers of religion have come to defend it from the Bible, and to claim for it a divine character and sanction [referring to Drs. Ross and Palmer of the South, of whom mention had been made] and now the cup of iniquity is full, and the vials of wrath will be poured out."

He went on still further, expressing his confidence in Divine Providence, declaring that "right is might," and that faith in God "is indispensable to successful statesmanship;" and that the support which a public man receives from these truths is grander than all other support. He freely announced his belief in the duty and power of prayer, and intimated that he had sought Divine guidance in his solemn and responsible position.

Mr. Bateman responded to him:—

"I have not supposed that you were accustomed to think so much upon this class of subjects. Your friends are ignorant of the fact that you entertain such pronounced sentiments on these topics as you have expressed to me."

"I am aware of that," Mr. Lincoln answered; "but I think more on these subjects than upon all others, and I have done so for years."

That Mr. Lincoln was a child of Providence, without knowing it, led and disciplined for graver responsibilities than any previous President had ever borne, not excepting Washington, is clear to the Bible student. His language was that of prophecy, and his spirit was that of a Christian hero and martyr.

Before leaving Springfield for Washington, Mr. Lincoln paid his mother and other relatives a visit. His mother was living with her daughter, Mrs. Moore, at Farmington. "The meeting between him and the old lady," says Mr. Lamon, "was of the most affectionate and tender character. She fondled him as her own Abe, and he her as his own mother."

Mrs. Lincoln returned with her son to Charleston that they might enjoy each other's company still longer. When the time arrived that Mr. Lincoln must leave, both he and his mother were deeply affected. Mr. Lamon continues:—

"The parting between Mr. Lincoln and his mother was very touching. She embraced him with deep emotion, and said she was sure she should never behold him again, for she felt that ' his enemies would assassinate him."

"No, no, mother; they will not do that. Trust in the Lord and all will be well; we shall see each other again.'

"Inexpressibly affected by this new evidence of her tender attachment and deep concern for his safety, he gradually and reluctantly withdrew from her arms, feeling more deeply oppressed by the heavy cares which time and events were rapidly augmenting."

Mrs. Lincoln was not alone in her fears that her son would come to an untimely end. Neighbors and friends in Springfield were equally anxious.

"They will throw the cars from the track," one suggested.

"Some one will stab him in the crowd," another.

"He will be poisoned before the fourth of March," still another.

"He will be shot from a housetop on inauguration day," a fourth.

"You ought to take a cook with you from your own female friends," suggested a fifth.

On the eleventh day of February, 1861, Mr. Lincoln left Springfield for Washington with his family. A multitude of friends and neighbors gathered at the depot for a parting hand-shake. From the platform of the cars, he addressed the company.

His journey to Washington was signalized by sincere demonstrations of respect and honor. His passage was like that of a conqueror. From the beginning to the end of his journey, it was one splendid ovation. At all the cities on the route, he addressed the vast multitudes assembled, and his sentiments were eagerly caught up and borne over the land; for the people were eager to obtain the least hint of his future policy. His speeches were characterized by that thoughtful, sound, solid, clear, and logical element that ever distinguished his best efforts.

The presidential party was met at Philadelphia by the son of Mr. Seward, with the startling intelligence that a plot had been discovered to assassinate the President-elect when he passed through Baltimore on the following day. Threats of assassination had been heard again and again, and now detectives supposed that they had discovered a veritable plot, and that speedy action alone could thwart the purpose of the conspirators.

A consultation with Mr. Lincoln followed, and it was arranged that, instead of going on the presidential train the next day, Mr. Lincoln should be taken through that night to Washington by the night express. At half-past six next morning he reached Washington, and the news of his arrival was flashed at once over the country by the telegraphic wires.

CHAPTER XXIV
LIFE IN THE WHITE HOUSE
Our purpose being to see the man Lincoln in the highest office, as we saw the boy

Abraham in his pioneer home, we shall not recount his public deeds in overthrowing the "Rebellion," which lasted during his entire life in the Executive Mansion. His remarkable success in marshalling the "Union Army" of more than two million men, controlling the perilous factions of the country, securing the confidence of every true patriot in the land, organizing victory upon a thousand battle-fields, creating a powerful navy, raising three thousand million dollars for the war, restoring the public credit, emancipating four million slaves, and restoring peace upon a stronger basis than ever, is well known to the world. These achievements caused M. Laboulaye to exclaim, at the College of France, before an immense audience of the site of the intellectual world, "Mr. Lincoln is a greater man than Cesar." To record a history of these achievements would require a volume instead of two or three chapters, and even then the real character of the man might not appear so clearly as it does in certain incidents of his presidential career. In his daily life, at the head of the nation, we are to find those qualities of mind and heart which made him truly great. Incidents will illustrate his ability, honesty, patriotism, industry, kindness, self reliance, firmness, tact, wit, genius, magnanimity, and influence, far better than declamation. For this reason we shall present his presidential career through the most instructive incidents of his life in the White House.

Mr. Lincoln was inaugurated on the fourth of March, 1861. A vast concourse of people assembled at Washington to witness the imposing ceremonies. Fears of an outbreak and the possible assassination of the President led General Scott to provide ample military defense of the city. President Lincoln closed his inaugural address with the following touching appeal to the enemies of the Government:—

"In your hands, my dissatisfied fellow-countrymen, and not in mine, is the momentous issue of civil war. The government will not assail you. You can have no conflict without being yourselves the aggressors. You have no oath registered in heaven to destroy the government; while I shall have the most solemn one to preserve, protect, and defend it. I am loath to close. We are not enemies, but friends. We must not be enemies. Though passion may be strained, it must not break our bonds of affection. The mystic chords of memory, stretching from every battle-field and patriot grave to every living heart and hearthstone all over this broad land will yet swell the chorus of the Union, when again touched, as surely they will be, by the better angels of our nature."

On that morning, Mrs. Lincoln relates, he read his inaugural address to his family; and after having read it, he requested to be left alone. The door stood ajar, and his friends distinctly heard him in prayer, commending himself, his country, and his family to the care and protection of God. The weight of responsibility laid upon him was too great for his human heart to bear alone. His Cabinet was William H. Seward, Secretary of State; Salmon P. Chase, Secretary of the Treasury; Simon Cameron, Secretary of War; Gideon Welles, Secretary of the Navy; Caleb B. Smith, Secretary of the Interior; Montgomery Blair, Postmaster-General and Edward Bates, Attorney-General—a body of advisers with whom the loyal people were well pleased.

A distinguished senator said to President Lincoln, just after his inauguration—

"You have as difficult a task in hand as Washington had, when he took command of the

American army and as little to do with."

"That is true, substantially," replied the President, "but then I have larger resources to draw from," a reply which showed that a hopeful, discriminating, thoughtful man had moved into the Executive Mansion.

"You are right, Mr. President," responded the Senator; "but my remark had reference to the weak condition of the government, as the out-going administration left it—no money, no army, no navy, no fire-arms, no nothing for you to begin with."

"But really, I have what is better, the patriotism of the loyal people," was the President's just and noble reply. Honorable Henry J. Raymond, speaking of a leading feature of Mr. Lincoln's administration, said:

"From the outset his reliance was upon the spirit and patriotism of the people. He had no overweening estimate of his own sagacity, he was quite sensible of his lack of that practical knowledge of men and affairs which experience of both alone can give; but he had faith in the devotion of the people to the principles of Republican government, in their attachment to the Constitution and the Union, and in that intuitive sagacity of a great community which always transcends the most cunning devices of individual men, and in a great and perilous crisis, more resembles inspiration than the mere deductions of the human intellect. At the very outset of his administration. President Lincoln cast himself, without reserve and without fear, upon this reliance." A man of less confidence in the ability and fidelity of the loyal people for such a crisis would not have been qualified for his position.

The senator referred to facts with which the country was familiar that is, that the National Government had been under the control of the South, especially during the previous administration, and that the cabinet had used their opportunity to prepare for civil war, by taking possession of its resources, that northern strength might be diminished. Howell Cobb was Secretary of the Treasury under the previous administration, and he was a slaveholder from Georgia. He left the public treasury without a dollar, and the national credit so much impaired that borrowing money was difficult, if not impossible. It was supposed that he used several million dollars of the public money in preparation for the rebellion. John B. Floyd was Secretary of War; and he was a slave holder from Virginia. He depleted northern arsenals, as Cobb depleted the treasury, and sent rifles, muskets, cannon, mortars, balls, powder and shells, to important posts in the South. The "Memphis Appeal," a disloyal journal of Tennessee, said that "seven hundred and seven thousand stand of arms, and two hundred thousand revolvers, were distributed at convenient points in the South, by the action of Secretary Floyd, at the commencement of the Rebellion." Isaac Toucey of Connecticut was Secretary of the Navy, and though not a slaveholder, he was as servile a tool in the hands of rebel manipulators as lived and he scattered our navy, ninety vessels, so widely that it could be of no immediate service to the government, when the South should rise up against it. Only two vessels of our entire naval squadron remained in northern ports when Mr. Lincoln became President. It was to this discouraging condition of affairs that the senator referred in addressing Mr. Lincoln. The latter closed the interview by telling a story.

"Did you read the prophecy which the papers say was spoken about my administration?" asked Mr. Lincoln.

The senator signified that he had not.

"Well," added Mr. Lincoln, "a prophet foretells that my administration will be the reign of steel. To which a wag replied, 'Buchanan's was the reign of stealing.'"

Mr. Lincoln's humor aided his hopefulness wonderfully in the very embarrassing circumstances in which he found the government, and thereby he was all the better fitted to rule the nation at such a time.

It was very important that a leading Democrat in Congress should stand squarely by Mr. Lincoln's administration and Senator Douglas, the President's old antagonist, was the man, above all others, to do it. Therefore Mr. Ashmun, of Massachusetts, called upon him on the day after the fall of Sumter, April 14th, 1861, just as the President was completing his proclamation and call for seventy-five thousand militia.

"No man can render greater service to the country than yourself now, Mr. Douglas," said Mr. Ashmun; "and I want you to go to the President and assure him of your cordial support in all necessary measures to subdue the rebellion."

"Mr. Lincoln has dealt hardly with me, in removing some of my friends from office," replied Mr. Douglas, "and I don't know as he wants my advice or aid."

"But Mr. Lincoln followed Democratic precedents in such removals," suggested Mr. Ashmun. "However, this is a time when the question of saving the Union towers above all party affiliations, and you can put the country under lasting gratitude to yourself, and show the people, also, that, in the hour of national peril, you can trample all party considerations under your feet."

"True, very true," responded Mr. Douglas, with considerable emotion; "and no man shall excel me in devotion to my country. My whole nature rises up to condemn this Rebellion."

Here, Mrs. Douglas, who was present, joined Mr. Ashmun in the most affectionate appeals to her husband, to take the important step suggested. The result was, that Senator Douglas accompanied his friend to the White House, where the two "giants" and former antagonists of the West were brought face to face. Grasping the President by the hand, Mr. Douglas said—

"You are my President, Mr. Lincoln, as well as the country's."

The President's heart was touched, and he shook the senator's hand heartily, thanking him for his cordial support, and assuring him that the administration would appreciate his patriotic position.

"Now permit me to read to you this important document," added Mr. Lincoln, taking up his proclamation in which he called for seventy-five thousand troops; "you understand the situation as well or better than I, and you will readily see the wisdom or unwisdom of the measure."

Senator Douglas signified his desire to hear the document read. Slowly, seriously, and distinctly Mr. Lincoln read it through, when, without waiting to be asked, Mr. Douglas said—

"Mr. President, I cordially concur in every word of that document, except that, instead of the call for seventy-five thousand men, I would make it two hundred thousand. You do not know the dishonest purposes of those men as well as I do."

Turning to a map hanging on the wall, he pointed out the many strategic points that should be strengthened at once, and closed by adding, that "the Government must pursue a firm and warlike course to crush the Rebellion."

On retiring from the President's room, Mr. Ashmun said—

"You have done justice to your own reputation and to the President and the country must know it. The proclamation will go by telegraph in the morning all over the country, and the account of this interview must go with it. I shall send it either in my own language or yours. I prefer you should give your own version."

Mr. Douglas consented to write the dispatch, and the following day the country knew that he stood side by side with Mr. Lincoln in saving the Union. From that time until Mr. Douglas died, the President numbered him among his true and tried friends. He rendered valuable assistance to Mr. Lincoln in learning the plans of the rebels and disclosing their real animus. The President regarded his death as a public bereavement.

These two incidents disclose the simplicity, hopefulness, patriotism, wisdom, magnanimity, and freedom from a partisan spirit, which proved so helpful to the President from the beginning of his rule.

Mr. Lincoln kept sacred the words of his inaugural address— "You can have no conflict without being yourselves the aggressors." But when the first gun was fired upon Fort Sumter, in Charleston harbor, the South became the aggressors. That was on the twelfth day of April, 1861. On the previous afternoon, General Beauregard, who commanded the rebel forces, ordered the commander of the fort—Major Robert Anderson—to surrender. The major replied:—

"My sense of honor and duty compel me to hold the fort for my government."

"Shall you treat the city as a hostile town?" he was asked.

"Only if I am compelled to do so," was his noble reply.

So careful had the President been of offering any provocation to the enemy to fire upon our flag, that he sent an unarmed vessel, instead of a man-of-war, with supplies to the .half-starved garrison; and the vessel was not allowed to deliver the supplies—the rebel troops prevented.

At half-past four o'clock on the morning of the twelfth, the bombardment was opened by twelve thousand troops, nearly twenty thousand more being spectators. It was more than two hours before the garrison replied, Major Anderson thus allowing the insurgents to prove unmistakably their treasonable designs to the world. All through the day and the following night, the terrible cannonade was continued, the gallant band within the fort standing by their guns until the barracks took fire, compelling them to roll ninety-six barrels of powder into the sea, and exhaust themselves in extinguishing the flames. In the afternoon of the thirteenth, the garrison surrendered upon terms perfectly satisfactory to Major Anderson, and they marched out of the fort with flags flying and drums beating, taking all their private property with them, and saluting the stars and stripes with fifty guns. The enemy had hurled two thousand three hundred and sixty-one shot and nine hundred and eighty shells at the fort, when it passed into their hands.

The news of the fall of Sumter flashed over the land, and awakened the loyal people to the dangers of the hour. The aggressors had settled what the policy of the President must be. War against the Government had begun, and the appeal to arms must be accepted. Hence the call for seventy-five thousand troops and the interview with Mr. Douglas to which reference has been made. From that time, President Lincoln was occupied in efforts to conquer the Rebellion—creating an army and navy; raising money to carry on warlike preparations; securing necessary legislation, and other things indispensable to the national defense. Not the least of all his labors was acquainting himself with military affairs and the best way of saving the Republic. For he was President, and no one else. While ever ready to accept advice, and even to seek advice from more experienced public servants in both civil and military life, by which he shaped or corrected his own opinions, he reserved the final decision to himself. A leading member of the cabinet remarked, on one occasion:

"The President is his own war-minister. He directs personally the movements of the armies, and is fond of strategy but pays much less attention to official duties than is generally supposed."

It was so with all measures, whether civil or military. While the head of each department was left untrammeled in his particular work, and was held responsible for the proper conduct of its affairs by the President, the latter never relinquished his right of judgment. For example, in his annual report to Congress, Senator Cameron advised arming the slaves that they might rise successfully against their masters—a measure that had been persistently urged upon the President. As Mr. Lincoln reserved the right of supervising affairs, knowing that the great public would hold him responsible, he carefully read the report. When he came to that recommendation, surprised and almost indignant, he drew his pen across it, remarking:—

"This will never do. Secretary Cameron must take no such responsibility. That is a question that belongs exclusively to me."

When the public heart was deeply touched by the sufferings of our soldiers, who had fallen into the hands of the rebels, and righteous indignation was aroused over the cruelties of Libby prison and Andersonville, there did not want public men who advised Mr. Lincoln to subject the rebel prisoners in Northern prisons to similar treatment by way of retaliation. But the proposition outraged his feelings, and he said to Mr. Odell:—

"I can never, never starve men like that. Whatever others may say or do, I never can, and I never will, be accessory to such treatment of human beings."

Many Republicans were dissatisfied with Mr. Cameron as a member of the cabinet and early in Mr. Lincoln's administration, a delegation of bankers from Boston and New York waited upon him to urge the removal of the War Secretary. The President heard them through, and was somewhat exercised over the weakness of their arguments and the persistency of their appeals. He cut short the interview by saying:—

"You talk very glibly, nevertheless I am not convinced. Now, gentlemen, if you want General Cameron removed, you have only to bring me one proved case of dishonesty, and I promise you his head; 'but I assure you I am not going to act on what seems to me the most unfounded gossip."

A congressional committee was appointed to examine a newly invented gun, and report upon the same. When the report was sent to Mr. Lincoln, who was conferring with Hon. Mr. Hubbard of Connecticut, upon the subject, he glanced at the voluminous document of many manuscript pages, and said—

"I should want a new lease of life to read this through!" Then throwing it upon the table, he added, "Why can't a committee of this kind occasionally exhibit a grain of common sense. If I send a man to buy a horse for me, I expect him to tell me his points, not how many friars there are in his tail."

An officer of the army had been cashiered from the service. Having prepared an elaborate, written defense of himself he appeared before the President and read it.

"According to your own statement of the case the facts do not warrant executive interference," said Mr. Lincoln.

The officer appeared the second and even the third time, going over substantially the same ground in his plea but with no better success. The President felt that he was justly cashiered.

"I see you are not disposed to do me justice, Mr. President," said the officer, at last, insultingly.

This was too aggravating for the even-tempered President and, rising from his seat, he seized the fellow by his coat collar, and thrust him out of the door, saying:

"Sir, I give you fair warning never to show yourself in this room again. I can bear censure, but not in suit!"

The officer begged for his papers which he had dropped.

"Begone, sir," replied the President; "your papers will be sent to you. I never wish to see your face again."

The second year of his administration brought personal sorrow, in addition to the perplexities and trials of his office. "I thought the war was all that I could bear, but this great affliction is worse than war," he said. His son, Willie, died, and "Tad" was in a dying condition at the time. We record the circumstances as related to us by Mrs. Rebecca R. Pomroy, a hospital nurse of rare experience, whose services in the family, at the time, were invaluable. Miss Dix recommended her to Mr. Lincoln on the last day of Willie's mortal life. Mrs. Pomroy had twenty or thirty sick soldiers under her charge, and eight of them were not expected to live through the day. "How can I leave them?" she said. "It is impossible." "But you must," answered Miss Dix: "the Lord's hand is plainly in it. I shall send for you in two hours;" and she did.

On arriving at the Executive Mansion, Miss Dix conducted her into the green room, where the lifeless remains of Willie had just been laid out. Thence, she was taken to Mrs. Lincoln's chamber, where she was lying quite sick. From Mrs. Lincoln's room she was led into an adjoining one where little "Tad" lay in a dying condition. The physicians had relinquished all hope of his recovery and he was not expected to live twenty-four hours. Mr. Lincoln was sitting by him "the very picture of despair." "Mrs. Pomroy, Mr. President," said Miss Dix. Mr. Lincoln arose, and very heartily shook her hand, saying:—

"I am glad to see you: I have heard of you. You have come to a sad house." His deep emotion choked further utterance and the tears streamed down his careworn cheeks.

Later both took seats beside "Tad's" cot —one on each side. The little sufferer lay unconscious, apparently very near death. Soon a telegram from Port Hudson was brought to the President.

"What news."" inquired Mrs. Pomroy.

"Oh, bad enough ; a terrible battle is going on at Port Hudson; we don't know how it v/ill turn. I hope God will give us the victory there: it will be a great gain for us."

"We must pray that God may give us the victory," replied Mrs. Pomroy. "There is nothing like prayer."

"True, very true," answered the President. "But between this terrible war and this sorrow I am having a sad time. Why is it? Oh, why is it?"

Later still the President looked up and inquired:

"What led you into the hospital service? You appear to be a feeble woman."

"God called me into the service. I took care of a sick husband almost twenty years."

"What about your family," urged the President; "let me hear about it."

"My husband and three of my four children are now on the other side. My living son is in the army."

"How mysteriously God deals with us!" answered Mr. Lincoln. "I trust that He will spare your son, and in due time return you both to your home again. But was this your call to the hospital service?"

"Yes: through this service for my sick family. God fitted me to take care of the soldiers, and he has wonderfully sustained me by giving me strength far beyond the expectation of my friends."

"How was it," continued the President, now greatly interested in her story. "Tell me all about it."

"My mother died, and then my brother, and then my little daughter,—my only daughter, the light of our home—and then two sons, and, last of all, my dear husband," Mrs. Pomroy answered calmly, as only a trusting Christian woman could, "When my husband passed away, our little cottage with all its furniture had to be sold in order to liquidate debts."

"How did you live?" eagerly inquired Mr. Lincoln at this point. "Tell me how you could bear so much?"

"Were you resigned."" interrupted Mr. Lincoln,

"I was not wholly resigned then."

"Did you feel rebellious?" he inquired, still more earnestly.

"Yes; I knew that 'whom the Lord loveth he chasten,' but I could not understand it. I did not think that He loved me—I could not. Finally, however, I was brought into a higher Christian experience, where I could say honestly, ' The Lord gave and the Lord has taken away, blessed be the name of the Lord.'"

"And how was that brought about.'" asked Mr. Lincoln, as if he were passing through a similar experience.

Mrs. Pomroy rehearsed how Christian friends interested themselves to take her to a camp-meeting, when her health was entirely prostrated. They thought that the change of scenes and the smell of the pine grove might aid her more than physicians. "And there," she added, "my soul was quickened, and I was led to see how tenderly God had dealt with me, and that his gracious discipline was suited to make me a more efficient worker in his vineyard, if I only would be true. From that time I have never even doubted that God loves me."

"Can others enjoy a similar experience?" the President inquired, "or is yours exceptional?"

"It is not exceptional, Mr. President; it is just what God promises to all who are willing to be led by His will."

"And how can we know that we are led by His will?"

"Through sincere, earnest prayer," replied Mrs. Pomroy. "Prayer has been everything to me, 'Let him that lack wisdom, ask of God, who giveth liberally, and upbraid not.'"

Much more was said in the same spirit, when the President reverted again to his own great sorrow — Willie dead and "Tad" not expected to live until sunrise, — and the burden of his country's perils weighing heavily on his heart.

"Prayer can do what armies cannot," suggested Mrs. Pomroy; "and never were so many prayers offered for a country as are offered for ours, and never so many offered for a ruler as are offered for you, Mr. President."

"I know it," answered Mr. Lincoln, deeply moved by the thought;" and it is great encouragement to me. Our cause is righteous, and I do believe that God will give us the victory; but this slaughtering of men is dreadful for both sides."

Mrs. Pomroy had proposed that he should retire to an adjoining room for rest, promising that she would call him at the least change in "Tad."

"Pray for me," he said, as he arose to leave the room and, looking down mournfully upon the little sufferer, he added, "and pray for him, that he may be spared, if it is God's will."

"And you pray yourself," responded Mrs. Pomroy. "There is nothing like prayer in trouble: do you not think so?"

"I surely do," was the President's reply, as he retired with weeping eyes and aching heart.

Very soon Mrs. Pomroy heard his own voice distinctly in prayer, commending himself, his family and his country to God. "From that moment," she says, "I felt that our cause would triumph. The President interceding with God for it assured me."

Scarcely had he fallen asleep when a messenger arrived with a telegram from Port Hudson. It was carried directly to his room, when he sprung from the bed, and, taking it to the door of the room where "Tad" was lying, that he might read it by the gas light, his eyes ran over it.

"Good news! good news! Mrs. Pomroy; Port Hudson is ours!" he exclaimed, forgetting all sorrow for the moment.

"There is nothing like prayer, Mr. President," responded Mrs. Pomroy.

"Yes, there is, praise," he promptly answered.

"Prayer and praise must go together."

"Tad" was somewhat improved on the following day and he continued to improve, and finally recovered. But Mr. Lincoln continued watching by his side for three days and nights— he on one side of the cot and Mrs. Pomeroy on the other — leaving only at brief intervals to recline upon the lounge or bed. His public duties were left to Mr. Seward and his private secretary. "It seemed as if he could not bear to leave 'Tad' for a moment," said Mrs. Pomeroy.

On the morning of Willie's funeral, Mrs. Pomeroy expressed her deep sympathy for him, and called his attention to the many prayers going up for him. "I am glad to hear that," he answered, wiping his tears: "I want they should pray for me. I need their prayers will try to go to God with my sorrows." Subsequently he said, "I wish I had that childlike faith you speak of, and I trust that God will give it to me."

On the second night of Mrs. Pomeroy's care of "Tad" about eleven o'clock, Mr. Lincoln remarked.

"You don't know how much good your conversation did me last night, Mrs. Pomeroy. I wish you would tell me your remarkable experience again."

She complied with his request, and rehearsed the whole of it over again, Mr. Lincoln interrupting her occasionally by inquiries, as if he were intent upon learning how to bear his own heavy burdens. Still again, on the third night, he requested another rehearsal of that Christian experience. Often afterwards, when riding to and from the Soldiers' Home, or to the hospital where Mrs. Pomeroy's sick soldier boys were, he would revert to that experience, and put some question, or say, "It did me so much good." Once a senator was going to the Soldiers' Home, where Mrs. Pomeroy and "Tad" were at the time; and Mr. Lincoln said to him:—

"I want you should see Mrs. Pomeroy, whose conversation did me so much good. Go and introduce yourself to her, and tell her that I want you should hear that experience."

At another time, on the way from the Soldiers' Home to the Executive Mansion, he said to Mrs. Pomeroy: "I don't know how I shall ever repay you for what you have done for me. If I live through the war, and retire from public life, I hope to be able to remunerate you in some way."

In common with many friends, she warned him one day against rebels in Washington who might assassinate him, when he replied:

"I am in God's hand; let Him do with me what seem good to Him."

He possessed his mother's old Bible, which he read so much in his boyhood, and he was wont to read it daily, usually just before he took his lunch. He would throw himself upon the lounge, and read a few moments. One day Mrs. Pomeroy entered his office while he was thus reading on the lounge.

"What portion of the Bible do you like best, Mrs. Pomeroy?" he inquired.

"The psalms are my favorite," Mrs. Pomeroy answered.

"Yes, the psalms have something for every day in the week, and something for every poor fellow like me," he responded.

He was accustomed to carry his mother's Bible back and forth from the Soldiers' Home, preferring to read from it rather than use another. Speaking of that Bible once, he added, "I had a good Christian mother, and her prayers have followed me thus far through life." Captain Mix, who was often in the family, says: — "Many times have I listened to our most eloquent preachers, but never with the same feeling of awe and reverence, as when our Christian President, his arm around 'Tad,' with his deep earnest tone, each morning read a chapter from the Bible."

He inquired very minutely into the method of speaking with sick and dying soldiers— what she said to them —how they answered her—how many of them became Christians? He accompanied her many times to the hospital and witnessed her effective management and talked with the soldiers and encouraged them. On learning that the managers of the hospital, who were Roman Catholics, had forbidden the Protestant nurses to pray with the soldiers, or read the Bible to them, he promptly removed the restriction, and allowed the Christian women henceforth to hold prayer-meetings, read the Bible to the "boys" and pray with them, as much as they pleased, adding:—" If there was more praying and less swearing it would be far better for our country, and we all need to be prayed for, officers as well as privates, and if I was near death I think I should like to hear prayer."

He took a lady to the Soldiers' Home in his carriage one morning, with Mrs. Pomeroy, and the horses became well-nigh unmanageable just where the severe shower of the previous night had flooded the road. The ladies were very much frightened, and Mr. Lincoln directed the driver to hold one of the horses and the footman the other, while he opened the door and jumped out. Stripping up his pants to his knees, he hastily brought three stones large enough to stand upon, and placing them so that the ladies could step upon them, from one to the other, he speedily helped them to the side-walk, remarking in a vein of humor, "All through life be sure you put your feet in the right place, and then stand army. Then, looking down upon his very muddy boots, he said:— "I have always heard of Washington mud, and now I shall take home some as a sample."

We have given somewhat in detail these incidents from Mrs. Pomeroy's experience, because they present so clear a view of the man. His simplicity, tenderness, affection, frankness, freedom from pride and ostentation, trust in Providence, and strong religious convictions—all appear unmistakably in these incidents that cluster about his stay in the White House and Soldiers' Home.

Willie died on Thursday, and, on the recurrence of that day for several weeks, Mr. Lincoln shut himself up in his room and indulged in excessive grief. Near friends spoke to Dr. Vinton of New York, who was visiting at Washington, of this practice, and urged him to see the

President. Accordingly he called upon him and told him frankly that it was sinful to indulge in such grief.

"Your son is alive in Paradise," said Dr. Vinton.

"Alive! Alive! " exclaimed the President, starting to his feet; "surely you mock me."

"No, my dear sir, believe me; Christ himself declares it."

Mr. Lincoln looked at him a moment, then throwing his arms about the clergyman's neck, and laying his head upon his shoulders, sobbed aloud, repeating: "Alive! Alive!"

Dr. Vinton comforted him by the words of Christ, and for an hour, labored and prayed with him, closing the interview by telling the President: "I have a sermon upon this subject which I think might interest you."

"Do send it to me as early as possible," Mr. Lincoln replied. Dr. Vinton forwarded the sermon, and the sorrowing President read it over and over, and then had it copied that he might enjoy the reading of it yet more. A member of the family says:— "From that time Mr. Lincoln's views in relation to spiritual things were changed."

Mr. Lincoln was a devoted father, and his great love for his children appeared in the White House in its tender simplicity, as it did elsewhere. No matter what dignitaries were about him, paternal affection asserted itself without let or hindrance. The Hon. W. D. Kelley, of Philadelphia, says:—

"His intercourse with his family was as beautiful as that with his friends. I think that father never loved his children more fondly than he. The President never seemed grander in my sight than when, stealing upon him in the evening, I would find him with a book open before him, as he is represented in the popular photograph, with little Tad beside him. There were of course a great many curious books sent to him, and it seemed one of the special delights of his life to open those books at such an hour that his boy could stand beside him, and they could talk as he turned over the pages, the father thus giving to the son a portion of that care and attention of which he was ordinarily deprived by the duties of office pressing upon him."

Mr. Carpenter writes:— "No matter who was with the President, or how intently he was absorbed, little Tad was always welcome. At the time of which I write, he was eleven years old, and of course rapidly passing from childhood into youth. Suffering much from an infirmity of speech which developed in his infancy, he seemed on this account especially dear to his father. 'One touch of nature makes the whole world kind and it was an impressive and affecting sight to me to see the burdened President lost for the time being in the affectionate parent, as he would take the little fellow in his arms, upon the withdrawal of visitors, and caress him with all the fondness of a mother for the babe upon her bosom!"

Several weeks after the death of Willie, Mr. Lincoln, with several members of his Cabinet, spent a few days at Fortress Monroe, watching military operations upon the Peninsula. He improved his spare time there in reading Shakespeare. One day he was reading "Hamlet," when he called to his private secretary:—

"Come here, colonel: I want to read you a passage." The colonel responded, when the President read the discussion on ambition between Hamlet and his courtiers, and the soliloquy, in which conscience debates about a future state. Then he read passages from "Macbeth," and finally opened to the third act of "King John," where Constance bewails her lost boy. Closing the book, and recalling the words. Mr. Lincoln said: "Colonel, did you ever dream of a lost friend, and feel that you were holding sweet communion with that friend, and yet have a sad consciousness that it was not reality? —just so I dream of my boy Willie." Overcome with emotion, he dropped his head on the table, and sobbed aloud.

Beautiful example of paternal love in the highest place of the land! The millions of fathers over whom he ruled found in him a worthy father to imitate!

President Lincoln's humor often exposed him to criticism. His frequent stories often elicited censure. Persons who did not understand him charged him with being light and trifling, when sadness and sorrow were more becoming. There was no ground for this censure. Mr. Lincoln told stories in the White House just as he did anywhere else. The simplicity of his character led him to be, when President, just what he was as a friend and neighbor. Then, he told stories for two reasons. First, he told them to point and enforce the subject in hand. Mr. Herndon, his law-partner for many years, remarks upon this peculiarity of the man:—

"It is said that Newton saw an apple fall to the ground from a tree, and beheld the law of the universe in that fall; Shakespeare saw human nature in the laugh of a man; Professor Owen saw the animal in its claw; and Spencer saw the evolution of the universe in the growth of a seed. Nature was suggestive to all these men. Mr. Lincoln no less saw philosophy in a story, and a schoolmaster in a joke. The world, fact, man, principle— all had their powers of suggestion to his susceptible soul. They continually put him in mind of something. He was often perplexed to give expression to his ideas: first, because he was not master of the English language and, secondly, because there were no words in it containing the coloring, shape, exactness, power, and gravity, of his ideas. He was frequently at a loss for a word, and hence was compelled to resort to stories, maxims, and jokes to embody his idea, that it might be comprehended.

"But more and better than that, in the White House he found recreation and relief in story-telling. He told them that he read Shakespeare and the 'Nasby Papers,' to help him endure the labors of his official position. He indulged in wit and humor when he felt more like crying. Indeed, he indulged them, often, in order to keep from crying as he said to a member of Congress when he was greatly distressed for the country. 'Were it not for this occasional vent I should die.' He kept a copy of 'Nasby Papers ' in his desk as an antidote for depression. He found relief in their perusal. He once said to a friend, 'I think of writing to 'Petroleum' to come down here, and I shall tell him, if he will impart his talent to me, I will swap places with him.'"

Speaking of this peculiarity of the President, a Congressman said, "It is his life preserver." He was severely criticized for it by the journals. Many stories and jokes were ascribed to him, which he never told. A volume of them was issued in New York, under the title, "Old Abe's Jokes." A friend submitted a copy of the work to him, with the request that he should report how many of the stories were genuine. His report was "six out of the whole number. Still, the attacks upon him only elicited more wit. After examining a gun so constructed as to prevent the escape of gas, he remarked, "I really believe this does what it is represented to do. But do any of you know of any machine or invention, for preventing the escape of gas from newspaper establishments. At a time when the public journals teemed with assaults upon him, for alleged acts and sayings that never occurred, Mrs. Secretary Welles called attention to certain reports. "The papers are not always reliable" responded one present. "That is to say, Mrs. Welles," interjected Mr. Lincoln, "they lie, and then they replied, "He" could bear censure," as he said, "but not insult." A friend proposed that he should contradict a particular false report in a leading journal but he replied, "Oh, no; if I were to try to read, much less answer, all the attacks made on me, this shop might as well be closed for any other business. I do the very best I know how— the very best I can and I mean to keep doing so until the end. If the end brings me out all right, what is said against me won't amount to anything. If the end brings me out wrong, ten angels swearing I was right would make no difference."

His grand magnanimity never appeared to greater advantage than it did when, after all his trials with General McClellan, before he removed him, and after he had facetiously remarked that he "would like to borrow his army if he had no use for it," and given as a reason why the General did not reply to the "Chicago letter," "he is entrancing" —he remarked to another, "so pleasant and scholarly a gentleman can never fail to secure personal friends.

Also, when Stonewall Jackson fell in battle, and the Washington Chronicle spoke well of him as a brave soldier but mistaken man, Mr. Lincoln wrote to the editor:—

"I honor you for your generosity to one who, though contending against us in a guilty cause, was nevertheless a gallant man. Let us forget his sins over his fresh-made grave."

His humor, kindness, and magnanimity appeared to go hand in hand, presenting one of the most unique, genial, and remarkable characters ever found in public life.

In this connection his art of putting things deserves attention. Mr. Lincoln understood it to perfection and these remarkable sallies often exposed him to severe criticisms. For example, the report of the capture of a Union brigadier and squad of cavalry, near Fairfax Court House, by rebel guerillas, was brought to him. The brigadier had proved to be incompetent.

"I am very sorry to lose the horses," responded the President, on receipt of the news.

"What do you mean?" inquired his informant, somewhat startled by his seemingly heartless words.

"Why," rejoined the President, " I can make a better brigadier any day; but those horses cost the government one hundred and twenty-five dollars apiece."

It was customary for the Secretary of State to write the President's speeches to foreign ministers, and, perhaps, home delegations. A messenger entered the President's room one day, saying, "The Secretary has sent the speech you are to make today to the Swiss minister." Mr. Lincoln received it, smiling, and then, as if to ridicule the practice, and intimate that he could make his own speeches, he remarked, loud enough for all present to hear:—

"Oh, this is a speech Mr. Seward has written for me, is it? I guess I will try it before these gentlemen and see how it goes." He proceeded to read it aloud, in a waggish manner, and remarked, as he closed it, "There, I like that. It has the merit of originality."

A delegation from the West waited upon him to protest against some of his measures.

After having listened to their complaints, he answered:—

"Gentlemen, suppose all the property you were worth was in gold, and you had put it into the hands of Blondin to carry across the Niagara river on a rope, would you shake the cable, or keep shouting out to him, 'Blondin, stand up straighter —Blondin, stoop a little more —go a little faster— lean a little more to the north— lean a little more to the south.' No, you would hold your breath as well as your tongue, and keep your hands off until he was safe over. The government is carrying an immense weight. Untold treasures are in their hands. They are doing the very best they can. Don't badger them. Keep silence and we will get you safe across."

Another delegation came to open his eyes to the "breakers ahead." Mr. Lincoln thought they magnified the perils; and so he told a story. "You remind me of the schoolboy," he said, "who found difficulty in pronouncing the Scripture names, 'Shadrach, Meshach, and Abednego.' The teacher had drilled him repeatedly in the pronunciation of these names. One day the teacher purposely took the same lesson in Bible reading, and managed to have this boy read the passages, containing these names, again. As the dull pupil came to them, he stopped, looked up, and said: 'Teacher, there's them three fellers again."

A clergyman remarked to him: "The Lord is on our side."

"I am not at all concerned about that," replied Mr. Lincoln; "for I know that the Lord is always on the side of the right. But it is my constant anxiety and prayer that and this nation should be on the Lord's side."

A whole volume of similar incidents might be furnished, not one of them showing that Mr. Lincoln was thoughtless and trifling but, on the other hand, that it was his unique, peculiar and pat way of putting the case clearly before those who approached him. In his felicitous handling of a subject, a story or witticism was often more convincing than argument. For this reason he employed them. The genius and real ability of the man often cropped out through this mode of speaking, so peculiarly his own. One of our best writers put the literary character of President Lincoln and his wonderful tact so tersely before the people that we quote it here. It was penned before the death of Mr. Lincoln and the paragraph is not only a faithful portrait of the man, but the style of the composition is more like his than any piece of composition we have seen.

Mr. Lincoln, like Washington, was continually showing, without design on his part, his sincere trust in Providence, as well as his great respect for the institutions of Christianity. After a serious defeat of the Union forces near Washington, he remarked to a friend, "I have done the best I could. I have asked God to guide me, and now I must leave the event with him." At another time, two hundred members of the Christian Commission called upon him, and George H. Stuart spoke, in their behalf, of the debt of gratitude the public owed him. Mr. Lincoln replied:—

"My friends: You owe me no gratitude for what I have done; and I—"(and here he hesitated as if he feared being misunderstood in what he was about to say) — "and I, I may say, owe you no gratitude for what you have done just as, in a sense, we owe no gratitude to the men who have fought our battles for us. I trust that this has been for us all a work of duty. All the gratitude is due to the great Giver of all good."

At another time he replied to Dr. J. T. Duryea and other members of the Commission as follows:—

"If it were not for my belief in an over-ruling Providence, it would be difficult for me, in the midst of such complications, to keep my reason on its seat. But I am confident that the Almighty has his plans, and will work them out and, whether we see it or not, they will be the wisest and best for us. I have always taken counsel of Him, and referred to Him my plans, and have never adopted a course of proceeding without being assured, as far as I could be, of his approbation."

At another time he said to friends, "I have been driven many times to my knees by the overwhelming conviction that I had nowhere else to go." And again, "I should be the most presumptuous blockhead upon this footstool, if I for one day thought that I could discharge the duties which have come upon me since I came into this place, without the aid and enlightenment of one who is wiser and stronger than all others."

In the early part of the war he issued an order for the better observance of the Sabbath in the army. In the order he said: "The importance for man and beast of the prescribed weekly rest, the sacred rights of Christian soldiers and sailors, a becoming deference to the best sentiment of a Christian people, and a due regard for the Divine Will, demand that Sunday labor in the army and navy be reduced to the measure of strict necessity."

The prevalence of profane swearing among the soldiers was rebuked in the same order and he said: "The discipline and character of the national forces should not suffer, nor the cause they defend be imperiled by the profanation of the day or name Of The Most High." And he enforced the order by the example of Washington, saying:—"At this time of public distress, adopting the words of Washington in 1776, 'men may find enough to do in the service of God and their country without abandoning themselves to vice and immorality.' The first general order issued by the Father of his Country after the Declaration of Independence indicates the spirit in which our institutions were founded and should ever be defended: 'The General hopes and trusts that every officer and man will endeavor to live and act as becomes a Christian soldier defending the dearest rights and liberties of his country.'"

Intemperance in the army he deeply deplored. Both by word and pen he sought to expose the perils of drinking habits among officers and privates, especially the former. His own example enforced his counsels with great power. For he continued to be the same uncompromising teetotaller at Washington that he had been elsewhere. The White House was run upon teetotal principles, as strictly so as his humble home in Springfield. In Washington circles, where the wine cup went round, he was always passed by out of respect to his temperance principles. At one time a delegation of the Sons of Temperance waited on him. In his reply, he said: "When I was a young man, long ago, before the Sons of Temperance, as an organization, had an existence, I, in my humble way, made temperance speeches and I think I can say that my example has never belied the position I then took." And when he read a petition from the women of Massachusetts, praying for the suppression of intemperance in the army, he exclaimed: "Dear, good souls! if they only knew how much I have tried to remedy this great evil, they would be rejoiced."

Notwithstanding his great weight of labors for the country. President Lincoln did not wholly neglect literary studies. He found necessary recreation in his books, and both poetry and prose often brought relief to him in seasons of depression and exhaustion. A California lady, who, with several other women, visited the cemetery at the Soldiers' Home in company with Mr. Lincoln, writes:—

"While we stood in the soft evening air, watching the faint trembling of the long tendrils of waving willow, and feeling the dewy coolness that was flung out by the old oaks above us, Mr. Lincoln joined us, and stood silent, too, taking in the scene.

"Now," said he, "this is all wrong. Richard, you remember, had been, and was then, plotting the destruction of his brothers, to make room for himself. Outwardly the most loyal to the newly crowned king, secretly he could scarcely contain his impatience at the obstacles still in the way of his own elevation. He appears upon the stage, just after the crowning of Edward, burning with repressed hate and jealousy. The prologue is the utterance of the most intense bitterness and satire."

Then, assuming the character, perhaps without design, he repeated Richard's soliloquy with so much effect, that Mr. Carpenter, who was present, says:—"It seemed like a new creation to me. Though familiar with the passage from boyhood, I can truly say that never till that moment had I fully appreciated its spirit."

A delegation of the "Christian Commission" waited upon him, and, in reply to their address, he said:—

"I desire, also, to add to what I have said, that there is one association whose object and motives I have never heard in any degree impugned or questioned [a sly rebuke at the unjust criticisms and faultfinding that prevailed]; and that is the 'Christian Commission.' And, as Shakespeare says," he added, "that is a record, gentlemen, of which you may justly be proud." Then, as if to correct himself, he remarked, "I believe, however, it is 'Jack Falstaff ' who talks about 'villainy,' though, of course, Shakespeare is responsible."

The particular circumstances of the country, or some phase of his personal experience, appear to have been the occasion generally of these and kindred drafts upon his literary resources.

Mr. Willis was both surprised and delighted with this evidence of familiarity with his writings, and the handsome compliment so gracefully tendered.

We do not design to speak at length of Mr. Lincoln's mental ability that has appeared, incidentally, from the beginning of our story. Enough has been quoted from his lip and pen to prove that Senator Trumbull's brief tribute was not exaggerated, "He is a giant and without the prefix 'Little ' to it, a giant ill intellect as well as in stature." In the light of what has been said, the words of that noted Englishman, Goldwin Smith, are pertinent: "He met the most terrible of all emergencies with ability and self-possession, as well, probably, as it would have been met by any European sovereign or statesman whom yon could have."

However, this chapter should not close without his eloquent and beautiful address at the dedication of the national cemetery at Gettysburg, November 18, 1863. Its originality and classic diction must commend it to the favorable consideration of the ripest scholars.

We have intentionally omitted President Lincoln's care of the soldiers and colored race during his life in the White House that we might devote a chapter to each subject, both on account of the intrinsic importance of each, and the clear and interesting view of his character which they afford.

CHAPTER XXV

HIS GREAT INTEREST IN SOLDIERS

From the time of President Lincoln's first call for troops, his life in the White House brought him into intimate relations with Union soldiers. At once he bestowed upon them his most tender regard, which they reciprocated with kindred heartiness. He was called by the endearing name of "Father Abraham" in the army; and they were called by him in the White House, "the boys." Our presentation of his public career would be very deficient without special attention to his fatherly service in their behalf. The controlling thought of his mind on this subject was expressed in the following words:

"This extraordinary war in which we are engaged falls heavily upon all classes of people, but the most heavily upon the soldier. For it has been said, 'all that a man hath will he give for his life; and, while all contribute of their substance, the soldier puts his life at stake, and often yields it up in his country's cause. The highest merit, then, is due to the soldier!"

He spoke somewhat from experience. His brief service in the "Black Hawk War," where the provisions for personal comfort were small, made him familiar with the hardships of soldier-life. He knew from personal experience how many and great privations are inseparable from army service; and no doubt this knowledge intensified the natural love in his heart for the loyal and patriotic "boys in blue."

Some public men claimed that the President ought not to be interrupted and annoyed by so many applications from soldiers and their friends—that some one of the military commissions, or a special one, should relieve him of this burden. But he would consent to no such arrangement. The "boys" belonged to his family, and he would enjoy a fatherly watch over them. There was reason for the suggestion, since his daily duties as President occupied every moment of his time, and, as we have seen, worried and wearied him beyond measure. The reader can scarcely understand how he could devote any time at all to the soldiers, when he reads the following description of his daily work, as given by parties who saw him every day.

"Mr. Lincoln is an early riser, and he thus is able to devote two or three hours each morning to his voluminous private correspondence, besides glancing at a city paper. At nine, he breakfasts; then walks over to the War Office to read such war telegrams as they give him, and to have a chat with General Halleck on the military situation, in which he takes a great interest. Returning to the White House, he goes through with his morning's mail, in company with a private secretary, who makes a minute of the reply which he is to make; and others the President retains, that he may answer them himself. Every letter receives attention; and all which are entitled to a reply, receive one, no matter how they are worded, or how inelegant the chirography may be. Tuesdays and Fridays are cabinet days; but, on the other days, visitors at the White House are requested to wait in the ante-chamber, and send in their cards. Sometimes, before the President has finished reading his mail, Louis will have a handful of pasteboard; and, from the cards laid before him, Mr. Lincoln has visitors ushered in, giving precedence to acquaintances. Three or four hours do they pour in, in rapid succession, nine out of ten asking offices; and patiently does the President listen to their application... The simple and natural manner in which he delivers his thoughts makes him appear "to those visiting him like an earnest, affectionate friend. At four o'clock, the President declines seeing any more company, and sometimes accompany his wife in her carriage to take a ride... He dines at six; and it is rare that some personal friends do not grace the round dining table, where he throws off the cares of office, and reminds those who have been in Kentucky of the old school gentlemen, who used to dispense generous hospitality there."

Another writer adds: "At night, from ten to twelve, he usually makes a tour all round—now at Secretary Seward's, and then at General Halleck's; and, if General Burnside was nearer, he would see him each night before he went to bed. Those who know his habits, and want to see him late at night, follow him round from place to place; and the last search generally brings him up at General Halleck's, as he can get the latest army intelligence there. Whoever else is asleep or indolent, the President is wide awake and around."

How a public servant, under such a constant pressure of care, could find time to listen to every complaint of soldiers and their friends, many of the cases requiring much time to investigate, and also visit hospitals and go to the front to "see how the boys are getting along," the reader can scarcely understand. But he did, as the very interesting incidents we shall relate abundantly show. There is evidence that his heart was not so thoroughly absorbed in any other department of his work as it was in this. He fully realized that the life of the nation hung upon the life of the soldier—that the appeal from the ballot to the bullet was a dire necessity— hence, he thought, "the highest merit is due to the soldier;" and he never belied that sentiment. To the day of his death, he treated soldiers as if they were really of more consequence, in the fearful crisis, than governors and senators. On one occasion, when there was so great a crowd at one of his receptions that hand-shaking was discontinued, the President stood and bowed his acknowledgments to senators and representatives; but finally, observing a wounded soldier enter with his poorly-clad mother, he hastily left his position, crowded his way to the couple, and taking them both by the hand, he gave them a most cordial welcome, congratulating the woman upon having so patriotic a son, and expressing his sympathy for the son in his disabled condition. It was a very affecting demonstration, and it brought tears to the eyes of many spectators. The President simply acted what he had said again and again, "the highest merit is due to the soldier." All who witnessed the hearty greeting were satisfied that Mr. Lincoln meant what he said.

In this and other incidents to be related, the true Republican simplicity of Mr. Lincoln's character appears. Official distinction obtruded no barrier between his own honest heart and that of the brave and true soldier.

One day he was going through a passageway to his private room for a cup of tea, when he heard the cry of a child. He returned immediately to his office, and rang the bell; Daniel responded promptly.

"Daniel, is there a woman with a baby in the anteroom?"

"There is, Mr. President; and she has been there three days," Daniel replied. "There has been no chance for her to get in."

"Go at once, and send her to me," he said, adding some words of regret that she had been overlooked.

The woman, with the baby in her arms, was soon in his presence, pleading for her husband, who was sentenced to be shot as a deserter from the army. There were several extenuating circumstances, and the President granted her request, writing his decision upon a slip of paper.

"There, my dear woman," he said, "you take that, and it will bring back your husband," at the same time directing her where to go with the document. Convulsive sobs of joy were all the response the glad woman could make, as she retired. Daniel went up to her, and pulled her shawl, saying, "Madam, it was the baby that did it."

Hon. W. D. Kelley said to the President, "There is a lad on the gunboat Ottawa, who has shown the mettle of a man in two serious engagements. Can you not send him to the naval school." You have the authority to send three boys there annually, who have served one year in the navy."

"Perhaps so," responded the President; "let me hear more about it." Mr. Kelley rehearsed, in detail, the heroic deeds of the boy.

"If the appointments for this year have not been made, let this boy be appointed," he wrote at once to the Secretary of the Navy, passing the message to Mr. Kelley. The appointment was made; but it was found the lad was not quite fourteen years of age. "I think the President can make it right," said Mr. Kelley to him; and he took the lad to Mr. Lincoln.

"Mr. President," said Kelley, "my young friend, Willie Bladen, finds a difficulty about his appointment. You have directed him to appear at the school in July, and he will not be fourteen until September." Willie bowed in a graceful, soldierly way to the President.

"Bless me!" exclaimed Mr. Lincoln, laying down his spectacles; "is that the boy who did so gallantly in those two great battles?" Why, I feel I should bow to him, and not he to me." Then, taking the order previously written, he changed it from July to September; and putting his hand lovingly on Willie's head, he said:

"Now, my noble boy, go home, and have a good time during the two months, for they are about the last holiday you will get."

Willie bowed himself out, remarking to an acquaintance, "I should like to have a game of romps with that man."

A small, pale, delicate-looking boy waited in the crowd to see the President. Observing him, Mr. Lincoln said, "Come here, my boy, and tell me what you want."

Advancing timidly, the little fellow placed his hand on the arm of the President's chair, and said:—

"Mr. President, I have been a drummer in a regiment for two years, and my colonel got angry with me, and turned me off. I was taken sick and have been a long time in the hospital. This is the first time I have been out, and I came to see if you could not do something for me."

His plea touched Mr. Lincoln's heart, and he replied by asking the boy—

"Where do you live, my son?"

"I have no home," the lad answered sadly,

"Where is your father?"

"He died in the army some time ago."

"Where is your mother?"

"My mother is dead also. I have no father, no mother, no brothers, no sisters, and," bursting into tears, "no friends—nobody cares for me."

Mr. Lincoln's eyes filled with tears, and his lips quivered for a moment, when he continued—

"Can't you sell newspapers?"

"No, I am too weak; and the surgeon told me I must leave the hospital, and I have no money, and nowhere to go to."

The President could say no more; and he drew forth a card, and wrote on it, "Take care of this poor boy," directing it to the proper official; then handed it to the lad, whose face lit up with a smile because he had found a true friend in the President.

A citizen of Washington tells the following:— "I was waiting my turn to speak to the President one day, when my attention was attracted by the sad patient face of a woman advanced in life, who in a faded hood and shawl was among the applicants for an interview.

"Presently Mr. Lincoln turned to her, saying in his accustomed manner, ' Well, my good woman, what can I do for you this morning?' 'Mr. President,' said she, 'my husband and three sons all went into the army. My husband was killed in the fight at I get along very badly since then, living all alone, and I thought I would come and ask you to release to me my oldest son.' Mr. Lincoln looked into her face a moment, and in his kindest accents responded, 'Certainly! Certainly! If you have given us all, and your prop has been taken away, you are justly entitled to one of your boys!' He immediately made out an order discharging the young man, which the woman took, and thanking him gratefully, went away.

"I had forgotten the circumstance," continued "till last week, when happening to be here again, who should come in but the same woman. It appeared that she had gone herself to the front, with the President's order, and found the son she was in search of had been mortally wounded in a recent engagement, and taken to a hospital. She found the hospital, but the boy was dead, or died while she was there. The surgeon in charge made a memorandum of the facts upon the back of the President's order, and almost broken-hearted, the poor woman had found her way again into Mr. Lincoln's presence. He was much affected by her appearance and story, and said: 'I know what you wish me to do now, and I shall do it without your asking; I shall release to you your second son.' Upon this, he took up his pen and commenced writing the order. While he was writing, the poor woman stood by his side, the tears running down her face, and passed her hand softly over his head, stroking his rough hair, as I have seen a fond mother caress a son. By the time he had finished writing, his own heart and eyes were full. He handed her the paper: 'Now,' said he, 'you have one and one of the other two left that is no more than right.' She took the paper, and reverently placing her hand again upon his head, the tears still upon her cheeks, said: 'The Lord bless you, Mr. Lincoln. May you live a thousand years, and may you always be the head of this great nation!"

Hon. Thaddeus Stevens accompanied an elderly lady to the President, to ask for the pardon of her son, who had been sentenced to death by a court-martial. Mr. Stevens knew that there were circumstances on which pardon could be reasonably based. After the President had listened to the woman's story, he turned to Mr. Stevens.

"Mr. Stevens, do you think this is a case that will warrant my interference?"

"Yes; I should have no hesitation in granting a pardon," Mr. Stevens replied.

"Then I will pardon him," and he proceeded to execute the papers. The mother's heart was too full for utterance. Her deep emotion, as she turned away, told how deep her gratitude was. On the way down stairs, when she could sufficiently control her feelings to speak, she broke out suddenly:—

"I knew it was a copperhead lie!"

"What do you refer to, madam?" inquired Mr. Stevens.

"Why, they told me he was an ugly-looking man, and it's a lie. He is the handsomest man I ever saw in my life."

Speaker Colfax interceded for the pardon of a son of one of his constituents, who had been sentenced to be shot. It was in the evening, and Mr. Lincoln was wearied by incessant calls, and wanted rest. He granted the request of Mr. Colfax, and said:—

"Some of our generals complain that I impair discipline and subordination in the army by my pardons and respites, but it makes me rested, after a hard day's work, if I can find some good excuse for saving a man's life, and I go to bed happy as I think how joyous the signing of my name will make him and his family and his friends."

Senator Harris, of New York, interceded for the reprieve of a young soldier, who was imprisoned at Elmira, N. Y., awaiting the sentence of death. His friends had been to the Secretary of War to intercede for the condemned young man; but the Secretary only replied:—

"Can do nothing for him; it is an aggravated case." True, it did seem like an aggravated case, for the fellow had deserted three times, and once attempted to poison his guards; but he had been of unsound mind. Evidence of his insanity was laid before Senator Harris, who became fully convinced that Executive clemency ought to save the soldier from death. It was twelve o'clock on Wednesday night when the senator went to the President, and the soldier was to be executed on Thursday. The President was in bed.

A messenger was sent to his room to announce that Senator Harris desired to see him upon important business.

"Let him come in," Mr. Lincoln said.

Senator Harris was soon at his bedside. "The boy is insane," he said; "there can be no question about it, —an irresponsible lad and his execution would be murder."

"And you are satisfied that these are the facts in the case?" replied Mr. Lincoln, inquiringly.

"Perfectly so. Besides, it is not a pardon that we ask, but a reprieve until a medical examination can be made."

"Well, that is reasonable and just," responded Mr. Lincoln. "The boy shall be reprieved."

He arose immediately, and ordered a telegram to be sent to Elmira at once, delaying the execution of the condemned. Early in the morning he sent another. And before the hour of execution arrived, he sent four telegrams by different lines, fearing that, by some misfortune, the reprieve might not reach him.

At another time, Judge Kellogg, of New York, interceded for the son of one of his neighbors, sentenced by court-martial to be shot the next day. It was near midnight when he reached the White House, and the President had retired. First, however, he went to the Secretary of War, thinking he might accomplish his purpose without disturbing the President.

"Too many cases of this kind have been let off now," replied the secretary; "it is quite time to make an example of somebody."

"But there are reasons enough for pardoning him," urged the judge; and he proceeded to enumerate them.

"Nevertheless, I shall not interfere," still insisted the unmoved secretary.

"Well, Mr. Secretary," exclaimed the judge, under much excitement, "the boy is not going to be shot, you may be sure of that."

He hurried away to the White House, where the sentinel intercepted him, saying:—

"My orders are to admit no one tonight."

"But I must go in: it is a case of life and death," urged the judge, persistently.

"That fact cannot modify my orders," answered the sentinel.

"I must go in; and I will take the responsibility," continued the judge. And he entered, going directly to the President's sleeping-room without the ceremony of sending his card. Opening the door, he said, hurriedly and excitedly:—

"Mr. President, a dispatch just received informs me that the son of one of my neighbors is to be shot tomorrow; and I want you to save his life."

"What is he to be shot for?" inquired Mr. Lincoln. "I don't know, and I can't help what he may have done. Why, he is an old neighbor of mine, and I can't allow him to be shot," Judge Kellogg continued, under increasing heat.

"Well," answered Mr. Lincoln, "I don't believe that shooting him will do him any good. Bring me a pen."

Without getting out of bed, he wrote a pardon for the judge to forward at once to the boy so near his doom.

Benjamin Owen, a young soldier of Vermont, was sentenced to be shot for sleeping at his post. The family was plunged into agony by the dreadful tidings. For some reason, a reprieve was granted him for several days, when he wrote the following letter to his father:

"Dear Father, — When this reaches you I shall be in eternity. At first it seemed awful to me, but I have thought about it so much now that it has no terror. They say they will not bind me, but that I may meet my death like a man You know I promised Jemmy Carr's mother I would look after her boy, and when he fell sick I did all I could for him. He was not strong when he was ordered back into the ranks, and the day before that night, I carried all his luggage, besides my own, on our march. Toward night we went in on double quick, and though the luggage began to feel very heavy, everybody else was tired, too; and as for Jemmy, if I had not lent him an arm new and then he would have dropped by the way. I was all tired out when I came into camp, and then, it was Jemmy's turn to be sentry, and I would take his place; but I was too tired, father, I could not have kept awake if I had had a gun at my head. But I did not know it until — well, until it was too late. Our good colonel would save me if he could. He says, forgive him, father, he only did his duty. And don't lay my death against Jemmy. The poor boy is broken-hearted and does nothing and entreats them to let him die in my stead. I can't bear to think of mother and sister. Comfort them, father! God help him, it is very hard to bear! Good-by, father! God seems near and dear to me; not at all as if he wished me to perish forever, but as if he felt sorry for his poor, sinful, broken-hearted child, and would take me to be with him and my Savior, in a better, better life! God bless you all!

His sister, who had read much about the President's tender heart, seized the letter, and quickly as steam could carry her was in Washington, in the presence of Mr. Lincoln.

"Well, my child, what do you want so bright and early this morning?" the President asked.

"My brother's life," she said, with much emotion.

"Who is he?"

She told him, and for what he was sentenced to be shot.

"Oh, yes, that fatal sleep," responded Mr. Lincoln; "thousands of lives might have been lost by that sleep."

"So my father said; but he was so tired carrying Jemmy's baggage;" and here she put his letter into the President's hand, saying that "would tell him all about it."

Mr. Lincoln read Benjamin's letter; when, with tearful eye and melted heart, he quickly wrote an order for his pardon, and, lest there might be some delay in the conveyance of the message, he ordered his own carriage and delivered it personally to the proper authorities. Before leaving his office, however, he said to the sister:

"Go home, my child, and tell that father of yours, who could approve his country's sentence, even when it took the life of a child like that, that Abraham Lincoln thinks the life far too precious to be lost."

He ordered a furlough for the soldier-boy, also, that he might return with his sister to

Vermont and when, subsequently, brother and sister came to the White House, the President, in his private room, fastened a badge of office upon his shoulder, saying, "the shoulder that could carry a sick comrade's baggage, and die for it so uncomplainingly, must wear that strap."

The father of a soldier applied to Congressman Kellogg, of whom we have spoken, for the pardon of his son, under sentence of death. Mr. Kellogg felt that it was a case where executive clemency ought to be exercised and he said to the distressed father, "you wait here until I go and see what can be done." He went directly to President Lincoln, and laid the case before him. When he reached that part of the narrative which related to a fearful charge across a bridge, wherein the soldier displayed remarkable heroism, Mr. Lincoln started up, and asked earnestly:—

"Do you say that the young man was wounded?" as if he were overjoyed to find a decent reason for saving another life.

"Yes, badly wounded," added Mr. Kellogg.

"Then he has shed his blood for his country?" suggested Mr. Lincoln.

"Yes, and shed it nobly," responded Mr. Kellogg.

"Kellogg!" continued the President, brightening up, "is there not something in the Bible about the shedding of blood for the remission of sins?"

"I think you are right," replied Mr. Kellogg.

"Well, it is a good point, and there is no going behind it," rejoined the President. And, taking up his pen, he wrote a pardon, which Mr. Kellogg bore to the now glad father.

With all his leniency towards erring soldiers and his passion for granting pardons, he had no patience with rebel sympathizers in places of trust. When Alexander Long, of Ohio, proposed, in the House of Representatives, to recognize the Southern Confederacy, General Garfield sprang to his feet, and denounced the "treason" in words of bitter detestation, comparing the author of the proposition to Benedict Arnold, who betrayed his country in the hour of its peril, and entreating loyal representatives not to believe that another such "growth on the soil of Ohio deformed the face of nature, and darkened the light of God's day." When news of this speech reached the President, he expressed his approbation in the most unqualified manner and subsequently thanked General Garfield for "flaying Long alive."

At one time the President called upon the head surgeon at City Point, and told him that he wanted to visit all the hospitals there, and shake hands with every soldier, as incidentally referred to on a former page.

"Do you know what a job you have undertaken, Mr. President?" responded the surgeon.

"How many have you in the hospitals?" Mr. Lincoln asked.

"From five to six thousand," answered the surgeon; "and you will be exhausted long before you get through all the wards."

Mr. Lincoln smiled as he continued, "I think I am quite equal to the task. At any rate, I can try and go as far as I can. I shall never see the boys again, probably, and I want they should know how I appreciate what they have done for the country."

The tour of the hospitals began, the surgeon leading the way, and the President stopping at every cot, extending his hand, with words of greeting to one, sympathy to another, and a kind inquiry of some—all glad to take his hand. In his rounds, he approached a cot on which lay a rebel soldier. Before the President had time to extend his hand the repentant soldier extended his, bursting into tears, and saying, "Mr. Lincoln, I have long wanted to see you, and ask your forgiveness for ever raising my hand against the old flag."

Mr. Lincoln wept, as he shook the penitent's hand kindly, assuring him of prompt forgiveness. And this recalls his remark to a public man who was complaining of his Amnesty Proclamation. "When a man is sincerely penitent for his misdeeds, and gives satisfactory evidence of the same, he can safely be pardoned, and there is no exception to the rule." The last clause, which we have put in italics, expresses the true Gospel idea of forgiveness better than most sermons of twenty pages.

After the tour of the hospitals had been made, and the President had seated himself in the surgeon's office, word came that, "one of the wards was overlooked, and the boys want to see the President."

"You are thoroughly tired, Mr. President, and so am I," said the surgeon, "and you had better not go; it will make no difference."

"But I must go," Mr. Lincoln replied; "I would not knowingly omit one, and the boys will be so disappointed if they do not see me."

He went, and completed the hand-shaking for that day, which consumed several hours, and returned perfectly satisfied, because he had carried joy and comfort to the "brave boys" whom he loved as a father.

His letters and public documents abound in expressions which show that the soldiers, officers and privates, were borne upon his mind constantly. He was invited to attend a large meeting in New York in honor of General Grant. He closed his reply with these words:—

"He and his brave soldiers are now in the midst of their great trial; and I trust that at your meeting you will so shape your good words that they may turn to men and guns moving to his and their support."

He closed his letter, accepting his second nomination, with the following:—

"I am especially gratified that the soldiers and seamen were not forgotten by the convention, as they forever must and will be remembered by the grateful country, for whose salvation they devote their lives."

If the people would but remember the soldier, they might withhold some of their praise for himself! News of the bloody slaughter of the "boys" always filled the heart of the President with grief.

"Terrible! terrible!"

How often this expressive word dropped from his lips! Often he could neither eat nor sleep, his soul was so wrought upon by bad news from the front. When the tidings of defeat with very heavy loss, in the Wilderness battles, reached him, he exclaimed:—

"My God! my God! Twenty thousand poor souls sent to their account in one day! I cannot bear it! I cannot bear it!"

One morning, Secretary Seward found him walking his room with a most distressed appearance in his face, when he inquired if the President was not well.

"This dreadful news from the days has banished sleep and appetite," he answered. "Not a moment's sleep last night, nor a crumb of food this morning!"

It was the grief of a father over his fallen sons—sincere and tender as that of a mother.

At another time, the news of a heavy loss in a hard fought battle caused him to bury his face in his hands, saying:—

"I shall never more be glad!"

Dr. Holland says of Mr. Lincoln and the soldiers:—

"With the soldiers who were fighting the battles of the country, he had the deepest sympathy. Whenever he was congratulated upon a success, he never failed to allude gratefully to the noble men who had won it. The trials of these men, — their sacrifices of comfort and health, of limb and life, —touched him with a sympathy that really sapped the foundations of his constitution. They were constantly in his thoughts and not a battle was fought to whose sacrifices his own vitality did not contribute. He admired the fighting man, and looked upon him as, in one sense, his superior. Although he did not plead guilty to the weakness of moral cowardice, he felt that the battle-field was a fearful place, from which, unaided by its special inspirations, he should run. Indeed, Mr. Lincoln did not give himself credit for the physical courage which he really possessed, though he had probably grown timid with his failing strength.

"This sympathy with the soldiers he manifested in many ways, and in none more than in the treatment of their offences against military law. In a letter to the author, a personal friend of the President says: 'I called on him one day in the early part of the war. He had just written a pardon for a young man who had been sentenced to be shot for sleeping at his post as a sentinel. He remarked as he read it to me:—

"I could not think of going into eternity with the blood of the poor young man on my skirts.' Then he added:—"

'It is not to be wondered at that a boy, raised on a farm, probably in the habit of going to bed at dusk, should, when required to watch, fall asleep and I cannot consent to shoot him for such an act.'

"This story with its moral is made complete by Rev. Newman Hall, of London, who, in a sermon preached after and upon Mr. Lincoln's death, says that the dead body of this youth was found among the slain on the field of Fredericksburg, wearing next his heart a photograph of his preserver, beneath which the grateful fellow had written, 'God bless President Lincoln!' From the same sermon another anecdote is gleaned, of a similar character, which is evidently authentic. An officer of the army, in conversation with the preacher, said: 'The first week of our command, there were twenty-four deserters sentenced by court-martial to be shot, and the warrants for their execution were sent to the President to be signed. He refused. I went to Washington and had an interview. I said: "Mr. President, unless these men are made an example of, the army itself is in danger. Mercy to the few is cruelty to the many."

"'Mr. General,' he replied, 'there are already too many weeping widows in the United

States. For God's sake, don't ask me to add to the number, for I won't do it.'"

As Dr. Holland intimates, President Lincoln was deeply impressed by deeds of daring, and he never lost sight of officer or private who distinguished himself in raid or battle. At a time when he was very much depressed in consequence of defeats, instead of victories, to the national arms, the news of successes in the Department of the West was brought to him. The battle of Chickamauga had been fought, and the bravery and exploits of General Garfield were rehearsed to him, such as his daring ride from General Rosecrans to General Thomas, and bringing supplies up the Big Sandy to his hungry soldiers.

"How is it," inquired Mr. Lincoln of an army officer who was present at the time, "that Garfield did in two weeks what would have taken one of your regular officers two months to accomplish?"

"Because he was not educated at West Point, as I was," replied the officer, laughingly, thinking the President designed to slur West Point graduates.

"No, that was not the reason," retorted Mr. Lincoln. "It was because, when he was a boy, he had to work for a living."

He made Garfield a major-general for his courage, tact, and efficiency and when, a few months later, Ohio proposed to transfer him to Congress and Garfield objected, the President said:—

"By all means, send him here. We need just such a man of military experience and skill in Congress."

He was often moved by the tales of sacrifice on the part of parents, wives, and sisters. He seemed to enter really into the feelings of patriotic mothers and wives, who cheerfully parted with their dear ones for the sake of their country. He was told of a mother in Boston who had lost five sons in battles, and he immediately sat down and wrote the following letter to her:—

"Executive Mansion, Washington, Nov. 21, 1864.

"Dear Madam: — I have been shown, in the files of the War Department, a statement of the Adjutant-General of Massachusetts that you are the mother of five sons, who have died gloriously on the field of battle. I feel how weak and fruitless must be any words of mine which should attempt to beguile you from the grief of a loss so overwhelming. But I cannot refrain from tendering to you the consolation that may be found in the thanks of the Republic they died to save. I pray that our Heavenly Father may assuage the anguish of your bereavement, and leave you only the cherished memory of the loved and lost, and the solemn pride that must be yours to have laid so costly a sacrifice upon the altar of freedom."

"Yours very sincerely and respectfully,

"Abraham Lincoln.

"To Mrs. Billy, Boston, Massachusetts."

His deep interest in the Union army caused him to hail every organization in behalf of the sick and wounded soldiers. The Sanitary Commission, the Christian Commission, and all soldiers' aid societies, won his heart. Any measure or enterprise that would carry comfort to the "boys" commanded his undivided support. In a speech at the close of a very successful fair in

Washington, for the benefit of soldiers, he said:—

"In this extraordinary war, extraordinary developments have manifested themselves, such as have not been seen in former wars and among these manifestations nothing has been more remarkable than these fairs for the relief of suffering soldiers and their families. And the chief agents in these fairs are the women of America. I am not accustomed to the use of the language of eulogy; I have never studied the art of paying compliments to women; but I must say that, if all that has been said by orators and poets, since the creation of the world, in praise of women were applied to the women of America, it would not do them, justice for their conduct during this war. I will close by saying, God bless the women of America!"

He was invited to preside at a meeting of the Christian Commission in Washington, but a pressure of duties prevented even his attendance. He wrote, however, to the chairman of the committee:—

"While, for reasons which I deem sufficient, I must decline to preside, I cannot withhold my approval of the meeting, and its worthy objects. Whatever shall be, sincerely and in God's name, devised for the good of the soldiers and seamen in their hard spheres of duty, can scarcely fail to be blessed. And whatever shall turn our thoughts from the unreasoning and uncharitable passions, prejudices, and jealousies incident to a great national trouble such as ours, and to fix them on the vast and long-enduring consequences, for weal or for woe, which are to result from the trouble, and especially to strengthen our reliance on the Supreme Being for the final triumph of the right, cannot but be well for us all."

These earnest words voice not only his abiding interest in the loyal army, but also his equally abiding confidence that God would give final victory to the right.

For the purpose of emphasizing his sympathy with the boys at the front, he attended soldiers' fairs in Baltimore and Philadelphia. Three years before he was obliged to pass through the former city in disguise to escape assassination. In its streets the Massachusetts Sixth had met with a bloody reception, on its way to protect Washington and left some of its heroic members dead. The city was then a hot-bed of treason. But a great change had been wrought there, and the chief attraction of the Soldiers' Fair was the presence of Mr. Lincoln. Alluding to the remarkable change that had been wrought he said, in his address—

"Calling to mind that we are in Baltimore, we cannot fail to note that the world moves. Looking upon the many people I see assembled here to serve as they best may the soldiers of the Union it occurs to me that three years ago those soldiers could not pass through Baltimore. I would say, blessings upon the men who have wrought these changes, and the women who have assisted them!"

In both these places, he spoke of the loyalty and sufferings of the "boys" with fatherly tenderness, and eulogized the women of the land for their self-denying and philanthropic labors in their behalf.

The proceeds of the Fair at Philadelphia amounted to one million three hundred thousand dollars, a result over which the President became enthusiastic. When he was told that the fairs in eleven cities netted nearly FIVE MILLION DOLLARS he exclaimed:—

"Was there ever such a country for patriotism and liberality? How much suffering will be prevented among the brave boys!"

When he was told that the Sanitary Commission, within ten days after the terrible battle of Antietam, sent 28,763 pieces of dry goods, shirts, towels, bed ticks, pillows, etc.; 30 barrels of old linen, bandages, and lint; 3,188 pounds of farina; 2,620 pounds of condensed milk; 5,000 pounds of beef-stock and canned meats; several tons of lemons and other fruit, crackers, tea, sugar, rubber-cloth, tin-cups, and 4,000 sets of hospital clothing all of which was tenderly distributed among the wounded by the scores of volunteer agents of the Christian Commission, language was not an ample vehicle to convey his overflowing gratitude; his unbidden tears told how full of joy his heart was.

We have said that Mr. Lincoln was opposed to the war-rule of retaliation but the suffering of our soldiers in Libby Prison, at Andersonville, Belle Isle, and at other points in the South, caused him to modify his views, and declare for retaliation, at least, under certain circumstances.

The investigation of the Congressional Committee on the "Conduct of the War," confirmed the most harrowing reports from rebel prisons, over which Mr. Lincoln's heart bled, and his indignation was aroused. Speaker Colfax said of him, "I doubt if his most intimate associate ever heard him utter bitter or vindictive language. He seemed wholly free from malignity or revenge, from ill-will or injustice." But the barbarous treatment of his "boys," who were prisoners in Southern stockades, came very near upsetting his famous motto, "With malice towards none; with charity for all." He could endure censure and even insult, and, "attacked ever so sharply, never answered railing for railing," but his whole soul was stirred over the treatment of Union soldiers by their captors.

The letter of Surgeon Chapel, who had charge of the "West's Buildings Hospital," Baltimore, to which many of our soldiers were sent, on returning from Southern prisons, caused him to weep, as if the sufferers were members of his own family. The letter was addressed to the Chairman of the Congressional Committee, and was as follows:—

"Dear Sir—I have the honor to enclose the photograph of John Breiring, with the desired information written upon it. I am very sorry your committee could not have seen these cases when first received. No one, from these pictures, can form a true estimate of their condition then not one in ten was able to stand alone some of them so covered and eaten by vermin that they nearly resembled cases of small-pox, and so emaciated that they were really living skeletons, and hardly that, as the result shows—forty out of one hundred and four having died up to this date. If there has been anything so horrible, so fiendish, as this wholesale starvation, in the history of this satanic Rebellion, I have failed to note it. Better the massacres of Lawrence, Fort Pillow, and Plymouth, than to be thus starved to death by inches, through long and weary months."

Mr. Lincoln could not consent to the starvation of rebel prisoners, nor to any approximation to cruel treatment. Retaliation must take some other form, or he would not endorse it. His real sympathy with soldiers, in their hardships and perils, extended even to rebel prisoners in our hands. At Frederick, Md., he visited a house in which there were a large number of Confederate wounded men. After viewing the scene, he said to them:—

"I should be pleased to take you all by the hand, if you have no objections. The solemn obligations which we owe to our country and posterity compel the prosecution of this war. Many of you, no doubt, occupy the attitude of enemies through uncontrollable circumstances. I bear no malice toward you, and can take you by the hand with sympathy and good feeling."

There was hesitation at first, but it was soon broken, and the Confederates stepped forward to shake the President's hand. Some of the numbers were too badly wounded to rise; Mr. Lincoln approached them, and, taking each one by the hand in turn, remarked—

"Be of good cheer, boys, and the end will be well. The best of care shall be taken of you."

It was a touching scene, and there were few dry eyes present. Many of the Confederates wept. It was evidently unexpected treatment to them. This was the kind of retaliation in which President Lincoln fully believed. It caused him unpleasantness and pain to be compelled to depart from it. He heartily enjoyed such a scene as was described to him after the battle of Antietam.

One of the agents of the Christian Commission found several wounded Confederate soldiers in a barnyard, deserted by their surgeons, and no one near to help them. They had been lying there with the dead for three days, without food or drink. The agent hurried food to them as soon as possible, and, with others, was proceeding to wash them when one of the number, from whose feet he was pulling his dirty stockings, began to cry violently.

"What's the matter? Do I hurt you?" inquired the agent.

"No, you don't," sobbed the man.

"What, then, can be the matter? Really, I can't go on with my work unless you tell me what is the matter?"

"Matter enough," ejaculated the Confederate. "You call us rebels, and I suppose we are; for I fought against the old flag; but, when we are wounded, you come to us here, not like angels, but like the Lord Jesus Christ himself, washing our feet and I can't stand it. I can't stand it."

Such treatment of enemies just suited Mr. Lincoln. The rehearsal of that single incident made him happy for a whole day.

In the light of such facts, W. H. Herndon, Esq., of Springfield, was right in saying—

"Through his perceptions—the suggestiveness of nature, his originality, and strength; through his magnificent reason, his understanding, his conscience, his tenderness, and kindness, his heart, rather than love—he approximated as nearly as most human beings in this imperfect state to an embodiment of the great moral principle? Do unto others as ye would they should do unto you?"

Thousands of the brave men who honored and loved Abraham Lincoln sleep on Southern soil. They went down to the graves of heroes from a thousand battle-fields, through four long, bloody, dreadful years and no heart throbbed with truer sympathy for them in their sufferings than the heart of the President and no eyes shed hotter tears for their loss than his. And when the nation's offering was complete, and there were no more human sacrifices to be laid upon the altar of liberty on gory fields, and the country was jubilant over the final victory and the return of peace, the chieftain himself was added to the hecatomb of loyal men, the tears and lamentations of a loving and afflicted people consecrating the unparalleled sacrifice!

Well may the Grand Army of the Republic cherish the memory of their heroic leader, whose thoughts were ever with them on the field of conflict. How ring his beautiful words, "The mystic chords of memory, stretching from every battle-field and patriot grave to every living heart and hearthstone all over this broad land, will yet swell the chorus of the Union, when again touched, as surely they wife be, by the better angels of our nature!

CHAPTER XXVI

HIS WORK FOR THE COLORED RACE

President Lincoln's life in the White House was distinguished by his work for the colored race. So providential and important were his relations to both free and enslaved negroes that justice could not be done to him or the subject without a separate exhibit of his work for them. He was, not only "The Savior of his Country," but, also, "The Liberator of a Race." While his great purpose was to save the Union, giving freedom to the slaves became absolutely necessary. He expressed his views in the following clear, forcible and characteristic way, after three years of war:—

"I am naturally anti-slavery. If slavery is not wrong, nothing is wrong. I cannot remember when I did not see, think and feel that it was wrong, and yet I have never understood that the Presidency conferred upon me an unrestricted right to act officially upon this judgment and feeling. I could not feel that, to the best of my ability, I had tried to preserve the Constitution, if, to preserve slavery or any minor matter, I should permit the wreck of the government, country and Constitution altogether. I claim not to have controlled events, but confess plainly chat events have controlled me. Now, at the end of three years' struggle, the nation's condition is not what either party or any man devised or expected; God alone can claim it. Whither it is tending seems plain. If God now wills the removal of a great wrong, and wills, also that we of the North as well as you of the South shall pay fairly for our complicity in that wrong, impartial history will find therein new cause to attest and revere the justice and goodness of God."

His memorable letter to Horace Greeley contained the following passages, which will appear more and more remarkable as the ages roll on:—

"If there be those who would not save the Union unless they could at the same time save slavery, I do not agree with them.

If there be those who would not save the Union unless they could at the same time destroy slavery, I do not agree with them. My paramount object is to save the Union, and not cither to save or destroy slavery. If I could save the Union without freeing any slave, I would do it —if I could save it by freeing all the slaves, I would do it—and if I could do it by freeing some and leaving others alone, I would also do that.

What I do about slavery and the colored race, I do because it helps to save the Union and what I forbear, I forbear because I do not believe it would help to save the Union.

I shall do less whenever I shall believe what I am doing hurts the cause, and I shall do more whenever I believe doing more will help the cause.

I shall try to correct errors when shown to be errors, and I shall adopt new views as fast as they appear to be true views.

I have here stated my purpose according to my view of official duty, and intend no modification of my oft-expressed personal wish that all men everywhere could be free.

For independent thought, invincible purpose, clearness of expression, model composition, and lofty sentiment, the foregoing was never excelled by American statesmen.

With these principles and aims, Mr. Lincoln grappled with slavery—the real cause of the Rebellion—and, finally, enlisted nearly two hundred thousand negroes as soldiers in the Union army, and gave liberty to every slave in the land.

Sojourner Truth was introduced to Mr. Lincoln as having "come all the way from Michigan to see you."

"I am very much pleased to see you," responded Mr. Lincoln, rising from his seat, and shaking the old lady's hand cordially, "Take a seat."

"Mr. President," replied Sojourner, "when you first took your seat I feared you would be torn to pieces, for I likened you unto Daniel, who was thrown into the lions' den; and if the lions did not tear you in pieces, I knew that it would be God that had saved you ; and I said if he spared me I would see you before the four years expired, and He has done so, and now I am here to see you for myself."

"I am truly glad that you have been spared to see this day," answered Mr. Lincoln.

"I appreciate you, for you are the best President who has ever taken his seat," added the old lady.

"I suppose you refer to the emancipation of your race," responded the President.

For half an hour the conversation continued with as much cordiality and politeness on the part of the President as he would have shown to the most refined white woman in Washington.

At one time he learned that Frederick Douglas, the distinguished ex-slave, was in Washington; and he sent his carriage to his boarding-place, with the message: "Come up and take tea with me."

Mr. Douglas accepted the invitation; and, for the first time in the history of our country, a colored man became an invited guest in the Executive Mansion. Mr. Douglas said of that interview, subsequently:—

"Mr. Lincoln is one of the few white men I ever passed an hour with, who failed to remind me in some way, before the interview terminated, that I am a negro."

The children of Concord, Mass., sent a memorial to him, praying for the freedom of all slave children. He replied to it as follows:—

"Tell those little people I am very glad their young hearts are so full of just and generous sympathy, and that while I have not the power to grant all they ask, I trust they will remember that God has; and that, as it seems, He wills to do it."

A citizen of Washington entered the President's office one day, and found him counting greenbacks.

"This is something out of my usual line," Mr. Lincoln remarked; "but a President of the United States has a multitude of duties not specified in the Constitution or acts of Congress."

The gentleman responded courteously, hinting that he would like to know what special duty was connected with that pile of greenbacks.

"This money belongs to a poor negro, who is a porter in the Treasury Department, at present very sick with the small-pox. He is now in the hospital, and could not draw his pay because he could not sign his name. I have been to considerable trouble in overcoming the difficulty, and getting it for him, and cutting red tape, as you newspaper men say. I am now dividing the money, and putting by a portion, labeled, in an envelope, with my own hands, according to his wish." Thus the kind-hearted man had turned aside from grave official duties to assist and comfort one of the humblest of God's creatures in his sufferings and sorrow.

A delegation of colored men from Louisiana waited upon the President to ask for some additional rights.

"I regret, gentlemen that you are not able to secure all your rights, and that circumstances will not permit the government to confer them upon you. I wish you would amend your petition so as to include several suggestions which I think will give more effect to your prayer, and, after having done so, please hand it to me."

"If you will permit me," replied the chairman of the delegation, "I will make the alterations here."

"Are you, then, the author of this eloquent production?" inquired Mr. Lincoln.

"Whether eloquent or not, it is my work," was the modest reply and the negro took his seat by the President's side, and made the alterations suggested. A Southern gentleman present concluded that Mr. Lincoln did not know that the delegation from Louisiana were "black men."

The rebel government inflicted inhuman barbarities upon Union colored soldiers at Port Hudson, Morris Island, and other places. The knowledge of the harrowing facts reaching the President, he immediately issued the following proclamation for the protection of colored soldiers:—

"Executive Mansion, July 30, 1863.

"It is the duty of every government to give protection to its citizens, of whatever class, color, or condition, especially those who are duly organized as soldiers in the public service. The law of nations, and the usages and customs of war, as carried on by civilized powers permit no distinction as to color in the treatment of prisoners of war as public enemies. To sell or enslave any captured person on account of his color, and for no offence against the laws of war, is a relapse into barbarism, and a crime against the civilization of the age. The Government of the United States will give the same protection to all its soldiers and if the enemy shall sell or enslave any one because of his color, the offence shall be punished by retaliation upon the enemy's prisoners in our possession. It is, therefore, ordered, that for every soldier of the United States killed in violation of the laws of war, a rebel soldier shall be executed and for every one enslaved by the enemy, or sold into slavery, a rebel soldier shall be placed at hard labor on the public works, and continued at such labor until the other shall be released and receive the treatment due to a prisoner of war."

"Abraham Lincoln.

"By order of the Secretary of War.

"E. D. Townsend, Adjutant-General"

Here, again, is proof of Mr. Lincoln's genuine interest in the soldiers. Retaliation was a war measure from which he shrank; his whole nature condemned it. And yet he adopted it, in the circumstances, as a dire necessity, to protect the soldier. In no case would he consent to starve or torture rebel prisoners by way of retaliation but he did consent to take life for life.

President Lincoln often expressed his admiration of the bravery and loyalty of colored soldiers, and once he said to Judge J. T. Mills, of Wisconsin:—

"There have been men base enough to propose to me to return to slavery the black warriors of Port Hudson and Olustee, and thus win the respect of the masters they fought. Should I do so, I should deserve to be damned in time and eternity. Come what will, I will keep my faith with friend and foe."

He was applied to for the pardon of a slave-dealer sentenced to five years' imprisonment and a fine of a thousand dollars. He had served the five years in Newburyport prison, Massachusetts, and was now held because he could not pay the fine. Parties interceded for the prisoner, and bore from him a very touching letter to the President. After having listened to the slave-dealer's advocate, and read his piteous letter, Mr. Lincoln said:—

"That is a very pathetic appeal to my feelings. You know my weakness is to be, if possible, too easily moved by appeals for mercy, and if this man were guilty of the foulest murder that the arm of man could perpetrate, I might forgive him on such an appeal but the man who could go to Africa, and rob her of her children, and sell them into interminable bondage, with no other motive than that which is furnished by dollars and cents, is so much worse than the most depraved murderer, that he can never receive pardon at my hands. No! He may rot in jail before he shall have liberty by any act of mine."

Before General Wadsworth was killed in the battle of the Wilderness, he wrote to Mr. Lincoln and inquired, "if universal amnesty should not be accompanied with universal suffrage in the event of complete success in the field."

Mr. Lincoln replied: "How to better the condition of the colored race has long been a study which has attracted my serious and careful attention; hence I think I am clear and decided as to what course I shall pursue in the premises, regarding it a religious duty, as the nation's guardian of these people who have so heroically vindicated their manhood on the battle-field, where, in assisting to save the life of the Republic, they have demonstrated in blood their right to the ballot, which is but the humane protection of the flag they have so fearlessly defended."

The reverence of the colored people for President Lincoln was always great, but its climax was reached when the proclamation of emancipation was issued. At one of his receptions, a large number of colored people gathered about the Executive Mansion, and waited two hours for the crowd of white visitors to pass. At length, they timidly advanced to the reception room, as if doubting whether they would be welcome, when Mr. Lincoln met them with one of his sweetest smiles, and encouraged them to take his hand. Their joy was unbounded, and they gave vent to their feelings in the wildest manner. An eye-witness says, "They laughed and wept, and wept and laughed—exclaiming through their blinding tears, God bless you!' 'God bless Abraham Lincoln!' 'God bless Massa Linkum!

Miss Canedy, of Fall River, Mass., was teaching the colored people at Norfolk, Va., and in her school-room was a plaster bust of Mr. Lincoln. One day she showed it to some colored men who were at work around the building, remarking about their benefactor. Their exclamations were as follows:—

"He's brought us safe through the Red Sea."

"He looks as deep as the sea himself."

"He's king of the United States."

"He ought to be king of the world."

"We must all pray to the Lord to carry him safe through, for it 'pears like he's got everything hitched to him."

"There has been a right smart praying for him, and it mustn't stop now."

President Lincoln's entrance into Richmond, after the rebel forces were driven out, was the signal for great rejoicing among the colored people. He entered the conquered city on foot, attended only by "Tad" and the sailors who rowed him up the James river. So quiet and unpretentious was his advent, that the negroes were taken by surprise and, when they found that the "Great Emancipator" was actually there, their joy knew no bound. Some of them shouted; many of them cried; all of them were frantic with delight. "Glory to God!" "Glory!" "Glory!" "Glory!" was the hearty tribute of the liberated slaves.

"I thank you, dear Jesus, that I behold President Linkum," exclaimed a woman on the street, crying like a child.

"Bless de Lord! Bless de Lord! Bless de Lord!" exclaimed several, jumping up and down as if bereft of their reason.

An eye-witness says, "An old negro cried out, "May de good Lord bless you. President Linkum!' while he removed his hat and the tears of joy rolled down his cheeks. The President removed his own hat, and bowed in silence; but it was a bow which upset the forms, laws, customs, and ceremonies of centuries. It was a death shock to 'chivalry,' and a mortal wound to caste."

Colonel McKaye, Robert Dale Owen, and one or two other gentlemen, were appointed by President Lincoln to investigate the condition of the freedmen on the coast of North Carolina. When they reported to Mr. Lincoln, Colonel McKaye related the following incident, as given by Mr. Carpenter:—

"He had been speaking of the ideas of power entertained by these people. He said they had an idea of God, as the Almighty, and they had realized in their former condition the power of their masters. Up to the time of the arrival among them of the Union forces, they had no knowledge of any other power. Their masters fled upon the approach of our soldiers, and this gave the slaves a conception of a power greater than that exercised by them. This power they called 'Massa Linkum."

"Colonel McKaye said that their place of worship was a large building which they called 'the praise house and the leader of the meeting, a venerable black man, was known as 'the praise man.' On a certain day, when there was quite a large gathering of people, considerable confusion was created by different persons attempting to tell who and what 'Massa Linkum' was. In the midst of the excitement the white headed leader commanded silence. 'Brederin,' 'said he, 'you don't know nose what you're talking 'bout. Now, you just listen to me. Massa Linkum, he very war. He know everything.' Then, solemnly looking up, he added, ' He walk like the Lord!'

"Colonel McKaye told me that Mr. Lincoln seemed much affected by this account. He did not smile, as another man might have done, but got up from his chair, and walked in silence two or three times across the floor. As he resumed his seat, he said, very impressively: 'It is a momentous thing to be the instrument, under Providence, of the liberation of a race.'"

The colored people of Baltimore presented the President with a very costly and beautiful copy of the Bible. Three colored clergymen and two laymen were the committee to present it. The address accompanying the gift was tender and reverential, to which President Lincoln replied in a characteristic speech, in which he said of the Bible:—

"It is the best gift which God has ever given to man. All the good from the Savior of the world is communicated to us through this book. But for that book we could not know right from wrong. All those truths desirable for men are contained in it. I return you my sincere thanks for the very elegant copy of the great Book of God which you present."

The Bible bore the following inscription:—

"To Abraham Lincoln, President of the United States, the friend of Universal Freedom. From the loyal colored people of Baltimore, as a token of respect and gratitude. Baltimore, July 4th, 1864."

A colored woman of Philadelphia presented him with a collection of wax-fruits, with an ornamented stem table — an elegant affair. Her pastor, Mr. Hamilton, made the presentation address, but closed by saying, "perhaps Mrs. Johnson would like to say a. few words." What Mrs. Johnson did is best told in her own words: "I looked down to the floor, and felt that I had not a word to say, but after a moment or two, the fire began to burn (laying her hand on her breast), and it burned and burned till it went all over me. I think it was the Spirit, and I looked up to him and said: 'Mr. President, I believe God has hewn you out of a rock, for this great and mighty purpose. Many have been led away by bribes of gold, of silver, of presents; but you have stood firm, because God was with you, and if you are faithful to the end, he will be with you.' With his eyes full of tears, he walked round and examined the present, pronounced it beautiful, thanked me kindly, but said: 'You must not give me the praise—it belongs to God.'"

Some public men desired Mr. Lincoln to issue his Proclamation of Emancipation long before he did. Delegations waited upon him to express their wishes in that direction. To a delegation of clergymen from Chicago, who urged the measure upon him, he replied:—

"I do not want to issue a document that the whole world will see must necessarily be inoperative, like the Pope's bull against the comet."

After some discussion, however, he assured them that "the subject was upon his mind night and day, more than any other;" and he added, "Whatever shall appear to be God's will, I will do."

He called a special Cabinet meeting two or three weeks before the battle of Antietam, and announced to the members:—

"I have prepared a proclamation of emancipation, believing that the time has come to issue it. I have not called you together for advice on the general subject, for I have settled that, I simply desire to inform you of my purpose, and receive such suggestions as you may make."

The members were somewhat surprised, but expressed a strong desire to hear it read. The President proceeded to read it in a slow, clear voice, evidently impressed with the grave responsibility he was taking upon himself. When he had finished reading the document, and opened the way for suggestions. Secretary Chase remarked:

"I would like to have the language stronger with reference to arming the blacks."

"I think it is bad policy to issue it now," said the Attorney General. "It will cost the administration the fall elections." It was then about the first of September, 1862.

"All these questions I have carefully considered, gentlemen," was Mr. Lincoln's response.

Secretary Seward remarked, at this point:—

"Mr. President, I approve of the proclamation, but I question the expediency of its issue at this juncture. The depression of the public mind consequent upon our repeated reverses is so great that I fear the effect of so important a step. It may be viewed as the last measure of an exhausted government—a cry for help —the government stretching forth its hand to Ethiopia, instead of Ethiopia stretching forth its hand to the government—our last shriek on the retreat. I think it would be best to delay it until it can be given to the country supported by military success, rather than after the greatest disasters of the war."

"That is a thought that has not occurred to me," immediately replied the President, "I shall adopt the suggestion at once, and await a signal victory."

Before the discussion ceased, however, Secretary Seward made another suggestion:—

"Mr. President, I think that you should insert, after the word 'recognize,' the words and maintain.'"

"I have fully considered the import of that expression," answered Mr. Lincoln; "but it is not my way to promise more than I am sure I can perform, and I am not prepared to say that I can 'maintain' this."

"Nevertheless that ground should be taken," continued the Secretary. "The dignity of the government and the completeness of the proclamation require it."

After a moment of serious thoughtfulness, the President responded, "You are right, Seward, and the words shall go in."

The proclamation v/as laid aside until the battle of Antietam was fought. Mr. Lincoln waited until he was satisfied that a valuable victory had been achieved, when he called the Cabinet together again, at a special meeting, and announced:—

"The time has come for emancipation to be declared; it cannot longer be delayed. Public sentiment will now sustain it, many of my warmest friends and supporters demand it, and I promised my God I would do it."

The last sentence was not quite understood by Secretary Chase, who asked for an explanation. Mr. Lincoln replied:—

"I made a solemn vow before God, that if General Lee was driven back from Pennsylvania, I would crown the result by the declaration of freedom to the slaved."

The Cabinet unanimously endorsed the President's decision, and the proclamation was issued September 22, 1862, promising, "That on the first day of January, in the year of our Lord one thousand eight hundred and sixty-three, all persons held as slaves within any State, or any designated part of a State, the people whereof shall then be in rebellion against the United States, shall be then, thenceforward and forever, free and the executive government of the United States, including the military and naval authority thereof, will recognize and maintain the freedom of such persons, and will do no act or acts to repress such persons, or any of them, in any efforts they may make for their actual freedom."

This proclamation offended many anti-slavery friends at the North, who wanted the President to strike an immediate and fatal blow at the institution, without warning or conditions. It is believed, however, that subsequent events caused them, and the civilized world, to concur in the President's judgment of the best method, in the circumstances. At the South, the excitement over the proclamation of promised freedom was intense, and the Rebel Congress enacted some violent threats. But the one hundred days of grace passed by, and the memorable first day of January, 1863, arrived, bringing the Proclamation of Emancipation, which deserves the highest place in the temple of American liberty. It merits the careful perusal of every citizen of the United States, old and young, and commends itself to the friends of humanity in every land.

President Lincoln signed the Proclamation after his public reception on January first, 1863. Mr. Colfax remarked to him—

"The signature appears somewhat tremulous and uneven."

"Not because of any uncertainty or hesitation on my part," answered the President; "but it was just after the public reception, and three hours' handshaking is not calculated to improve a man's chirography. The South had fair warning, that if they did not return to their duty, I should strike at this pillar of their strength. The promise must now be kept, and I shall never recall one word."

Mr. Carpenter's noble conception of a painting to commemorate the act of Emancipation enlisted the President's deepest interest. When the work was nearly completed, the artist remarked to him—

"I am very proud to have been the artist to have first conceived the idea of the design of painting a picture commemorative of the Act of Emancipation."

"Yes," answered the President, "as affairs have turned, it is the central act of my administration, and the great event of the nineteenth century."

When Mr. Carpenter's work was done, and he was about to take leave of the White

House, the President said—

"Well, Mr. Carpenter, I must go with you and take one more look at the picture before you leave us."

The parting interview with the artist before the picture was very interesting and President Lincoln closed it in his familiar way, by saying:—

"Mr. Carpenter, I believe that I am about as glad over the success of this work as you are."

This chapter would be incomplete without the Proclamation of Emancipation, which must ever be a memorable document in the future history of our country.

Speaker Colfax said of Mr. Lincoln and his proclamation, when the great man died:—

"The great act of the mighty chieftain, on which his fame shall rest long after his frame shall molder away, is that of giving freedom to a race. We have all been taught to revere the sacred characters. Among them Moses stands pre-eminently high. He received the law from God, and his name is honored among the hosts of heaven. Was not his greatest act the delivering three millions of his kindred out of bondage? Yet we may assert that Abraham Lincoln, by his proclamation, liberated more enslaved people than ever Moses set free, and those not of his kindred or his race. Such a power or such an opportunity, God has seldom given to man. When other events shall have been forgotten; when this world shall have become a network of republics; when every throne shall be swept from the face of the earth ; when literature shall enlighten all minds; when the claims of humanity shall be recognized everywhere, this act shall be conspicuous on the pages of history. We are thankful that God gave to Abraham Lincoln wisdom and grace to issue that proclamation, which stands high above all other papers which have been penned by uninspired men."

CHAPTER XXVII
STILL IN THE WHITE HOUSE

Mr. Lincoln was renominated for a second term in the summer of 1864. There were not wanting leaders who opposed his renomination. He was too slow and too kind to suit them. But their opposition was short-lived. When the National Convention assembled in Baltimore, the current of enthusiasm for Mr. Lincoln swept away all opposition. Intelligence from the army proved that one feeling pervaded the rank and file—the "boys" demanded the renomination of "Father Abraham." The colonel of a regiment on the Potomac, in which were many Democrats, reported a conversation among his men, as follows:—

"Who are you for, Joe?" inquired one of a Democrat.

"Father Abraham, of course; a new man would upset things," was the reply.

"Who knows but a new man might hurry up the end of this Rebellion!" interjected another.

"But we know who we have now for President," responded the Democrat; "but when you have a new man you must wait to find out."

"That's so," loudly answered a comrade, "no time for an armistice now."

"Soldiers think too much of Lincoln to swap him off now for somebody else," remarked another.

And so the discussion proceeded, until a German, who had remained a silent listener, spoke:

"I goes for Fader Abraham," he said. "Fader Abraham, he likes the soldier-boy. On he serves tree years he gives him four hundred dollar, and re-enlists him von veteran. Now Fader Abraham, he serve four years. We re-enlist him four years more, and make von veteran of June."

The German settled the question in that regiment; and it was about a fair representation of the feeling throughout the Union army.

In the convention, the votes of every State except Missouri were cast for Mr. Lincoln. Her twenty-two votes were cast for General Grant, but, immediately upon the announcement of the ballot, they were transferred to Mr. Lincoln.

In less than two months after his renomination, the President resolved to issue a call for five hundred thousand more troops. On laying the subject before his Cabinet, objections were provoked at once.

"It will prove disastrous," said one.

"It will defeat your re-election, Mr. President," suggested another.

"It will furnish material for your enemies to use against you; the people are tired of the war," added the first-named speaker.

For quite a while the measure was discussed and the President listened with his accustomed deference, occasionally dropping a word. At length, however, he settled the matter beyond controversy. Rising from his seat, and assuming that commanding attitude so usual when he was about to make a noble stand, he remarked, with profound seriousness, as well as emphasis:—

"Gentlemen, it is not necessary that I should be re-elected, but it is necessary that our brave boys at the front should be supported, and the country saved. I shall call for five hundred thousand more men, and if I go down under the measure, I will go down like the 'Cumberland' with my colors flying."

God crowned his noble decision with success. He did not go down like the "Cumberland" or any other riddled gunboat. Opposition hid itself before the onward march of his popularity. He was re-elected by the largest majority ever known in presidential elections. His popular majority was 411,428, in a total vote of 4,015,902; and he had 212 of the 233 votes in the electoral college. On being publicly congratulated upon this emphatic endorsement. President Lincoln said: —

"I am thankful to God for this approval of the people. But, while deeply grateful for this mark of their confidence in me, if I know my heart, my gratitude is free from any taint of personal triumph. I do not impugn the motives of any one opposed to me. It is no pleasure to me to triumph over any one; but I give thanks to the Almighty for this evidence of the people's resolution to stand by free government, and the rights of humanity."

The re-election of President Lincoln was equal to the addition of five hundred thousand more soldiers to the Union army. It destroyed the last hope of the Rebellion. It was staggering when the day of the election arrived and from that time its fall was rapidly accelerated.

On the fourth day of March, 1865, his second inauguration as President of the United States occurred. A great concourse of people witnessed the imposing ceremonies, and listened to his remarkable inaugural address. According to the national custom, Mr. Lincoln kissed the open Bible, after having taken the oath of office. Mr. Middleton, who passed the Bible to him, instantly marked the verses touched by the President's lips. They were the 26th and 27th verses of the Fifth chapter of Isaiah, and read as follows:—

"And he will lift up an ensign to the nations, and will hiss unto them from the end of the earth and, behold, they shall come with speed swiftly; none shall be weary nor stumble among them; none shall slumber nor sleep; neither shall the girdle of their loins be loosed, nor the latchet of their shoes be broken."

The speedy overthrow of the Rebellion furnished a remarkable interpretation of these words and they are choice words of prophecy to be forever associated with President Lincoln's memory.

His inaugural address on that occasion has been declared to be the most remarkable State paper extant.

It has often been classed with the "Farewell Address" of Washington; as it proved, indeed, the farewell address of Lincoln to the American people. And as Washington's life would be incomplete without the former, so Lincoln's life would lack an essential fact without the latter.

Charles Sumner said of this address: "The Inaugural Address which signalized his entry for a second time upon his great duties was briefer than any similar address in our history but it has already gone farther, and will live longer, than any other. It was a continuation of the Gettysburg speech, with the same sublimity and gentleness. Its concluding words were like an angelic benediction."

The subject of Civil Service Reform, which provokes so much discussion at the present time, engaged the attention of Mr. Lincoln at the time he entered upon the second term of his presidential career. He remarked to Senator Clark of New Hampshire:—

"Can't you and others start a public sentiment in favor of making no changes in offices except for good and sufficient cause."

"It would be an excellent measure," answered the senator. "You would remove or appoint no one for party considerations alone?"

"Exactly, it seems as though the bare thought of going through again what I did the first year here, would crush me."

"I am not surprised to hear that remark," continued Mr. Clark. "Nine-tenths of your callers are office seekers, or persons without any important business."

"Besides, it is all wrong to remove public servants who deserve to be retained, for the sake of promoting politicians who have done well for their party." Then, referring to applicants for office, he added, "It seems as if every visitor darted at me, and, with thumb and finger, carried off a portion of my vitality."

The senator laughed over this figure of a "carcass," carried off by birds of prey; and the President went on:—

"I have made up my mind to make very few changes in the offices in my gift for my second term. I think now that I will not remove a single man, except for delinquency. To remove a man is very easy, but when I go to fill his place, there are twenty applicants, and of these I must make nineteen enemies."

Senator Clark endorsed these sentiments as belonging to true statesmanship, and hoped that the President would be able to reduce his theory to practice. The latter closed the interview with the following rather sharp remark:—

"Sitting here, where all the avenues to public patronage seem to come together in a knot, it does seem to me that our people are fast approaching the point where it can be said that seven-eighths of them are trying to find how to live at the expense of the other eighth."

Three weeks after Mr. Lincoln entered upon his second term of office, he went to City Point, partly to recruit his wasted energies, and partly to be near the base of military operations now hastening to a crisis. The "boys in blue" greeted him with an enthusiasm that showed their strong love for the man.

A grand review had been arranged for the twenty fifth of March, in honor of the President; but General Lee attacked and captured Fort Stedman, on that morning, requiring a hard-fought battle, instead of a review, to drive out his forces—a feat that was triumphantly accomplished within a few hours. President Lincoln visited the field of carnage soon after the battle, and, on hearing regrets expressed that the grand review did not occur, he said—

"This victory is better than any review."

Immediately a council of war was held at City Point, attended by the President and Generals Grant, Sherman, Sheridan, Meade, and Ord; and it was followed by those three memorable days of battle, Friday, Saturday, and Sunday, sealing the doom of Richmond.

Mr. Lincoln remained at City Point, receiving dis patches from the front and forwarding them to Washington.

This was not reckless daring on his part, but his philosophical way of viewing the danger, as we shall learn more particularly in the next chapter.

On Monday, President Lincoln entered the fallen city without parade. Usually, conquerors have taken possession of captured cities and fallen thrones with the proudest display of exultation, bearing along with them the trophies of war. But true to himself, Mr. Lincoln found it more congenial to his heart to enter the subdued rebel capital without even fife or drum. Unheralded by brilliant cavalcade, he threaded his way as a common man through the streets to the headquarters of Jefferson Davis, who had become a voluntary fugitive. And though he took possession of the traitor-city without ostentation or military parade, history records his entrance as a triumphal march, and patriot fathers tell the story of it to their children in honor of Lincoln's greatness.

President Lincoln remained in Richmond until Tuesday morning, occupying the house so unceremoniously vacated by the arch-traitor of the Rebellion. The loyal people trembled for his safety when they heard he was there. Many pronounced his going to Richmond "a foolhardy act." All deprecated his unnecessary exposure of life, as they regarded it, and were greatly relieved when the telegraph informed them that he was back again in Washington.

Speaker Colfax expostulated with him upon his seeming disregard of danger, to which the President replied:—

"I should have been alarmed myself if any other person had been President and gone there; but I did not feel in any danger whatever."

Before reaching Washington, on his return, he read aloud twice from his copy of Shakespeare the words which Macbeth uttered about the murdered Duncan, calling the special attention of his friends to them:—

The friends who listened to his remarks upon this striking passage could but recall the singular circumstances, after his assassination.

The fall of Richmond was celebrated throughout the North and West by bonfires, illuminations, speeches, music, ringing of bells, and general rejoicing. Everywhere Mr. Lincoln was remembered and eulogized for his wisdom, patriotism and achievements.

Just one week from the time the news of the fall of Richmond was flashed over the land, the tidings of Lee's surrender at Appomattox Court-house followed, magnifying the general joy tenfold, if possible. The war was ended, and Constitutional Liberty maintained. Over the western portico of the Capitol at Washington was inscribed, with a beautiful banner waving over it:—

"This is the Lord's doing; it is marvelous in our eyes."

Over the door of the State Department was the following:—

"The Union saved by faith in the Constitution, faith in the People, and trust in God."

The day of jubilee had come—"the greatest day," said one, "since the Resurrection."

The welcome news of "Peace" spread over the land with the rapidity of light, and flashed under the ocean to foreign countries, where glad millions joined in festivities over the end of the conflict and the triumph of freedom. As when Cornwalls surrendered, and the War of Independence was over, the people became wild with joy; so the news— Lee has surrendered— awaked almost frantic demonstrations of delight. All modes of expressing exultation were inadequate, and yet all were employed. Sextons rushed to the churches to ring the bells; gunners added the peal of cannon; acquaintances met in the streets and embraced each other; some wept, others laughed, all were jubilant. Never before were so many bells run together, so many cannon fired, so many shouts of victory raised, so many bands of music waked, to many banners waved, and so many bonfires and illuminations kindled, to celebrate the return of peace and the nation saved.

The praise of Lincoln was on every lip, and has continued to be from that day to the present time. The nation delights to honor his memory, and one of the recent acts of the National Government is a tribute to his memory by a generous increase of his widow's pension.

Mr. Lincoln had accomplished the purpose of his administration — he had crushed the Rebellion and saved the Union

Charles Sumner said of President Lincoln's administration: "The corner-stone of National Independence is already in its place, and on it is inscribed the name of George Washington. There is another stone which must have its place at the corner also. This is the Declaration of Independence, with all its promises fulfilled. On this stone we will gratefully inscribe the name of Abraham Lincoln.

"Each was at the head of the Republic during a period of surpassing trial; and each thought only of the public good, simply, purely, constantly, so that single-hearted devotion to country will always find a synonym in their names. Each was the national chief during a time of successful war. Each was the representative of his country at a great epoch of history."

"The part which Lincoln was called upon to perform resembled in character the part which was performed by Washington. The work left undone by Washington was continued by Lincoln. Kindred in service, kindred in patriotism, each was naturally surrounded at death by kindred homage."

CHAPTER XXVIII
SHOT OF THE ASSASSIN

From the time of Mr. Lincoln's nomination for the Presidency, as we have seen, fears of his assassination prevailed among his friends. The President himself had reason to believe that he was in danger of being shot, for he had a package of threatening letters, which he had appropriately labeled, "Assassination Letters," and laid away. His attention was often called to the subject by anxious friends. On being remonstrated with for unnecessarily exposing himself, he replied, without denying his danger:—

"Soon after I was nominated at Chicago, I began to receive letters threatening my life. The first one or two made me a little uncomfortable, but I came at length to look for a regular installment of this kind of correspondence in every week's mail, and up to Inauguration Day I was in constant receipt of such letters. It is no uncommon thing to receive them now; but they have ceased to give me apprehension."

Surprise was expressed that he could be indifferent to a peril that his friends considered imminent, and he answered:

"Oh, there is nothing like getting used to things!"

A cavalry guard was once placed at the gates of the White House, but was removed at his request, "I worried until I got rid of it," he said to a friend.

He once remarked to Colonel Halpine, "It will never do for a President to have guards with drawn sabres at his door, as if he fancied he were, or were trying to be, or were assuming to be, an emperor."

Once he went to General Halleck's private quarters and protested against a detachment of cavalry, detailed, without his request, by General Wadsworth, to guard his carriage going to and from the Soldiers' Home. He remarked, facetiously, yet earnestly:—

"Why, Mrs. Lincoln and I cannot hear ourselves talk for the clatter of their sabres and spurs and some of them appear to be new hands and very awkward, so that I am more afraid of being shot by the accidental discharge of a carbine or revolver, than of any attempt upon my life by a roving squad of Stewart's cavalry."

Very much in the same vein he replied to Colonel Halpine, who was trying to show him his exposure even in the White House, saying:—

"There are two dangers, the danger of deliberate political assassination, and the mere brute violence of insanity."

The President replied, as related by Mr. Carpenter:

"Now as to political assassination, do you think the Richmond people would like to have Hannibal Hamlin here any better than myself? In that one alternative, I have a insurance on my life worth half the prairie land of Illinois. And beside," —this more gravely—"if there were such a plot, and they wanted to get at me, no vigilance could keep them out. We are so mixed up in our affairs, that—no matter what the system established—a conspiracy to assassinate, if such there were, could easily obtain a pass to see me for any one or more of its instruments.

"To betray fear of this, by placing guards or so forth, would only be to put the idea into their heads, and perhaps, lead to the very result it was intended to prevent. As to the crazy folks, Major, why I must only take my chances—the most crazy people at present, I fear, being some of my own too zealous adherents. That there may be such dangers as you and many others have suggested to me, is quite possible; but I guess it wouldn't improve things any to publish that we were afraid of them in advance."

At one time, there was undoubted proof of a rebel plot to abduct Mr. Lincoln, or kill him in the attempt, as there was at one time to capture or kill George Washington and when the facts were laid before him, he replied:—

"Well, even if true, I do not see what the rebels would gain by either killing or getting possession of me. I am but a single individual, and it would not help their cause, or make the least difference in the progress of the war."

On the morning of April 14, 1865, the President's son, Capt. Robert T. Lincoln, returned from the army, and spent an hour in giving his father a detailed account of Lee's surrender. At the same time, also, he received a letter from General Owen Allen, of New York, entreating him not to expose his life again, as he did by going to Richmond, to which he replied:

"I intend to adopt the advice of my friends, and use due precaution."

The 14th of April was a holiday for the loyal people for it was the anniversary of the evacuation of Fort Sumter, just four years before and the day had been set apart for the restoration of the old flag to its former place over the fort. The ceremony, with speeches, music, cannon, and other demonstrations of joy, at Charleston, S. C, was witnessed by a great concourse of loyal men from every part of the land.

A special programme for the evening of that day was announced at Ford's Theatre, and President Lincoln, General Grant, and other public men in the city were invited; and it was announced in the public journals that these dignitaries would be present.

Mr. Ashmun and Mr. Colfax were with him when his carriage was driven to the gate. The latter gentleman was to leave in the morning for California. Mr. Ashmun had important business to lay before the President and, before entering his carriage, the latter wrote upon a card:—

"Allow Mr. Ashmun and friend to come in at nine A. M. tomorrow.

"A. Lincoln."

These were the last words he wrote. Passing out to his carriage, he said to Mr. Colfax:—

"Do not forget to tell the people of the mining regions what I told you this morning about the development when peace comes."

After being seated in his carriage and the horses started, he added, "I will telegraph you, Colfax, at San Francisco."

It was twenty minutes to nine o'clock when he entered the theatre, accompanied by Mrs. Lincoln, Miss Harris and Major Rathbone. General Grant had been called to Philadelphia.

The vast audience rose to their feet, and made such a demonstration in honor of their chief, as was possible only by those who appreciated the end of the war and the reign of peace.

An hour afterwards, the crack of a pistol startled the audience, although, at first, many thought it was a part of the entertainment. A shriek from Mrs. Lincoln, and the leap of the assassin from the President's private box to the stage, however, assured them that a real tragedy had been enacted. The murderer exclaimed, as he leaped to the stage:—

"Sic semper tyrannis!" [Thus let it ever be with tyrants] Then brandishing a gleaming dagger he added, "The South is avenged," and escaped.

For a moment the audience was paralyzed, scarcely realizing the tragic situation.

"John Wilkes Booth!" shouted a man in the audience.

"Shoot him!" "Shoot him!" "Hang him!" screamed a hundred men, awaking to the fact that it was the shot of an assassin which startled them.

Women screamed and fainted; men gesticulated and threatened; everybody was filled with consternation and dismay; hundreds wept in fright and horror. The scene beggared description. From the highest peak of joy, the audience was plunged in a moment down to unutterable sorrow. To add to the terrible fear and apprehension the tidings were brought, as the excited assembly were issuing from the building, that Secretary Seward and Vice-President Johnson were assassinated, also. At once, hundreds caught up the idea that the oft-repeated rebel threats to assassinate the members of the Cabinet and take forcible possession of the Government were being executed. All sorts of rumors of violence and blood spread through the city, creating the apprehension that republican institutions were dissolving into anarchy and that horrid butchery would destroy what treason had failed to overthrow.

The reports proved to be true, as far as Secretary Seward was concerned. One of the conspirators, Lewis Payne, an infamous character, had entered the secretary's chamber and stabbed him three times in bed. Mr. Seward was helpless at the time, from the effects of a serious injury and, but for the courage and great strength of his attendant, the assassin would have killed him on the spot. Mr. Seward's son was present, and was badly wounded, with four others, by the villain, before he escaped from the house.

The unconscious form of the President was borne across the street to the house of Mr.

Peterson, where the best medical and surgical talent of the city came to his relief. It was soon manifest that the good and great man was beyond the skill of physicians. He was shot through the back of the head, the ball entering on the left side behind the ear, passing through the brain, and lodging just behind the right eye.

By midnight all the members of the Cabinet stood around the couch of the dying President, together with Mrs. Dixon, for whom Mrs. Lincoln had sent, Miss Harris, Major Rathbone, Captain Robert Lincoln, and his almost distracted mother, with other friends. At the announcement of Surgeon-General Barnes, that there was "not a ray of hope," Secretary Stanton burst into tears, saying—

"Oh, no! General, no, no!"

Senator Sumner stood holding one of the President's hands, sobbing as if parting with his father. Mrs. Lincoln walked to and fro from room to room, wringing her hands in despair, exclaiming—

"How can it be so? Why did he not shoot me instead of my husband?"

Again and again she would leave the room, but soon return, wringing her hands in agony, reiterating—

"Why is it so? I must go with him!"

Captain Robert Lincoln bore himself with great firmness, comforting his mother in the most affectionate manner, and entreating her to look to God for support. Occasionally, unable to control his feelings, he retired to the hall, and gave vent to his deep sorrow for a moment, and then returned with renewed strength, to assuage the grief of his mother.

Such a night of woe and anguish was never known before in Washington. The weary hours dragged heavily because of their weight of sorrow. The murdered one lay unconscious of his sufferings and the grief of friends around his bed, through all the dismal night. Before eight o'clock in the morning, Secretary Stanton sent the following telegram over the land:—

"Abraham Lincoln died this morning at twenty-two minutes after seven o'clock."

But we must return to the assassin. He was known to some persons who saw him and heard his voice, after the fatal shot—John Wilkes Booth—a worthless, dissipated fellow, in full sympathy with the rebel cause. Immediate efforts were put forth by the authorities to capture him and his fellow-conspirators. It was soon ascertained that Booth had been busy laying his plans during the previous day, and that several accomplices were engaged with him. There was unmistakable evidence that other members of the Cabinet were singled out for assassination, and that General Grant would have been a victim had he remained in the city. A letter was found in Booth's trunk which showed that the assassination was planned for March 4—the day of Mr. Lincoln's inauguration, and that it failed because the accomplices refused to proceed "until Richmond could be heard for."

Colonel Baker, with his picked men, pursued Booth to the farm-house of one Garrett, in Lower Maryland, in whose barn he was found, with Herold, one of his accomplices. Herold gave himself up, but Booth refused to surrender, whereupon the barn was set on fire, and he was shot by Boston Corbett, in his attempt to escape. Lewis Payne, who made the attempt upon the life of

Secretary Seward, George A. Atzerodt, to whom was assigned the murder of Vice-President Johnson, Michael O'Laughlin, Edward Spangler, who aided Booth at the theatre, Samuel Arnold, Mary E. Surratt, and Dr. Samuel A. Mudd, were the conspirators arrested and tried by a military commission. Herold, Atzerodt, Payne, and Mrs. Surratt were sentenced to be hanged, and were executed on the seventh day of July.

We stop here to record a fact about the assassin that has never been published. A retired sea-captain of New Bedford, Mass., remarked, when he read that J. Wilkes Booth had murdered President Lincoln:

"I am not at all surprised; just what I should expect!"

"Why do you say that?" inquired a listener.

"I will tell you," replied the captain; "when J. Wilkes Booth was about ten years old, I was running a vessel from Liverpool to New Orleans, and I brought J. Wilkes, with his father and family, from the former to the latter place. That boy, John Wilkes, was the most ungovernable and impudent fellow of his age I ever met with. Like most boys who go to ruin, he was disrespectful and saucy to his mother. She could do nothing with him. One day she was correcting him for his usual impudence to her, when Mr. Booth, her husband, made his appearance. Observing what his wife was about, he cried out at the top of his voice, 'What! treating that boy so? He never will make a man if you treat him so.' "The captain added: "I am not surprised that such a boy should become an assassin."

Before his assassination, President Lincoln was often likened to William of Orange, whose subjects called him "Father William," as we were wont to call our beloved President "Father Abraham." But when treason had done its worst, and our Lincoln was assassinated, as William of Orange was assassinated, the comparison with that "purest and best-loved ruler of his times" became a remarkable and affecting coincidence.

By midnight, April 14, the tidings of President Lincoln's assassination began to flash over the wires. Long before sunrise the large cities and towns of the country, having night telegraphic connection with Washington, were startled by the terrible news. Governors, mayors and other officials were called from their beds to receive the dreadful announcement. By the time men and women went to the business of the morning the sad news met them everywhere and speedily followed Mr. Stanton's telegram announcing the President's death.

Never was there such sorrow in the Republic before. The people had been rejoicing over the close of the war for several days, and the praise of President Lincoln, for his wise and successful administration, was on every lip. The heights of national joy had been reached and now to plunge therefrom into the lowest depths of sorrow, was a fearful change. The popular heart sunk under the burden of grief. Strong men wept as they went about the streets. Great men buried their faces in their hands and cried as if a member of their own families had been stricken down. The marts of trade were turned to houses of mourning. The transaction of business ceased. Neither rich nor poor had any heart to traffic or labor. Neighbor accosted neighbor — "terrible! terrible!" and burst into tears. The sorrow was universal. Both old and young felt its oppressive weight.

A few weary, sad hours passed, and people began to gather in halls and churches to carry their case to the Lord. There was no help in man for such a trial. When stalwart men bear about so great a sorrow, that they meet only to speak in tears, the only relief is found at the throne of grace. And so men left their business and women their homes to gather round a common altar; rich and poor, learned and unlearned, meeting together before the Most High. There were hundreds and thousands of such assemblies on the afternoon of that sorrowful Saturday, April 15, 1865. Words of comfort, prayers, and tears, brought some relief to the mourning people.

The next day was the holy Sabbath and such a Sabbath! Already the symbols of grief had appeared on churches and public buildings, stores and dwelling houses. As if by a general impulse, the people everywhere began on Saturday to drape their homes and places of business with the habiliments of sorrow. The markets were exhausted of every fabric that could be used to express the sadness of human hearts. Houses of worship were crowded on Sunday with honest mourners. In pulpits heavily draped with crape, preachers discoursed upon the great sorrow, and led their sorrowful congregations to the Lord. The day will never be forgotten by the multitude who mingled their common grief.

In some localities the grief expressed itself in the form of vengeance. It assumed that form early on Saturday morning in the city of New York. Armed men gathered in the streets threatening speedy death to disloyal citizens. Their numbers rapidly increased, until fifty thousand assembled in Wall street Exchange, bearing aloft a portable gallows, and swearing summary vengeance upon the first rebel sympathizer who dared to speak. One thoughtless fellow remarked that "Lincoln ought to have been shot long ago; and he was struck dead instantly. The grieved and vengeful crowd seethed towards the office of the World, a disloyal paper, with mutterings of violence on their lips. It seemed scarcely possible to prevent violent demonstration. A bloody scene appeared to be imminent. At that critical moment a portly man, of commanding physique and voice, appeared upon the balcony of the City Hall, from which telegrams were read to the people, and raising his right hand to invoke silence, he exclaimed, in clear and sonorous tones:—

"Fellow-citizens: Clouds and darkness are round about Him! His pavilion is dark waters and thick clouds of the skies! Justice and judgment are the habitation of His throne! Mercy and truth shall go before his face! Fellow-citizens: God reigns, and the government at Washington still lives!"

The effect of this serious address was magical. The raging populace subsided into repose. A hushed silence pervaded the vast assembly, when the voice of the speaker ceased, as if they had listened to a messenger from the skies. The change was marvelous. The speaker was General James A. Garfield, who became President sixteen years afterwards, and was shot by an assassin four months later! How strange that the inhabitants of that metropolis, who listened to the gifted statesman so gladly, April 14th, 1865, should be shocked by the news of his assassination on July 2, 1881!

No class of citizens was more sincere mourners for the illustrious dead than the colored race. They went about the streets of Washington wringing their hands and weeping as Rachel did for her children. They gathered in groups on the streets and bewailed their loss in pitiful lamentations. Many of them appeared to be inconsolable. More sincere and profound sorrow never bowed human hearts.

A correspondent of the New York Tribune, writing from Charleston, S. C, said:—

"I never saw such sad faces or heard such heavy heart-beatings as here in Charleston the day the dreadful news came! The colored people — the native loyalists —were like children bereaved of an old and loved parent. I saw one old woman going up the street wringing her hands and saying aloud as she walked, looking straight before her, so absorbed in her grief that she noticed no one: 'O Lord! O Lord! O Lord! Massa Sam's dead! Massa Sam's dead!'"

'Who's dead, Aunty?' I asked her.

"'Massa Sam,' she said, not looking at me, renewing her lamentations.

"'O Lord! O Lord! O Lord! Massa Sam's dead!"

"Who is Massa Sam?" I asked again.

"Uncle Sam,' she said.

"'O Lord! Lord! Lord!" she continued.

"I was not quite sure that she meant the President, and I spoke again:—

"Who's Massa Sam, Aunty?"

"Mr. Lincum!' she said, and resumed wringing her hands and moaning in utter hopelessness of sorrow. The poor creature was too ignorant to comprehend any difference between the very unreal Uncle Sam and the actual President but her heart told her that he whom Heaven had sent in answer to her prayers was lying in a bloody grave, and she and her race were left— fatherless.

A friend of the writer was in a city of North Carolina when the news of the assassination reached the colored people there. In their profound grief they followed their leader to their humble place of worship, filling it to overflowing. Our friend went thither, and found the whole congregation upon their knees, giving vent to their feelings in convulsive sobs and piteous moans. Even their patriarchal leader was too full for utterance and, on his knees, he was crying with his afflicted people. At length, an old woman, bowed with age and trembling with emotion, rose to express her grief in words. Clasping her dusky hands together, and lifting her streaming eyes heavenward, she exclaimed:—

"Bless de Lord ! bless de Lord ! They have killed Massa Linkum, but they can't kill God!"

"Amen!" "Amen!" "Amen!" was the response from every part of the house, showing, not only the greatness of their bereavement, but, also, their gladness that God was left. From that moment their tongues were loosed, and they found relief in the inspiring thought, "they can't kill God."

The Atlantic Cable flashed the terrible news across the sea, "President Lincoln Assassinated," startling foreign governments, and eliciting expressions of profound sympathy.

Queen Victoria instructed Earl Russell to convey her unfeigned sorrow to the government of the United States, and, at the same time, with her own hand, she addressed a letter of touching condolence to Mrs. Lincoln.

The London "Spectator" declared that all England wept for "the noblest President whom America has had since the time of Washington; certainly the best, if not the ablest, man ruling over any country in the civilized world."

The Empress Eugenie, wife of Napoleon, the Emperor of France, addressed a letter of true sympathy to Mrs. Lincoln and the French government seconded the address of the Emperor to the United States, expressing the deepest sorrow over our national bereavement.

The governments of Russia, Italy, Prussia, Belgium, Turkey, Austria and Switzerland, were equally demonstrative in their expressions of grief and condolence.

Hon. George Bancroft, the historian, said, "The echoes of his funeral knell vibrate through the world, and the friends of freedom of every tongue and in every clime are the mourners."

CHAPTER XXIX

FUNERAL CEREMONIES

Immediate preparations were made for the obsequies. The dead body of the President was removed to the White House, where it was embalmed and placed in a costly casket resting upon an elaborate catafalque. On Monday, a meeting of Congressmen, with other notable persons in Washington, was held in the Capitol, when Charles Sumner of Massachusetts was appointed Chairman of a Committee to arrange for the funeral ceremonies. At four o'clock in the afternoon this Committee reported Wednesday for the time of the funeral, and the names of six Senators and six Representatives for pall-bearers, and one gentleman from each State and Territory as a National Committee to attend the remains to Springfield, Illinois.

On Tuesday morning the White House was thrown open to the tens of thousands anxious to behold once more the face of their beloved ruler. All day, until far into the evening, a steady stream of visitors, of all ages and classes, passed into the presence of the dead. Thousands were unable to gain admittance to the Executive Mansion during the day, on account of the multitude, and they turned away in disappointment.

When the hour of the funeral arrived on Wednesday, the city, with all its public buildings, was elaborate draped in black. The symbols of mourning were of the most varied and expensive character. Decorative art was taxed to its utmost to express the sentiment of grief that pervaded the city. A public man, looking at the sable drapery, remarked:—

"As it should be. The nation would have it so. It tells the real sorrow of the people."

The funeral services were conducted in the East Room, where the family and relatives of the President, with many distinguished men, were seated. Mrs. Lincoln was too much prostrated to attend the funeral service. Many governors, senators, judges, representatives, and other men of note, were present from different parts of the Union. Governors Fenton of New York, Andrew of Massachusetts, Brough of Ohio, Parker of New Jersey, Oglesby of Illinois, and Buckingham of Connecticut, were there. The ceremonies were simple and touching, very appropriate for the truly Republican statesman for whom the nation mourned. Rev. Dr. Gurley paid a just and eloquent tribute to the dead.

At the close of the services in the presidential mansion, the body was conveyed to the Capitol, followed by a larger and more imposing procession than had ever been seen in Washington. The grand avenue leading from the White House to the Capitol was one dense mass of human beings, and all the neighboring streets of the city were thronged with tearful spectators. As the hearse, which was drawn by eight gray horses heavily draped in black, approached the Capitol grounds, several bands joined in a mournful requiem, answered by minute guns from the fortifications. The casket was deposited in the rotunda, resting upon a grand catafalque, when Dr. Gurley conducted further ceremonies suited to the place and the occasion. Then the doors were thrown open, that the remains might be viewed by the tens of thousands who had failed to gain access to the Executive Mansion. From that time, all through the night, and far into the next day, a tide of people flowed in and out of the rotunda, to view the face of the President whom they had honored and loved. Of the pageant of that day, Dr. Holland says: "In many of its aspects, it was never paralleled upon this continent. Nothing like it—nothing approaching it—had ever occurred in this country, if, indeed, in the world."

The same day was set apart, throughout the land, for funeral ceremonies, in honor of the deceased President. In hundreds and thousands of towns and cities, churches and public halls were thrown open, and the clergy and other professional gentlemen as well as laymen, addressed the assembled multitudes, and led them to the throne of grace.

The funeral train left Washington on the morning of April 21. Along with the casket of the President, was borne that of Willie—father and son united in death in the journey homeward, as they were united in life, four years before, on their journey thitherward. The train was elaborately draped, from the locomotive to the last car.

At Baltimore, where conspirators sought the President's life, four years before, on his journey to Washington, thus obliging him to pass through the city by night, a vast concourse of people assembled to pay their tribute of respect to the dead. The city was almost as profusely draped as Washington itself and when the casket was opened to the public, for a brief time, as honest tears were shed by the multitude about his remains as were wept in any other part of the land.

The inhabitants of every village through which the funeral train passed, gathered at the depots, and, with uncovered heads, watched it as it swept by, while the tolling of bells, and sometimes the solemn dirge by a band, together with sable draperies on buildings and flags, added pathos to their grief.

At York, six ladies entered the funeral car, bearing an immense floral tribute, which they laid upon the coffin so tenderly, and with so much emotion, that all witnesses were moved to tears.

The funeral cortege reached Philadelphia on Saturday evening, and the remains were conveyed to Independence Hall, followed by a procession of one hundred thousand people, while from three to four hundred thousand more were spectators. In the solemn shadows of night, moving to the measure of funereal music, the departed President was laid in the historic hall, which was one mass of flags, drapery, and flowers.

After the addition of a few more words, he added:

"I have said nothing but what I am willing to have by and if it be the pleasure of Almighty God, to die by."

How wonderful his words in view of the appalling fact, that the enemies of the Declaration of Independence finally took his life!

From Saturday night until Monday morning, the face of the murdered President was viewed by three hundred thousand people—an eager, orderly, mourning procession, moving in and out of Independence Hall, night and day, to pay their sincere tribute of respect to the dead.

In the city of New York more than one hundred thousand people were in the procession, twenty thousand of whom were soldiers. One hundred bands of music played during the march. Nearly a million people witnessed the pageant. Public services were held in Union Square, where Hon. George Bancroft delivered the eulogy, and Dr. J. P. Thompson read the President's last inaugural address.

Of the ceremonies in New York, Morris said: "The funeral ceremonies of the first Napoleon, in the streets of Paris, when his remains were transferred from St. Helena to the Invalides by Louis Philippe, were regarded as the greatest pageant the world had ever known, but the pageant in New York far exceeded it."

At Dunkirk, upon a tastefully draped platform was "a group of thirty-six young ladies, representing the States of the Union. They were dressed in white, each with a broad black scarf resting on the shoulder, and holding in her hand a national flag."

At Cleveland and Columbus, Ohio, one hundred and eighty persons a minute saw the remains, "two rows of spectators were constantly passing, one on each side of the coffin." Flowers wrought into every conceivable device, to express affection and respect for the dead, literally covered the coffin and platform harps, wreaths, bouquets, crosses, anchors, and crowns.

At Piqua ten thousand people assembled at midnight, with uncovered heads, as distinctly seen under the blaze of torches and bonfires as under the light of mid-day, and thirty-six ladies in white, with black sashes, upon a draped platform, sang a plaintive tune amidst a hushed silence that was oppressive. As they closed, a band followed with a touching dirge. The effect of these ceremonies at midnight baffles description.

The body of the President lay in state at Indianapolis over the Sabbath of April 30, and was viewed by over one hundred thousand people, among whom were five thousand Sabbath-school scholars who came in a body with flowers to scatter upon the bier.

At Chicago, the preparations for funeral ceremonies were too elaborate to be described. Thirty-six young ladies in white, with black sashes, bareheaded and with a black velvet wreath over the brows, a star in front, their arms full of flowers—immortelles and garlands—met the procession before it reached the court-house, and laid their floral tributes upon the funeral car. As the coffin was deposited in the spacious hall, a hundred singers, overhead and invisible, sang a funeral dirge with melting effect. Speaker Colfax delivered an eloquent eulogy.

During the two days the remains reposed in Chicago, five hundred thousand mourners paid their tributes of respect to their lamented fellow-citizen and neighbor.

But at his home, in Springfield, among his former intimate friends and townsmen, the most touching scenes occurred. Many sobbed aloud as they looked upon his familiar face in death. Old men and women, young men and maidens, mourned as for a brother and father. From the country around, for fifty miles and more, people came wearing badges of mourning—so many thousands that the town could scarcely contain them. And when the body was conveyed to the Oak Ridge Cemetery, where Bishop Simpson delivered a funeral oration, acres of ground were one vast "sea of upturned faces." In just two weeks from the time the funeral cortege left Washington, upon its march of sixteen hundred miles, the remains were deposited in the grave, over which a grateful country has reared a costly monument.

The closing paragraph of Bishop Simpson's eloquent eulogy shall close our story of him who worked his way from his pioneer home to the White House:—

"Chieftain! Farewell! The nation mourns thee. Mothers shall teach thy name to their lisping children. The youth of our land shall emulate thy virtues. Statesmen shall study thy record and learn lessons of wisdom. Mute though thy lips be, yet they still speak. Hushed is thy voice, but its echoes of liberty are ringing through the world, and the sons of bondage listen with joy. Prisoned thou art in death, and yet thou art marching abroad, and chains and manacles are bursting at thy touch. Thou didst fall not for thyself. The assassin had no hate for thee. Our hearts were aimed at, our national life was sought. We crown thee as our martyr—and humanity enthrones thee as her triumphant son. Hero, martyr, friend, farewell!

CHAPTER XXX

ORATION BY HON. GEORGE BANCROFT

Our grief and horror at the crime which has clothed the continent in mourning, find no adequate expression in words, and no relief in tears. The President of the United States of America has fallen by the hands of an assassin. Neither the office by which he invested by the approved choice of a mighty people, nor the most simple-hearted kindliness of nature, could save him from the fiendish passions of relentless fanaticism. The wailings of the millions attend his remains as they are borne in solemn procession over our great rivers, along the seaside, beyond the mountains, across the prairie, to their resting-place in the valley of the Mississippi. His funeral knell vibrates through the world, and the friends of freedom of every tongue and in every clime are his mourners.

Too few days have passed away since Abraham Lincoln stood in the flush of vigorous manhood, to permit any attempt at an analysis of his character, or an exposition of his career. We find it hard to believe that his large eyes, which in their softness and beauty expressed nothing but benevolence and gentleness, are closed in death; we almost look for the pleasant smile that brought out more vividly the earnest cast of his features, which were serious even to sadness. A few years ago he was a village attorney, engaged in the support of a rising family, unknown to fame, scarcely named beyond his neighborhood; his administration made him the most conspicuous man in his country, and drew on him first the astonished gaze, and then the respect and admiration of the world.

Those who come after us will decide how much of the wonderful results of his public career is due to his own good common sense, his shrewd sagacity, readiness of wit, quick interpretation of the public mind, his rare combination of fixedness and pliancy, his steady tendency of purpose; how much to the American people, who, as he walked with them side by side, inspired him with their own wisdom and energy and how much to the overruling laws of the moral world, by which the selfishness of evil is made to defeat itself. But after every allowance, it will remain that members of the government which preceded his administration opened the gates to treason, and he closed them that when he went to Washington the ground on which he trod shook under his feet, and he left the republic on a solid foundation that traitors had seized public forts and arsenals, and he recovered them for the United States, to whom they belonged that the capital, which he found the abode of slaves, is now the home only of the free that the boundless public domain which was grasped at, and, in a great measure, held for the diffusion of slavery, is now irrevocably devoted to freedom that men then talked a jargon of a balance of power in a republic between slave States and free States, and now the foolish words are blown away forever by the breath of Maryland, Missouri, and Tennessee; that a terrible cloud of political heresy rose from the abyss, threatening to hide the light of the sun, and under its darkness a rebellion was growing into indefinable proportions now the atmosphere is purer than ever before, and the insurrection is vanishing away the country is cast into another mould, and the gigantic system of wrong, which had been the work of more than two centuries, is dashed down, we hope forever. And as to himself, personally: he was then scoffed at by the proud as unfit for his station, and now, against usage of later years, and in spite of numerous competitors, he was the unbiased and the undoubted choice of the American people for a second term of service. Through all the mad business of treason he retained the sweetness of a most placable disposition and the slaughter of myriads of the best on the battle-field, and the more terrible destruction of our men in captivity, by the slow torture of exposure and starvation, had never been able to provoke him into harboring one vengeful feeling, or one purpose of cruelty.

How shall the nation most completely show its sorrow at Mr. Lincoln's death? How shall it best honor his memory? There can be but one answer. He was struck down when he was highest in its service, and, in strict conformity with duty, was engaged in carrying out principles affecting its life, its good name, and its relations to the cause of freedom and the progress of mankind. Grief must take the character of action, and breathe itself forth in the assertion of the policy to which he fell a victim. The standard which he held in his hand must be uplifted again higher and more firmly than before, and must be carried on to triumph.

Above everything else, his proclamation of the first day of January, 1863, declaring, throughout the parts of the country in rebellion, the freedom of all persons who had been held as slaves, must be affirmed and maintained.

Events, as they rolled onward, have removed every doubt of the legality and binding force of that proclamation. The country and the rebel government have each laid claim to the public service of the slave, and yet but one of the two can have a rightful claim to such service.

That rightful claim belongs to the United States, because every one born on their soil, with the few exceptions of the children of travelers and transient residents, owes them a primary allegiance. Every one so born has been counted among those represented in Congress; every slave has ever been represented in Congress; imperfectly and wrongfully, it may be—but still has been counted and represented. The slave born on our soil always owed allegiance to the general government. It may in time past have been a qualified allegiance, manifested through his master, as the allegiance of a ward through its guardian, or an infant through its parent. But when the master became false to his allegiance, the slave stood face to face with his country and his allegiance, which may before have been a qualified one, became direct and immediate. His chains fell off, and he rose at once in the presence of the nation, bound, like the rest of us, to its defense. Mr. Lincoln's proclamation did not take notice of the already existing right of the bondman to freedom. The treason of the master made it a public crime for the slave to continue his obedience; the treason of a State set free the collective bondmen of that State.

This doctrine is supported by the analogy of precedents. In the times of feudalism, the treason of the lord of the manor deprived him of his serfs; the spurious feudalism that existed among us differs in many respects from the feudalism of the middle ages, but so far the precedent runs parallel with the present case for treason the master then, for treason the master now, loses his slaves.

In the middle ages, the sovereign appointed another lord over the serfs and the land which they cultivated in our day, the sovereign makes them masters of their own persons, lords over themselves.

It has been said that we are at war, and that emancipation is not a belligerent right. The objection disappears before analysis. In a war between independent powers, the invading foreigner invites to his standard all who will give him aid, whether bond or free, and he rewards them according to his ability and his pleasure, with gifts or freedom but when at a peace he withdraws from an invaded country, he must take his raiders and comforters with him or, if he leaves them behind, where he has no court to enforce his decrees, he can give them no security, unless it be by the stipulations of a treaty. In a civil war, it is altogether different. There, when rebellion is crushed, the old government is restored, and its courts resume their jurisdiction. So it is with us; the United States has courts of their own, that must punish the guilt of treason, and vindicate the freedom of persons whom the fact of rebellion has set free.

Nor may it be said, that because slavery existed in most of the States when the Union was formed, it cannot rightfully be interfered with now. A change has taken place, such as Madison foresaw, and for which he pointed out the remedy. The constitutions of States had been transformed before the plotters of treason carried them away into rebellion. When the Federal Constitution was framed, general emancipation was thought to be near and everywhere the respective legislatures had authority, in the exercise of their ordinary functions, to do away with slavery. Since that time the attempt has been made, in what are called slave States, to render the condition of slavery perpetual and events have proved, with the clearness of demonstration, that a constitution which seeks to continue a caste of hereditary bondsmen through endless generations is inconsistent with the existence of republican institutions.

So, then, the new President and the people of the United States must insist that the proclamation of freedom shall stand as a reality. And, moreover, the people must never cease to insist that the Constitution shall be so amended as to utterly prohibit slavery on any part of our soil for evermore.

Alas! that a State in our vicinity should withhold its assent to this last beneficent measure: its refusal was an encouragement to our enemies equal to the gain of a pitched battle and delays the only hopeful method of pacification. The removal of the cause of the rebellion is not only demanded by justice; it is the policy of mercy, making room for a wider clemency; it is the part of order against a chaos of controversy; its success brings with it true reconcilement, a lasting peace, a continuous growth of confidence through an assimilation of the social condition. Here is the fitting expression of the mourning of today.

And let no lover of his country say that this warning is uncalled for. The cry is delusive that slavery is dead. Even now it is nerving itself for a fresh struggle for continuance. The last winds from the South waft to us the sad intelligence that a man who had surrounded himself with the glory of the most brilliant and most varied achievements, who but a week ago was counted with affectionate pride among the greatest benefactors of his country and the ablest generals of his time, has initiated the exercise of more than the whole power of the Executive, and, under the name of peace, has, perhaps unconsciously, revived slavery, and given the hope of security and political power to traitors, from the Chesapeake to the Rio Grande. Why could he not remember the dying advice of Washington, never to draw the sword but for self defense or the rights of his country, and, when drawn, never to sheathe it till its work should be accomplished. And yet, from this ill-considered act, which the people with one united voice condemn, no great evil will follow save the shadow on his own fame and that, also, we hope will pass away. The individual, even in the greatness of military glory, sinks into insignificance before the resistless movements of ideas in the history of man. No one can turn back or stay the march of Providence.

No sentiment of despair may mix with our sorrow. We owe it to the memory of the dead, we owe to the cause of popular liberty throughout the world, that the sudden crime which has taken the life of the President of the United States shall not produce the least impediment in the smooth course of public affairs. This great city, in the midst of unexampled emblems of deeply-seated grief, has sustained itself with composure and magnanimity. It has nobly done its part in guarding against the derangement of business or the slightest shock to public credit. The enemies of the republic put it to the severest trial but the voice of faction has not been heard doubt and despondency have been unknown. In serene majesty, the country fuses in the beauty, and strength, and hope of youth, and proves to the world the quiet energy and the durability of institutions growing out of the reason and affections of the people.

Heaven has willed it that the United States shall live. The nations of the earth cannot spare them. All the worn-out aristocracies of Europe saw in the spurious feudalism of slaveholding their strongest outpost, and banded themselves together with the deadly enemies of our national life. If the Old World will discuss the respective advantages of oligarch or equality of the union of church and state, or the rightful freedom of religion of land accessible to the many, or of land monopolized by an ever decreasing number of the few—the United States must live to control the decision by their quiet and unobtrusive example. It has often and truly been observed, that the trust and affection of the masses gather naturally round an individual if the inquiry is made, whether the man so trusted and beloved shall elicit from the reason of the people enduring institutions of their own, or shall sequester political power for a superintending dynasty, the United States must live to solve the problem. If a question is raised on the respective merits of Timoleon or Julius Caesar, or of Washington or Napoleon, the United States must be there to call to mind that there were twelve Caesars, most of them the opprobrium of the human race, and to contrast with them the line of American Presidents.

The duty of the hour is incomplete our mourning is insincere, if, while we express unwavering trust in the great principles that underlie our government, we do not also give our support to the man to whom the people have entrusted its administration.

Andrew Johnson is now, by the Constitution, the President of the United States, and he stands before the world as the most conspicuous representative of the industrial classes. Left an orphan at four years old, poverty and toil were his steps to honor. His youth was not passed in the halls of colleges; nevertheless, he has received a thorough political education in statesmanship, in the school of the people, and by long experience of public life. A village functionary; member successively of each branch of the Tennessee Legislature, hearing with a thrill of joy the words, "The Union, it must be preserved; " a representative in Congress for successive years; governor of the great State of Tennessee, approved as its governor by re-election; he was at the opening of the rebellion a senator from that State in Congress. Then at the Capitol, when senators, unrebuked by the government, sent word by telegram to seize forts and arsenals, he alone of that southern region told them what the government did not dare to tell them, that they were traitors, and deserved the punishment of treason. Undismayed by a perpetual purpose of public enemies to take his life, bearing up against the still greater trial of the persecution of his wife and children, in due time he went back to his State, determined to restore it to the Union, or die with the American flag for his winding-sheet. And now, at the call of the United States, he has returned to Washington as a conqueror, with Tennessee as a free State for his trophy. It remains for him to consummate the vindication of the Union.

To that Union Abraham Lincoln has fallen a martyr. His death, which was meant to sever it beyond repair, binds it more closely and more firmly than ever. The blow aimed at him was aimed not at the native of Kentucky, not at the citizen of Illinois, but at the man, who, as President in the executive branch of the government, stood as the representative of every man in the United States. The object of the crime was the life of the whole people ; and it wounds the affections of the whole people. From Maine to the southwest boundary of the Pacific, it makes us one The country may have needed an imperishable grief to touch its inmost feeling. The grave that receives the remains of Lincoln, receives the costly sacrifice to the Union; the monument which will rise over his body will bear witness to the Union; his enduring memory will assist during countless ages to bind the States together, and to incite to the love of our one undivided, indivisible country. Peace to the ashes of our departed friend, the friend of his country and of his race. He was happy in his life, for he was the restorer of the republic he was happy in his death, for his martyrdom will plead forever for the Union of the States and the freedom of man.

Made in United States
North Haven, CT
11 June 2024